T0308512

Phillies
1980!

Phillies 1980!

MIKE SCHMIDT, STEVE CARLTON, PETE ROSE, AND PHILADELPHIA'S FIRST WORLD SERIES CHAMPIONSHIP

LEW FREEDMAN

SPORTS
PUBLISHING

Sports Publishing books may be purchased in bulk at special discounts for sales promotion, corporate gifts, fund-raising, or educational purposes. Special editions can also be created to specifications. For details, contact the Special Sales Department, Sports Publishing, 307 West 36th Street, 11th Floor, New York, NY 10018 or sportspubbooks@skyhorsepublishing.com.

Sports Publishing® is a registered trademark of Skyhorse Publishing, Inc.®, a Delaware corporation.

Visit our website at www.sportspubbooks.com.

10 9 8 7 6 5 4 3 2

Library of Congress Cataloging-in-Publication Data is available on file.

Cover design by 5mediadesign
Jacket photo credits: Getty Images

Insert photos credit: Getty Images

Print ISBN: 978-1-68358-310-3
Ebook ISBN: 978-1-68358-311-0

Printed in the United States of America

To former *Philadelphia Inquirer* sports editor Jay Searcy. And a thank you to the media relations departments of the Philadelphia Phillies and Kansas City Royals for those organizations' assistance.

TABLE OF CONTENTS

INTRODUCTION

BY 1980, THE Philadelphia Phillies had been playing big-league baseball for nearly a century. To that point, the club had never won a world championship.

Philadelphia was a rabid sports town, represented by the Phillies in Major League Baseball, the Eagles in the National Football League, the 76ers in the National Basketball Association, and the Flyers in the National Hockey League. For a half-century-plus, once the American League was formed, the City of Brotherly Love (as the biggest city in Pennsylvania is nicknamed), was also represented on the diamond by the Philadelphia Athletics.

Before the A's fled Philadelphia for Kansas City and then moved on to Oakland (where they currently reside), the Athletics, under the nearly exclusive ownership and field stewardship of Connie Mack, won five World Series titles and eight American League pennants.

Philadelphia Phillies rooters loved their baseball as much as soft pretzels and cheesesteaks, but they did not gain as much satisfaction as they did from the eats, or for that matter, over the decades, from the Athletics.

The club was founded in 1883. But going into the 1980 season, the Phillies had won exactly two pennants: in 1915 and 1950. Baseball teams have endured long droughts, longer than teams in other American professional sports leagues because baseball has been around longer. When the Boston Red Sox won the World Series in 2004, it was the club's first title triumph in eighty-six years. When the Chicago Cubs won the World Series in 2016, it was the franchise's first championship in 108 years.

The difference between the Phillies of 1980 and the Cubs and Red Sox is that the Phillies had NEVER won a title. Much like those other two teams, during their forever-drought, or ninety-seven years, the Phillies had recorded some horrifyingly bad seasons that led their fans to near despair, or at least to stay home from the ballpark for years at a time.

For most of the twenty years leading up to the 1950 pennant winners, called "The Whiz Kids," the Phillies were the worst team in baseball. Between 1930 and 1948, Philadelphia recorded just one winning record—by two games—in 1932. During that stretch, the club lost at least 100 games eight times and four times recorded sub-.300 winning percentages. (The team's record over this stretch was 1084–1821, with an overall winning percentage of .373.)

After the 1950 surge, when the team won 91 games and was swept in the World Series, 4–0, by the New York Yankees, it receded into mediocrity—and worse—for another two decades. The exception occurred in 1964 when the Phillies won 92 games yet blew a sure-thing pennant in the final week of the season.

However, by the late 1970s, Phillies fans and players shared a different type of heartbreak. During the latter half of the decade, the team emerged as one of the best in the National League, one that could win more than 100 games in a season. But it was also a team that could not go the distance, could not get beyond the National League Championship Series.

This was a new art form of vexation. The Phils glittered in the regular season, but were overwhelmed in the playoffs. They seemed to be just a player or two shy of fielding a championship club. Phillies followers wearied of almosts.

That was the prevailing mood amongst supporters and those wearing the uniforms when spring training began in Clearwater, Florida, in 1980. Pessimists who paid for seats in Veterans Stadium feared their team would never win it all.

Jaw-set Phillies fans believed their time had finally come. The 1980 season, they were sure, was going to be their year, the long (very long)-awaited prized moment when the Philadelphia Phillies were crowned kings.

The city, the franchise, the ballplayers were hungry.

In 1979, the Phillies hired as manager no-more-Mr.-Nice-Guy Dallas Green, whose personality seemed more like one belonging to a hard-nosed football coach, as a disciplinary leader.

In 1979, too, the Phillies hired the legendary Pete Rose off the free-agent market, hoping he was the missing cog, the type of always-hustling on-field leader to spark the lineup. That season had produced a disappointing backwards step. Now it was time for a revival.

During the 1980 baseball season, from March to October, there was no such thing as too much attention showered on this baseball team, and during that year there were four Philadelphia daily newspapers providing coverage.

The *Philadelphia Daily News*, the short-lived *Philadelphia Journal* (in existence between 1977 and 1981), the soon-to-die afternoon *Philadelphia Bulletin*, and the *Philadelphia Inquirer* competed for scoops. I was a member of the *Inquirer* sports department at the time, an occasional fill-in at games and part of the all-hands-on-deck late-season and World Series coverage packages.

On the night the Phillies won their title in six games over the Kansas City Royals, I was in the locker room, writing the Most Valuable Player story on third baseman and future Hall of Famer Mike Schmidt as the celebration commenced. I also covered the pivotal regular-season-ending Los Angeles Dodgers-Houston Astros series that determined who the Phillies' opponent would be in the National League Championship Series. There were no wild-card playoff qualifiers in those days.

This was a season where Mike Schmidt and Pete Rose shined the brightest on the field and Steve "Lefty" Carlton and reliever Tug McGraw—the player I knew best—were the most reliable arms on the mound. A trio of rookies, pitchers Bob Walk and Marty Bystrom and outfielder Lonnie Smith, enjoyed the season of their lives and such clutch hitters as Greg Gross and Del Unser played critical roles.

The rest of the regulars, from Greg Luzinski to Bake McBride and Garry Maddox, from Larry Bowa to Manny Trillo, and hurler Dick Ruthven, took turns as difference makers.

The Phillies were anointed the best team in baseball that year, but it was a bumpy ride at times, featuring histrionics in the clubhouse, with Green emphasizing he was the boss, not a pal.

There were struggles reaching the finish line first in the Eastern Division and against both Houston in the NCLS and Kansas City in the Series. There were times one could doubt the final result unless you were one of the guys on the roster. They forged a faith built over the hot summer and at long last it truly was the Philadelphia Phillies' year.

—Lew Freedman
February 2020

1

GLORY

WHEN THE LAST pitch was hurled and the last out was recorded to make history, Tug McGraw, the clever and pixyish relief pitcher always counted on by the Philadelphia Phillies to save the day, showed his hops.

McGraw made one great leap for mankind, showing the vertical leap of an NBA star as he tried to touch the night sky above Veterans Stadium. Arms outstretched, glove on his right hand pointed upward, legs as straight as a Kenyan Maasai warrior performing his tribal dance, McGraw was captured midair in iconic photographs, the perfect and ultimate joy-of-celebration picture that symbolized a Phillies triumph nearly a century in the making.

The date was October 21, 1980. A fall night to be remembered. A culmination of both a journey begun with the franchise in 1883 and also seven months earlier during spring training in Clearwater, Florida. It was very much a pothole-riddled journey, too. Winning the first championship for a club that predated the creation of the World Series was something to be savored for eternity.

Oh, what a moment for Philadelphia, the Phillies, and McGraw.

Only twice before had the often woebegone Phillies even won a pennant, in 1915 and in 1950, and man, there had been rocky years—even rocky decades—since then.

So the night of revelry was well earned. Even the last minutes of waiting, the culmination of the ninety-seven years, were not without suspense. It was not as if, on this special night, the Phillies had things on cruise control.

This was Game Six of the World Series versus the Kansas City Royals, with the champs of the American League facing the champs of the National League. Philadelphia came into the evening leading the best-of-seven series, three games to two. The Phillies had laboriously built that one-game margin in a series of tight games, most of which could have concluded with the opposite result.

The Royals were veritable newcomers. The team was not founded until 1969, just eleven years prior, and this was their first run for the roses. The team had zero world titles on its résumé, but that was not particularly surprising given the youth of the organization—a mere eyeblink of time compared to what Phillies fans had endured, with generations of diehard spectators passing on to heaven after watching too much hellishly subpar baseball.

One could easily say that the Kansas City Royals baseball club and its fans had not suffered enough to deserve a world championship in 1980. Compared to the Phillies, Chicago Cubs, and Boston Red Sox, they were callow punks who had not paid their dues. That did not mean they did not present a dangerous threat in 1980. Their season's accomplishments were very real and their players were very capable.

Negotiating the first five games of the Series was a minefield for the Phillies. They had earned the right to be confident, but had no history to back up such an attitude. Most of the players were battle-tested, fighting their way to divisional crowns in the late 1970s, but falling short of winning the flag and gaining a place in the World Series. They were seasoned by demoralizing close calls.

However, management had tinkered—worked hard to add missing pieces, to fill holes. So while most of the Phillies' key players had competed together for a few seasons, some key new faces were added—players who had been around, players who had won elsewhere.

The big add, the big plus in the daily lineup, was the great Pete Rose. Admired for his hustle and versatility, ability to come through in the clutch, and inbred winning outlook, Rose had made his reputation with the Cincinnati Reds and their Big Red Machine of the early and mid-1970s. Rose was on an improbable quest to break one of the oldest and most revered records in Major League Baseball—Hall of Famer Ty Cobb's mark of 4,191 hits. He accomplished the feat five years later, on September 11, 1985, after rejoining the Reds.

Although he joined the Phillies in 1975, McGraw fit the profile of a player who knew how to win. He had been there. In 1969, the New York Mets, founded as a hapless expansion team in 1962, stunned the baseball world by capturing a World Series over the favored Baltimore Orioles. The Mets were founded as a civic endeavor and in retribution in a sense, to guarantee that New York City, which until the late 1950s was home to three big-league teams before the Giants and Dodgers fled to California, was represented in the National League.

Those 1962 Mets lost 120 games and are considered the worst team in the modern era of baseball. It took the organization the whole decade—but a short one at that—to build a champion. McGraw was a big part of that success, finishing the 1969 season with a 9–3 record, 12 saves, and a 2.24 earned run average.

The Mets had to outlast the Chicago Cubs to make believers of the National League, and then the Baltimore Orioles, on their own joyride. Perhaps no one has been better equipped to lap up the joy in the sport than McGraw. He was witty, demonstrative, oftentimes in stressful moments on the field flapping his glove against his chest to signify the fluttering of his heart, and during his heyday in New York he actually authored a comic strip with a partner called "Scroogie." There was no mystery about the identity of the protagonist, a pitcher who made wry observations and frequently found himself in small difficulties. Highlights of those comic strips were collected into two books.

McGraw was playful and enjoyed the heck out of playing what Hall of Famer Roy Campanella told baseball fans is essentially a little boys game.

In the middle of the 1980 season, the *Philadelphia Inquirer*—one of four daily newspapers in the City of Brotherly Love feverishly covering every move the club made that year—ran a lengthy feature story about McGraw. The headline read "Forever Young." The subhead read, "McGraw Enjoys His life, His Job, Himself."[1] That was a neat summary of the pitcher, especially at that point in his life as a thirty-five-year-old (going on thirty-six) veteran in his 15th major-league season and on his way to his second world championship.

Frank Edwin McGraw Jr. was born on August 30, 1944, in Martinez, California. Not the only talent in the family, his brother Hank also became a ballplayer and his son Tim became a world-famous country singer, although Tug was long into adulthood before he acknowledged he had fathered this child during what he said was a one-night stand.

McGraw stood 6 feet tall and played at 170 pounds. His hair was sandy blond and his demeanor was impish. It was noted once that even during pregame workouts, that looking into McGraw's brown eyes appeared to reveal a boy caught with his hand in a cookie jar. He broke into the majors at age twenty with the Mets, young for the job—especially someone who seemed to retain that youthfulness even well into his career. While on that 1980 run, McGraw admitted he pretty much always wore his uninhibited emotions on his sleeve, and those emotions almost always tilted toward having fun.

"It's just that I never learned to hide my feelings," McGraw said. "And, I'm not trying to, either. I have a lot of fun being myself."[2]

That comment probably came as a relief to fans. That's what they saw, and that's what they wanted to believe. It would have disappointed Phillies supporters if they discovered this character really sat at home on offdays and in the offseason in his mansion-like home in the Philadelphia suburbs reading Aristotle, or brooding as he stared into the fireplace.

After all, the comic strip was named "Scroogie," and McGraw had written a book titled *Screwball*. That was seen as a double entendre, describing both his best pitch and the person as well. McGraw, hyperactive on the mound, slapping his glove against his thigh, never held back in making postgame comments—whether he was the star who closed out the win, or those times when he gave up the winning run.

McGraw was a chatterbox at heart, and while he recognized that some people just didn't get him, he felt it was their loss not appreciating his enthusiasm which was merely part of his dedication to the game.

"It's a shame they don't enjoy me as much as I enjoy me," he once said. "Sometimes it's so much fun to plan a series of pitches and have everything go right, it makes you go crazy."[3]

Sometimes baseball can be a stuffed-shirt sport, and it was certainly accused of such while Bowie Kuhn was commissioner back then. Just musing one day, McGraw, who was facing impending free agency, suggested if he could not stay with the Phillies he might like to rejoin the Mets. Kuhn viewed that as self-tampering or something and chided McGraw for making the statement. And they call the NFL the "No Fun League."

Those who took the sport too seriously, or resented McGraw for having too much fun at various times, referred to him as a flake or a blithe spirit, as if those were insults. He was also called an Irish rogue because of his Irish roots, his love of potatoes, and professed desire to visit Ireland. Or maybe teammates held his preference of playing Elvis Presley music in the locker room against him.

Until this current era when managers sometimes start games with relievers, past bullpen experts knew the manager was never going to call on them until the later innings except in case of emergency. That made for a lot of downtime (aside from actually paying attention to how the game was unfolding). While employed by the Mets, McGraw made some legendary moves while waiting for the phone to ring. Once, he sent out to a nearby delicatessen to order spare ribs. Knowing he wasn't likely to be warming up until the latter innings, for one period of time McGraw set himself to plotting a garden and growing tomatoes in the bullpen dirt.

During an exhibition game, meaningless by definition, on St. Patrick's Day in 1979, McGraw chose to celebrate his Irish heritage in flashy fashion. He stripped off his Phillies uniform to reveal a pair of shorts, green long johns, green socks, and a green T-shirt featuring a picture of a leprechaun and decorated with the words "Ya Gotta Believe."

It didn't seem to matter that the Phillies' manager's name was Green—as in Dallas Green—who was not the type to be overly amused by antics. Green, more of a disciplinarian than many skippers, seemed to have as dulled a sense of humor as Kuhn.

"A lot of people are always looking for an angle on good bullpen stories," McGraw said, "but generally speaking it's boring out there."[4] Boring enough that McGraw usually spent the first six innings hanging out in the dugout before drifting to the pen for possible late-game insertion. "I have a lifetime of being a show-off guy, but that doesn't make me a bad guy."[5]

For all the time McGraw spent playing the jester, he invested considerable time in helping others. Much of his off-field attention was focused on assisting children who got a bad break, often visiting hospitals. He also regularly spoke at Little League banquets. Naturally, that made him the object of admiration for kids. He gave his approval when some young people wanted to found a Tug McGraw Fan Club, but he required that their dues go to help an American Indian family in New Mexico. He also served on the national board of the Muscular Dystrophy Foundation.

McGraw came by his nickname Tug as a baby. Everyone called his dad Frank, and it was too crowded in the house for two Franks. He happened to be a vigorous breastfeeder, and his mother said he was always tugging away. The nickname was originally Tugger, and everyone in the family called him that. Tug was the diminutive of that.

That was all he knew, and when the teacher called roll in kindergarten and asked if any student had been missed, he raised his hand. She had called out a Frank McGraw, and Tug didn't even realize she was referring to him. When the search of the room was narrowed down to him, McGraw actually said Frank was his "daddy, and he's already been to kindergarten."[6] Tug stuck.

No doubt a bunch of McGraw's future major-league teammates wondered if he was still attempting to graduate from kindergarten. One of the zany things McGraw did regularly was give other nicknames to his pitches, mostly a variety of fastballs, in addition to his screwball. One fastball was his "John Jameson" because the ball was thrown "straight, like I drink it." Another pitch was named for Bo Derek, who had posed nude for *Playboy* and In 1979, Derek had famolusly starred in the movie *10.* because "it had a nice little tail on it." A third was called his Peggy Lee because "Is that all there is?" as in the name of her hit song. Presumably, batters had less of a challenge connecting with that one.[7]

Many years later, under the microscope, in the spotlight, with 65,838 Veterans Stadium fans wondering if they dared inhale, the most important play in Philadelphia Phillies history was about to unfold 2 hours and 59 minutes into a tense evening.

Steve "Lefty" Carlton had presided over an excellent seven innings of pitching against Kansas City in that sixth World Series game when he gave way on the mound to McGraw for the eighth. Just getting out of that frame was a bit of an adventure, but McGraw was left in for the ninth as well. Modern relief pitchers hardly ever throw two innings in close, late-game situations, but it was indeed a different time.

The Phillies led the Royals, 4–1, in the top of the ninth. There were two outs, and Kansas City outfielder Willie Wilson was at the plate with the bases loaded—three ducks on the pond—all courtesy of pitches thrown by McGraw. Wilson, who batted .326 that season, could stroke a hit and spark a tying rally—even smash a grandslam for the lead—putting tremendous pressure on the Phillies in the bottom of the ninth.

McGraw worked the count to 1-2 in the anything-can-happen moment. He was weary and didn't know what kind of power he had left on his fastball. But he threw it, flung it as hard as he could, and Wilson swung and missed ... and it was over. McGraw became a jumping jack, fans roared and hugged, Phillies players ran out on the field and mimicked berserk children at recess.

Of course, in his postgame review, McGraw casually dismissed loading the bases.

"With all of those people watching on television, I hate to make the game boring."[8] McGraw had made it clear earlier in the season he felt an obligation to fill any vacuum attributable to boredom.

Still, McGraw figured if he did not get Wilson out, he was toast. Dallas Green would have certainly lifted him, he thought, and he even would have recommended such a course of action himself because "I had nothing left. Nothing."[9]

Instead, McGraw became the author of the most exhilarating page in the Phillies' history book.

2

SPRING TRAINING

BOB WALK WAS just one of many rookies whose talents were being evaluated by upper management when he showed up for Phillies spring training camp in Clearwater, Florida, in March 1980.

He was not regarded as a fresh, hot prospect. He was only a slightly better betting favorite to make the big-league roster than any one of the three-year-old thoroughbreds who would qualify for the Kentucky Derby in early May. In other words, there were more than enough horses vying to fill the starting gate, just as there were more than enough pitchers seeking a major-league spot with the Phils.

At that point, Walk, who was born in Van Nuys, California, in 1956, was twenty-three years old—far from a peach-fuzzed draft pick right out of high school like his counterparts. He had been in the minor leagues since 1977, competing in such places as Spartanburg, South Carolina; Peninsula in the Carolina League; Reading, Pennsylvania; and he was basically earmarked for the Phillies' AAA farm club in Oklahoma City. That could be his make-it-or-break-it stop, halted one step shy of the bigs, or he could show enough stuff to make the jump.

The same could be said of the Phillies themselves this season. They had been on the cusp of grabbing the National League pennant and reaching the World Series in 1976, 1977, and 1978. Each season they lost in the Championship Series, the first two years after winning 101 regular-season games.

Team management was frustrated. This oh-so-close business was getting old. That's why the club played the free-agent market for Pete Rose. That's why they installed Dallas Green as the new manager before the 1979 season concluded. There was no doubt they had collected a talented group of ballplayers. Nobody had to tell them that. Winning more than 100 games in a season announces that fact to the world. Nice years, all of them, but what really mattered was advancing in the playoffs.

In 1979, with the team floundering compared to those recent successful seasons, manager Danny Ozark was fired and replaced by Green for the final 30 games of a season (going 19–11) that concluded with an 84–78 record and without a division title. The team wanted better results in a hurry, and that was Green's task.

In those days, Ruly Carpenter owned the Phillies and the general manager was Paul Owens, nicknamed "The Pope." Owens and Green collaborated on personnel discussions and decisions while Carpenter paid the bills. In the context of the times, four decades ago, Rose commanded an almost unheard-of amount of money. He was pursued by the Kansas City Royals and Milwaukee Brewers, whose offers approached $4 million. These days, the weakest starter in the lineup may make that amount per season.

The Phillies won the sweepstakes with a four-year, $3.25-million deal. Rose wanted to go with a winner, and the Phillies wanted him to be the difference between almost winning and winning. But Green and Owens were in the marketplace for more, to fill any small hole that might prevent the team from going all the way.

"I'd like to think that our work ethic, as well as our ability to have a good time, earned us respect around the majors," Green said in connection with a Christmas party story he was telling. "At the annual winter meetings our suite became a command center for 14-hour workdays. Pope always left the door to the suite open so that anyone who wanted to talk about a trade, or baseball in general, could come in and bend our ears. We also worked to make sure all our minor-league affiliates felt connected to the major-league club. The officials who ran those teams were welcome to join in those discussions."[1]

Some fairly big names began the 1979 season with the Phillies—all of them aging players, who were gone from the club early on. Jim Kaat went 1–0 before departing to complete the final chapter of his career that ran into his forties. Onetime Cy Young Award winner Jim Lonborg retired after going 0–1 in 1979. Outfielder Jose Cardenal did not last the season, either. If all of those players had been Phillies in their primes, or had been able to contribute more regularly, the Phils would have been a juggernaut.

One thing Green needed was some maturing players coming up from the farm system or obtained otherwise. In March, this was an unknown factor. Outfielder Lonnie Smith had two years of brief cameos behind him, but no one knew what he could accomplish if he played on a regular basis. To a large extent,

Smith (and several others) were seen as potential contributors, but perhaps nobody to count on for a pennant-chasing club. If only some of them came through to supplement the All-Star cast of regulars, the front office would be pleased.

* * *

Clearwater is a beautiful community on Florida's Gulf Coast, near Tampa, a retirement haven that has been the Phillies' spring training home since 1955. Jack Russell Stadium was replaced as the team's park for exhibition games in the Grapefruit League in 2004, and the Phils' average attendance has run between 7,000 and 9,000-plus per game in recent years at new Spectrum Field. Unlike many other big-league teams, which have hopped around communities in Florida and Arizona for their spring headquarters, the Phillies have retained allegiance to Clearwater for more than sixty years.

Clearwater is assuredly a part of Phillies history, a place where careers were made and broken, where players were first noticed or where they sometimes threw their last pitch or took their last at-bat. It is a playground resort for vacationers seeking to elude winter, but a place of very serious business for young players whose focus is making it to the majors.

Suffice it to say, the Bob Walks, Lonnie Smiths, and others were not in Clearwater to go jet skiing on Tampa Bay. They were there to make an impact on Dallas Green. The veterans, too, were on the prowl to see what young talent might be added to the club, as some of them were hurting from those near-miss playoff losses, results difficult to stomach and reconcile with since they believed in their own abilities and yet had ended recent seasons as also-rans.

There was no particular rallying cry in Clearwater, no blackboard messages pronouncing a theme to the season, a catchy phrase to latch onto. But there was an attitude: Our time is now.

"I sort of had that feeling when I first got over there in '79," said Greg Gross, a lefty-hitting pinch-hitter extraordinaire. He thinks the turning point for the Phillies was the acquisition of Rose. It was a statement that management was willing to up the ante to chase the crown. "When they added him it was thinking maybe he was the kind of guy who could handle the pressure. He was a great teammate. With him, there wasn't any class system."[2]

By that, Gross meant there were not really any cliques, no hierarchy of stars and benchwarmers. Rose was a common link who treated everyone the same. This would prove to be a valuable characteristic as key members of the 1980 Phillies were nothing if not naturally inclined to be grumpy. There were often caustic relations with the press, primarily newspaper reporters in those days, and it wasn't as if everyone was buddy-buddy with each other. Rose and Tug McGraw crossed all lines, as did such players as Gross, Del Unser, and infielder John Vukovich.

A sportswriter venturing into a pregame Phillies locker room never knew what snarling or "no comment" might be encountered. That was also true in a postgame locker room, especially if the game ended in defeat.

The ace of the pitching staff was Steve Carlton, by all definitions a star. Carlton won 329 games during his Hall of Fame career, second-most among southpaws behind Warren Spahn's 363. But for such a key figure on the team, he was virtually invisible except in those hours taking his regular turn on the mound.

Like Greta Garbo, he wanted to be alone, an early propo-
nent among ballplayers of hiding in the trainer's room to
avoid discussing his performance or his team's showing with
members of the media. The situation was such that whoever
was Carlton's catcher on a given day was often asked to act as
a translator of his pitching, explaining whether it was a curveball or a change-up that struck a batter out, or just what he
threw for the game-losing home run. That was Carlton being
Carlton.

Relief pitcher Ron Reed was a gifted enough athlete to also
play professional basketball in the NBA for the Detroit Pistons,
a much-admired achievement that could have made him a
popular figure in town. But sometimes Reed would aggressively
growl at sportswriters for no apparent reason and was skeptical
of Green's methods.

At one point in the season, Green issued a high-decibel rant
in the clubhouse that could be heard by writers in the hallway
outside. He loudly lectured players to get their acts together
during a losing stretch. This became a legendary pep talk in
Phillies annals.

General manager Owen also got fed up at one point and
visited the clubhouse to personally ream out individual players,
although the content of his speech was not overheard.

Feisty shortstop Larry Bowa at times openly feuded with
Green, once appearing on a radio show where he disparaged
the manager for benching slumping veterans in favor of untried
rookies.

Outfielder Bake McBride appeared at his locker one game
with adhesive tape over his mouth. It was his way of advertising

he did not want to talk to reporters, a reasonably blatant signal difficult to misinterpret.

By 1980, Philadelphia center fielder Garry Maddox was known as "The Secretary of Defense" because he so brilliantly covered ground. During his 15-year career, Maddox won eight Gold Gloves.

But Maddox was uncomfortable with Green's gruff managerial style from the beginning and wasn't sure the new man appreciated his skills and wanted him on the team. During spring training of 1980, Maddox was unsure about his status with the Phillies. He was about to start his option year and worried he might be traded. He wanted to remain with the team, but also wanted long-term security from his next contract. Maddox was looking for a solid raise from his $425,000 a year.

His agent, Jerry Kapstein, announced in mid-March that there was an impasse in negotiations. Maddox did not like the position he was in. Carpenter, the owner, reached out to meet privately with Maddox, not including his GM, manager, or Maddox's agent, but taking it upon himself to soothe the player's feelings. Carpenter told Maddox he might not be able to get the largest offer from the Phillies, but the club wanted and needed him. Maddox wanted to stay in Philadelphia, and this human interaction was welcomed.

"I asked him to do everything in his power to keep me with the Phillies," Maddox said of subsequently urging Kapstein to cut a deal.[3] He did sign a long-term contract with a raise to $675,000, but said the disruption was unsettling. "As I look back, that whole spring ordeal cost me. I didn't really get a chance to train, to get myself ready for the season the way I usually do. It ended up hurting me, but I didn't blame anyone for it."[4]

There was always something going on off the field with the 1980 Phillies, pretty much from the first moment to the last between March and October. Sometimes it was soap opera stuff. Sometimes it was the business of baseball. Once in a while it even involved baseball.

The phrase "City of Brotherly Love" did not apply inside the team's clubhouse. Of course, when any group of thirty or so men (players, manager, and coaches) are thrust together for months there are going to be testy times. The Phillies just seemed to have more of those fractious moments than other teams. Since they were simultaneously trying to cooperate their way to a pennant, it sometimes came off as unseemly. It seemed legitimate to ask why those guys weren't having more fun. They were playing baseball for a living, winning baseball, and the longtime goal appeared to be within their grasp.

Manager Danny Ozark was out, despite leading those winning teams into the playoffs, and Green, who had been the club's farm system director, was in to mold the talent into fighters who could go the extra mile, win the next round, and advance to the World Series.

After managing those last 30 games of the 1979 season, following Ozark's 65–67 run, Green had formed opinions about the veterans. As an indicator of what he thought about their approach, when players reported to Clearwater for spring training they were greeted by signs reading, "We, Not I." This was not a subtle statement, even if it was something that might more commonly be messaged to a high school or college team. Hmm. Enough said.

Green's formidable size as a 6-foot-5, 210-pound man with a deep voice and a stare that could compete with Superman's X-ray vision made some players uncomfortable. They knew he had evaluated them the preceding season and even though they were still present in the spring of 1980, they had been reading the Hot Stove rumors over the winter.

"If they want to trade me, then get it over with and trade me," said Bake McBride. "This whole winter, every time the phone would ring, I would think it was Owens calling to tell me I'd been traded. It got to the point where I wouldn't answer the phone."[5]

He was likely not alone in thinking that way during the off-season, but the Phillies did not make any major trades between seasons, so mostly the same old gang was gathered in Clearwater to give it another shot.

"We knew we had the best team in our division," said catcher Bob Boone, who at seventy-one in 2019 was still in the game as a vice president of the Washington Nationals. "We thought we had the best team in the National League. I knew we had a great team. I knew we were going to be there."[6]

Bob Walk was less convinced he was going to be there, as in Philadelphia, at any point during the 1980 season. He was a walk-on, so to speak, hoping to climb the last step to the majors by showing well in Clearwater.

There was uncertainty about the starting pitching, however, after 1979. Steve Carlton stood by himself, No. 1 in the rotation. Still, he was thirty-five and coming off an 18–11 season with a 3.62 earned run average, not his finest work. Was it possible Lefty was showing his age? Nonetheless, he needed assistance.

For the '79 team, Nino Espinosa went 14–12, while Ron Reed actually had the next-best record on the staff, although his 13–8 mark was formed in relief and his earned run average was a troublesome 4.15 for a guy whose job it was to come to the rescue. Randy Lerch went 10–13. The Phillies were looking for more out of Larry Christensen and Dick Ruthven. But the vagueness of how the slots were shaping up also meant there was opportunity for a guy like Walk.

When Walk became a professional ballplayer after being drafted in the fifth round of the amateur draft by the Phillies in 1976 out of College of the Canyons in Santa Clarita, California, he was excited just for the chance to do some traveling away from that community where he had also attended high school. He said his first thought was not of working his way up to the majors from those low-minor teams in South Carolina and North Carolina, but the perk of seeing other parts of the United States.

"I'm getting out of the small town I grew up in," Walk said thirty-nine years later, after his journey to the Phillies landed him in the majors. "I'd never traveled in my life. It was an adventure."[7]

It was not until Walk reached the Double A level of play that he even considered the prospect of possibly becoming a big-league pitcher.

"It was, 'Hey, I've got a chance to go to the big leagues,'" he said. "A year ago [after playing in A ball] I was pumping gas at a Texaco station."[8]

Trying to sort through the candidates, Green was not yet convinced Walk was ready for "The Show" and when the team went north to start the 1980 season, Walk went west to play for Triple-A Oklahoma City.

"I got off to a really good start in Oklahoma," Walk said, recalling what propelled him to Philadelphia.[9]

Walk went 5–1 with a 2.94 earned run average in 49 innings in Oklahoma City when he thought he might have sunk himself into a problematical situation. One night on the road, he drank at a bar in Des Moines until 2:30 a.m.

"They have bars there, too," Walk said. "I broke curfew pretty badly." When he was summoned to meet with manager Jim Snyder, he thought he was in for it, and mulled, *You might be in big trouble.* Instead, he was informed he was headed to the majors.[10]

This was not only good news for Walk, but for the Phillies and Green. They did not anticipate the value they would receive from the rookie.

One thing a young player like Walk was not going to do was mix it up with the veterans, take sides, or make waves in the clubhouse. He was thrilled to be there in Philadelphia and every minute counted to prove he should be kept around permanently. As every rookie knows—especially those not heralded in advance—the path between the big-league club and the club's high minors can be a two-way street.

In Walk's case, he was there for the duration, an emerging key figure relied on for the rest of the season. Bringing Walk up from the minors after cutting him in Clearwater turned out to be one of the most important personnel moves the Phillies made all season.

3

WHEN HOPE SPRINGS ETERNAL

SPRING IS WHEN the baseball fans are at their most optimistic. When all teams are 0–0, no one is in last place, and everybody is in first place. So when teams break from their spring training homes, everybody is happy. Until the games begin there is no cause for disappointment.

If believers in the Phillies prospects for a fine 1980 season could be quantified, it would be the companies that invested in the team's super boxes at Veterans Stadium.

At the rate of $20,000 to $25,000 a year, corporations leased one of the 23 spots to be assured they would not miss a pitch of what could become a special season. This was before the real proliferation of luxury boxes, sky boxes, and private boxes taking over sports teams' budgeting plans. There was a waiting list to obtain one of these.

The information was imparted in a *Philadelphia Inquirer* story the day before the season began, the implication being the average fan knew nothing of this. It was a wave of the future, though these particular super boxes were actually gussied up lousy seats.

The companies saw the potential, though, and as has become a staple of these types of seating, they wined and dined customers, gave seats to employees as perks, and generally used them for entertainment.

"We supply the paper goods," said Phillies vice president Bill Giles, "but they bring in their own booze, setups and beer. The boxes are catered either by Nilon or the Friendly Caterers. There is also a concession stand near there."[1]

This quaintly presumed there were still some fans who would eschew higher-class fare for the staple ballpark hot dog.

When one is attending a ballgame, it is assumed the game is the main event. Luxury boxes can serve as insurance entertainment if the home team is bad. But this season, the added benefit was the expectation the Phillies would be providing world-class entertainment with frequent victories.

The mood was certainly upbeat in Philadelphia. The Phillies, the comparatively so-so season of 1979 notwithstanding (it had still been a winning year!), gave off good vibes. They had a lineup dotted with stars, a new manager, and strong signals sent by management that a winner was to be expected.

Nor was this misplaced optimism. On paper, the Phillies looked to be as strong as anyone in the National League. The Los Angeles Dodgers had been an aggravation in recent years, besting the Phillies 3–1 in the best-of-five National League Championship Series twice in a row, in 1977 and 1978. That was after the Phillies lost the 1976 NLCS, 3–0, to the Cincinnati Reds, pretty much the wrap-up season for the Big Red Machine. There was no shame in winning the NL Eastern Division three times in a row—that was an accomplishment. But it was frustrating being unable to clear that last hurdle and stake a claim to even one pennant.

Del Unser, who rejoined the Phillies in 1979 after playing for them in 1973 and 1974, said the veterans who endured those losses seemed to have a particularly intense resolve at the beginning of the 1980 season.

"I thought all the pieces were there to do it," said Unser, who in 2018 concluded a half-century career in the majors as a player, coach and scout (40 of them with the Phillies). "There was a whole lot of experience. It was an experienced team that didn't need a whole lot of rah-rah"[2]

Younger baseball fans who do not know the sport's history, may not be aware that between 1876 (when the National League was founded) and 1968, there were no postseason playoffs aside from the World Series. Baseball did not establish the National League Championship Series and American League Championship Series until 1969, and has tweaked the format since, adding wild-card play and a Division Series.

Formed in 1883, the Phillies were originally known as the Quakers. Whether it was as the Quakers or Phillies, the nineteenth century was not a particularly good one for the Philadelphia-based franchise. That first year, the Quakers went 17–81. Some may have called that foreshadowing. A few half-decent years were mixed in, leading up to the modern structure of baseball as we know it with the American League's establishment in 1901 as a rival to the National League. When it became clear neither league was going to fold, the World Series began in 1903. This really did not affect the Phillies' lives much because the team was involved in a string of mediocrity, typically placing fourth or fifth—neither horrible nor victorious.

Then came 1915, when the Phillies won the first pennant in their history. Finishing with a 90–62 record, they earned the right to compete in the World Series against the Boston Red Sox. This was a pitching-dominated team under manager Pat Moran, with just one .300 hitter, first baseman Fred Luderus (who batted .315). He is not remembered as one of the team greats.

However, Grover Cleveland Alexander, who finished 31–10 with a 1.22 earned run average that season, is. The right-handed Alexander is one of the greatest pitchers of alltime, winner of 373 games, the-third-most ever along with Christy Mathewson. Boston had five 15-game winners, including Babe Ruth—still hurling more than swinging—who won 18. Future Hall of Famer Tris Speaker hit .322 while patrolling center field. The Red Sox won the Series handily, four games to one.

There were numerous grim seasons before the Phillies won another pennant and returned to the World Series thirty-five years later in 1950. In between, the Phillies were one of the most hapless long-term clubs in baseball history. First, they were periodically horrible. Then, they were consistently horrible. The word *winning* might as well have been spoken in a foreign language.

In 1921, the Phillies' record was 51–103. It was 50–104 in 1923, 51–103 in 1927, 52–102 in 1930, and 54–100 in 1936. Then things really got bad.

In 1938, the club sunk to 45–105 and the next year finished 45–106. A couple of rainouts not made up kept the schedule under 154 games. Starting in 1938, the Phillies lost more than 100 games five seasons in a row, with the low point being 1941 when their record was 43–111. However, in 1942, Philadelphia won just 42 games while losing 109.

When the 1949 team finished over .500 at 81–73, it was the first time in sixteen years the Phillies had posted a winning record. When the 1950 team actually claimed the National League pennant with a 91–63 record, the fans were delirious. It was a Phoenix-style resurrection of a long-moribund franchise.

The success was a shock to the baseball world, and the team was nicknamed the "Whiz Kids" because the roster was populated with so many outstanding young players just making their mark. Managed by Eddie Sawyer, the Phillies had future Hall of Famer Richie Ashburn (batting .303) in one outfield slot and Del Ennis (hitting .311) in another. Shortstop Granville Hamner hit .270 and fielded marvelously. None were over twenty-five years of age, with Ashburn just twenty-three.

Righty Robin Roberts, another future Hall of Famer, was also just twenty-three. His record was 20–11 and was complemented by Curt Simmons, who won 17 games at age twenty-one. The Phillies had a bigger lead, but won the pennant by just two games over the Brooklyn Dodgers. Simmons missed some time when his National Guard unit was called up because of the Korean War.

But the true revelation of the season was relief pitcher Jim Konstanty at a time when relievers were not such important figures. Konstanty, then thirty-three, put up his season of a lifetime. He finished 16–7 with 22 saves and a 2.66 earned run average in an astonishing 74 games and won the Most Valuable Player Award. Those 74 appearances were, at the time, a major-league record. Konstanty, son of a farmer in upstate New York, did not break into the majors until he was twenty-seven and never approached the results of his 1950 season again. He was only fifty-nine when he died, and is buried in Oneonta, New York, roughly 25 miles from the National Baseball Hall of Fame in Cooperstown.

That victory total for Roberts in 1950 made him the Phillies' first 20-game winner since Alexander won 30 in 1917. Roberts won 286 games in his 19-year career, and was a powerhouse of stamina on the mound, throwing 305 complete games in an era when pitchers were expected to go nine innings each time they were handed the ball. A seven-time All-Star, Roberts won more than 20 games in a season for the Phillies four times.

"It was a wonderful time for me," Roberts said of his stay in Philadelphia, when the team was winning more than losing.[3]

Konstanty was a one-hit wonder, though the face of a pennant-winning team, but Ashburn was on his way to winning two batting titles, and over a 15-year career would be a lifetime .308 hitter with six All-Star selections. A star on the 1950 pennant-winners, Ashburn, who was affiliated with the Phillies for nearly fifty years, was a broadcaster in 1980 and an in-the-stadium human reminder of the 1950 pennant so many gray hairs ago.

The Whiz Kids were dominated by the New York Yankees that season, dropping the Series in four games. Afterwards, Ashburn was so upset he disdained eating or drinking anything. "I couldn't swallow a corn flake," he said.[4]

Thirty years later, in 1980, Ashburn was a witness to the season unfolding. In those days, Ashburn—always popular with the Philadelphia faithful—also wrote a column for the *Philadelphia Bulletin*, an afternoon newspaper that was a local institution (though it went out of business in 1982, before the players on the championship team were exiting the sport).

Ashburn was a revered figure in Philadelphia. Once a player, he was now seen as being on the other side of the fence. He was a broadcaster for thirty-four years and was a writer, too. His boss wasn't the manager, but his audience was the same—the fans. He was just using different skills to entertain them.

"From a broadcaster's standpoint you cannot deceive the fans," Ashburn said. "Philadelphia fans are vocal, but they are knowledgeable. They know what's going on and I would be a fool to try to deceive them.[5]

Ashburn understood his changed relationship with the team.

"When I left the field and went into broadcasting, I still felt like a player and a jock. But I think from day one when I went into the booth the players did not consider me a player anymore."[6]

Still, Ashburn was at ground zero in 1950 and in 1980 was someone with a unique perspective on Phillies history.

* * *

If there was hunger in the Phillies lineup as the season began, there was just as much anticipation in Philadelphia. A Firestone tire advertisement in the *Philadelphia Inquirer* featured "Big League Bargains."[7] Also, much ado was made about the Phillie Phanatic's more formalized relationship with the team.

The Phanatic, one of the most beloved mascots in baseball history, first appeared on the diamond in 1978. Human-sized in height, the big, green, furry figure of considerable girth also somewhat resembled a *Sesame Street* character. Kid friendly, but also capable of making adults laugh, the Phanatic was a bird that did not fly, but one that entertained by waddling around and performing humorous antics.

A prominent baseball predecessor to the Phanatic was the esteemed San Diego Chicken. In 1977, the Phillies decided they wished to go the anthropomorphic route, and that was how the Phanatic was born. The Phillies put the New York City creative marketing firm of Harrison/Erickson with their connections to the Muppets to work to invent something fresh for their franchise.

The story goes that Phillies vice president Bill Giles was offered a deal paying $5,200 for the creation, plus the copyright, or paying $3,900 for just the Phanatic. Not foreseeing the tremendous popularity of the Phanatic, Giles opted for the lower cost. Five years later, Giles was part of a new team ownership group. The organization then brought the copyright at a cost of $250,000.

Normally, the human identity is kept secret as a colorful mascot (like a masked super hero) cavorts, but it was known early on that the Phanatic's alter ego was David Raymond of Delaware, then in his early twenties. Raymond was the son of the University of Delaware's prominent football coach, Tubby Raymond. For the 1980 season, David Raymond signed a contract to make 200 personal appearances inside and away from the ballpark. He had already been to Japan before the season started.

"They laughed at things that weren't funny to Philadelphia fans anymore," Raymond said. "They especially liked an imitation I had of sumo wrestlers."[8]

Raymond, and his longtime successor, Tom Burgoyne, always talked about the Phanatic in the third person, preserving the illusion for children that the Phanatic was a distinct individual and that the men were just good friends with the creature.

One way the Phanatic's act was enhanced was by scooting around the field on an ATV. That was introduced in 1980, too.

Raymond, his close, personal friend, let it slip as a sneak preview about the season that the Phanatic was going to be gifted a surprise vehicle.

Initially, Raymond said he had difficulty keeping his persona and the Phanatic's separate, but had come to terms with it by 1980. He said being funny was the crux of the whole routine, but he was sure the allegiance to the Phanatic would eventually run its course. Raymond was wrong about that. He stayed in the role through 1993, the Phanatic is still going strong, and a replica Phanatic is even on display in the National Baseball Hall of Fame in Cooperstown.

In spring training 2020, the Phillies, not content to let their popular mascot alone, began tinkering with the big green guy's design slightly.

During its lead-up to Opening Day, the *Philadelphia Inquirer* featured star third baseman Mike Schmidt in a story that explored why he was not more famous in the sport, concluding he may have been a tremendous player but was shortchanged in the charisma department.

By then, Schmidt was one of the best players in the game. He was on his way to slugging 548 home runs, had won four Gold Gloves in the 1970s, and was a regular on the All-Star team, but fans did not genuflect at his feet the way they had in the presence of Mickey Mantle and Willie Mays.

Schmidt was not seen as playful or fun-loving, not a wink-and-a-smile show business type, but as a serious guy. Yet his performance was the equivalent of a doctorate in academia or a Pulitzer Prize in journalism, for sure. He had the work ethic of a steel worker as well.

"The thing I really enjoy about the game," Schmidt said on the cusp of the season, "is the constant challenge of hitting a line drive. It looks so easy and it comes so easy sometimes, but technically, it's the most difficult thing to do in sports. There's so many variables against the hitter. To me, that's what makes the game challenging."[9]

Schmidt put together a 45-homer, 114-RBI season in 1979, so he was already a star, but by the end of 1980 he would be much more highly rated by the average baseball fan.

As the 1980 season opened, Pete Rose, beginning his second season as a Phillie, was sixth on Major League Baseball's all-time hits list with 3,372. Rose, thirty-nine that year, was fighting time as he sought to break an unbreakable record. Ty Cobb's total of 4,191 hits had been the standard since the Hall of Famer's retirement in 1928. There were still other players to pass along the way such as Honus Wagner, Tris Speaker, Stan Musial, and Hank Aaron, but Rose had long before cast his gaze to the horizon where Cobb stood.

After batting .331 with 208 hits in 1979—his debut year with the Phillies—Rose did not appear to be slowing down. He needed just 144 hits to surpass Speaker and Wagner, but that year couldn't reach Musial, who in his lengthy career with the St. Louis Cardinals set the National League record of 3,630 hits. Rose, who is the most versatile All-Star of all time, with selections at five positions, was slotted to play first base.

It was a good time to be Pete Rose. He owned a Rookie of the Year Award, a Most Valuable Player Award, was chasing one of the most hallowed records in the game, and after being part of two World Series championship teams with his hometown

Cincinnati Reds, he was now a key man on a potential pennant-winner in Philadelphia.

Harboring great optimism, the Phillies opened the 1980 season on April 11 at Veterans Stadium against the Montreal Expos. Steve Carlton was on the mound for Philadelphia and Steve Rogers, a very adept pitcher, was throwing for the Expos.

Starting the season off strong, the Phillies scored three runs in the home half of the first inning and added two more in the seventh, which was enough for a 5–3 victory. Carlton went the distance, striking out six while only walking one. But left fielder Greg Luzinski's bat basically won the game for the 48,460 fans in attendance. He accounted for those three first-inning runs with a homer, bashing a 2-2 slider to left.

"I guess if you would fantasize, that would be 'Fantasy Island' right there," Luzinski said.[10]

Luzinski stood 6-foot-1 and weighed 220 pounds. Adorned with the nickname "Bull," he had been with the Phillies since 1970 when he was just nineteen years old. But after a 35-homer, 101-RBI season in 1978, he dropped off to 18 and 81 the following year. In the offseason, after '79, he began to shed some weight.

"He worked so hard to get weight off," catcher Bob Boone said of Luzinski. "This year is very important to him. So for him to respond in the normal Bull way—well, I'm really pleased for him."[11]

The players had already been around Green for a couple of slices of time; for those 30 games at the end of the 1979 season and through spring training. Yet on Opening Day he made copies of a list of rules to be followed during the season, emphasizing where he was coming from. They included a dress code, a rule against drinking on the team plane without his authorization, and a set of curfews—one a.m. following day games and 2:00 a.m. following night games. He also prohibited card games and in sternly worded phrasing, declared: "Any player acting unprofessionally, or who embarrasses me or the organization will be fined at my discretion."[12]

There was more. He didn't say anything about taking away their scholarships, but he seemed to cover everything else. This was Green the baby-sitter/general issuing orders.

This was all made public in a column by the *Philadelphia Inquirer*'s Frank Dolson, who focused his season-opening piece on Green making his seasonal debut as a manager and winning his first game, but also reminding the public of the nature of the man in charge of the club.

"The new era had begun," Dolson wrote. Then he quoted Green, saying, "I think we have great ability. We've proven in the past we can win. We've also proven we haven't won the whole ball of wax. The only ingredient I can come up with comes down to the true character of the team.

"This team has told me they want to stay together as a team and win the world championship. To do it, we've got to search ourselves, forget the 'I,' forget our own petty problems. We've got to be able to set those aside and think of the team for a year."[13]

After the high of the opening-night home victory, the Phillies promptly began drifting. Although Carlton was 3–0, by the end of April the team was just 6–9, in fourth place in the division, and 4 ½ games out of first place. No other Phils pitcher had more than one win. No regular was hitting .300. Could the Phillie Phanatic hit? Or pitch? The arrow was pointed toward last place, not first.

4

STEVE CARLTON AND THE
PITCHING STAFF

APRIL 11 WAS a satisfying day at Veterans Stadium. Steve Carlton, the fastballing left-hander with the exceptional slider, was the Phillies' opening-game pitcher and he was the winner in the 5–3 decision over the Montreal Expos.

This was Carlton at his routine best, not his overpowering best. This was exactly what manager Dallas Green and the Phillies front office expected from their ace.

Carlton had been with the Phillies since 1972 after starting his major-league career with the St. Louis Cardinals in 1965. He had been in the bigs since he was twenty years old, and was best known for both the speed of his best pitch and his stamina, going the distance as often as possible.

During Carlton's last season with the Cardinals, in 1971 he finished 20–9. His first season with the Phillies was one of the most spectacular pitching seasons of all time—within context. In his 41 starts, Carlton went 27–10, the most wins in Major League Baseball, while also leading with 30 complete games. His earned run average was a NL-leading 1.97, as was his 346 1/3 innings and 310 strikeouts. That work was good enough to win him the NL Cy Young Award, but that was only part of the story. Carlton accomplished this superior pitching for a truly terrible team. The Phillies finished with a 59–97 record, some 37 ½ games behind the Pittsburgh Pirates in the National League East standings. It was basically a goliath effort for a team of Davids.

Carlton had followed that stupendous season with some uneven ones, but also won 20 games for the Phillies in 1976 and 23 in 1977. In 1979, Carlton went 18–11, so he was still a prime cut heading into the 1980 campaign.

In April, when the 1980 Phillies of such confidence did falter, Carlton did not. On April 16, Carlton bested the Cardinals, 8–3, going 8 1/3 innings. He won his third game on April 26, shutting out the Cardinals, 7–0. That was a complete game one-hitter, a masterful showing. Catcher Ted Simmons's second-inning single was the only safety. Simmons also reached on Carlton's only walk of the game.

On May 1, Carlton moved to 4–1 as Philadelphia beat the New York Mets, 2–1. Tug McGraw came out of the bullpen in that one and threw 2 1/3 innings, the kind of work closers do not often tackle in today's game.

Carlton was born on December 22, 1944, and was thirty-five during the 1980 season; a 6-foot-4, hard-throwing 210-pounder who seemed to have his most impressive muscle residing in his left arm. It was quite the versatile left arm, indeed. Even when he was young, Carlton could throw—although not always in the manner baseball stars develop. He liked to hunt and once killed a rabbit at 90 feet with a rock after his rifle jammed. Another time he decapitated a quail by flinging an ax at it.

He studied Eastern philosophy on his own and played basketball and baseball in high school. After attending Miami Dade Junior College, Carlton signed with the St. Louis Cardinals for a $5,000 bonus, certainly a bargain. He made his major-league debut in a 1965 game against the Chicago Cubs—in relief. As Carlton matured on the mound, the development of a slider to complement his fastball at times made him unhittable. He did not welcome the trade to the Phillies from St. Louis for pitcher Rick Wise, and protested vigorously. He had no recourse in an era before free agency, but Carlton then gained his greatest fame and recorded his greatest achievements with the Phils.

Carlton was traded to Philadelphia when he was battling with the Cardinals for more money over a new contract for a second time after settling for a two-year, $40,000 per year deal that had expired. Wise was seeking bigger bucks from the Phillies as well. At the time, analysts viewed the trade as an even-up deal. Looking back now, they were obviously wrong. Wise was a very good pitcher, winning 188 games in his career, but he was not a Hall of Famer.

"I was shocked at first," said Carlton, who was still talking to sportswriters at the time of the trade. "I hate to leave the Cards. I wish I had known they were considering a trade. It might have changed my mind. But I'm sure there was a bitter taste left over from two years ago."[1]

The Phillies gave Carlton a one-year contract at $65,000 for 1972, the amount he said he was seeking from St. Louis. That's peanuts by current league standards. After Carlton slashed and burned his way through National League hitters that season, the Phillies upped his salary to $165,000 in one swoop.

Except for the numbers written next to his name in the record books, however, Philadelphia fans and sportswriters never really got to know him. That was his choice.

In 1973, Carlton retreated into a cone of silence with the press (with the exception of the team's radio broadcasters with whom he conversed sometimes on non-baseball topics). Occasionally, some theorized on why Carlton remained incommunicado. The only statement that floated out from his bunker in the trainer's room inside the clubhouse was that talking to reporters interrupted his concentration and if that happened his ability to pitch well was affected. It was also said that Carlton had been once burned by a journalist and held it against the entire profession. The "Carlton Rules" persisted for the last 12 years of his career, so no one was going to glean insights on how he felt about his swift 1980 start and the Phillies' slow start.

This was particularly irksome to the media, since Carlton was such an important member of the team and how it fared. Hardly any other ballplayers went to such extremes of walling off all reporters. George Hendrick, who was a solid-hitting outfielder with the Cardinals and played in the majors for 18 years, was also mum, even during the 1980 season when he slugged 25 home runs and drove in 109 runs while batting .302. Veteran Associated Press sportswriter Ralph Bernstein observed that year it would be a sportswriters' worst nightmare if Carlton had a no-hitter going with two outs in the ninth inning and Hendrick broke it up with a base hit.

A year later, with the policy of silence still being enforced, Atlanta Braves broadcaster Ernie Johnson noted that during that 1981 season of Fernandomania, the two best pitchers in the National League "don't speak English: Fernando Valenzuela (who was from Mexico) and Steve Carlton."[2]

Not immediately before or after games did Carlton talk to writers or broadcasters about his career, though sometimes, much after the fact, he did. When Hal Bodley, a Phillies beat writer for the *Wilmington News-Journal* in Delaware was working on a book commemorating the 1980 season, Carlton did grant him an interview.

One thing they spoke about was Carlton's extraordinary 1972 season. Even he acknowledged how remarkable it was.

"I'm never going to have a year like 1972 again," Carlton said. "I know that. That was a matter of precision. I made pitches during that year that were unbelievable. I was able to put the ball where I wanted to. Sometimes they caught the corner by a fraction of an inch. This is a game of inches. I was able to throw breaking balls when I was behind in the count. I threw some nasty sliders."[3]

It may have been true that Carlton believed it was impossible to match his 1972 season, but the Phillies were hoping for something close to it … and he delivered a season that was probably the runner-up in his career—right from the start of the 1980 schedule. Whenever it was Carlton's turn to pitch, his teammates had no worries. Much was expected of him because he had set such a high standard.

"I can only remember him coming out of a game one time before an inning was over," Bob Walk, a rookie at the time, recalled years later. "That was the absolute stud he was. He was just an incredible pitcher."[4]

What the Phillies needed in 1980, though, were more Carltons, or at least pitchers who were worthy complements in the rotation. That was a Dallas Green–prompted search heading into the season, and in the earliest days of the campaign he saw little that reassured him. While Carlton was winning nearly every time out, it was not clear what might happen on the days he did not start.

Right-hander Dick Ruthven, from Fremont, California, was twenty-nine that season. He broke in as a Phillie in 1973, went to Atlanta, and then rejoined the Phillies in 1978. Throwing for the two teams combined in '78, Ruthven had his best season at 15–11, with 13 of those wins for the Phillies. Philadelphia was waiting for him to truly blossom.

On the second day of the 1980 season, when the Phillies beat Montreal to go to 2–0. Ruthven was the winner, but it would be his only victory of the month. By the time he got another one, on May 6, he was 2–2—too soon to tell what the season held.

Larry Christenson picked off one of the April victories, too, fighting to make himself an integral part of the rotation. He also bested Montreal, though in a different series. Another right-hander, Christenson, who was born in Everett, Washington, had been with the Phillies since 1973, winning 11 games in 1975, 13 in 1976 despite being removed from a game on a stretcher with back spasms incurred while he was trying to avoid a high and inside pitch, and won a career-best 19 in 1977, with 13 more in 1978. Christenson then slumped to 5–10 in 1979 due to an elbow injury and a broken collarbone, but was being counted on to regain his old form in 1980.

Christenson was 3–0 when his elbow failed him again and he underwent surgery, losing the bulk of the season to recovery, although he did somehow return to pitch late in the regular season and compile a 5–1 record, as well as participating in the playoffs. The loss of Christenson early carried the potential to be a major blow.

That problem meant there was more reliance on Ron Reed, the 6-foot-6, 215-pound former professional basketball player who had played two professional sports at once for a while. Reed, who came out of Notre Dame, began his major-league career as a starter and maintained the role from 1966 through 1975, mostly with the Braves (though briefly with the Cardinals). From the time Reed joined the Phillies in 1976 he was a reliever, though one who threw many more innings than most relievers do in today's game.

Reed appeared in 59, 60, 66, and 61 games for the Phillies out of the bullpen between 1976 and 1979, throwing a high of 128 innings and a low of 102. He also filled holes when starters gave up too many runs. But Reed was now thirty-seven years of age, and Green was not going to rely on him to be an everyday starter.

Initially, Reed did not relish this new role. He believed starting was the be-all—not relieving.

"I always felt that once you're sent to the bullpen, the next step is out the back door," Reed said in 1979. "But, boy, was I wrong about that." Reed even admitted that when then-manager Danny Ozark asked him to relieve he was upset. "I'll be the first to admit I wasn't always a 'we' player. The only thing I used to be concerned with was myself. It was just a matter of youth and immaturity. But I don't have that problem anymore and the Phillies are the reason."[5]

Selfishness was precisely the trait Green was trying to eradicate, so in 1980 he would not have tolerated the previous Reed.

As it was, life was not always harmonious between the pitcher and skipper.

The third of Christenson's spring victories came on May 17, he allowed two earned runs over five innings, as the Phillies topped the Houston Astros, 4–2. After Philadelphia's weak April and slowness to recover, the team was just two games over .500.

Then Christenson was gone. Probably for the season, it was initially thought, but definitely for the foreseeable future. Meanwhile, Bob Walk was tearing it up in Oklahoma City with his 5–1 record. The need for starting pitching was acute, and he got the call.

Walk made his major-league debut on May 26, 1980, against the Pittsburgh Pirates—a team that would figure prominently in his future. When he was called up, Walk arrived for a day game and pulled on his new No. 41 jersey.

"I walked through the old tunnel at the Vet and I remember how amazing the uniform felt," Walk recalled years later. "The first thing I saw in my big-league career was Mike Schmidt and Greg Luzinski going back-to-back [hitting homers]."[6]

The Pirates were a tough team at the time, featuring Willie Stargell, Dave Parker, and Bill Madlock in the batting order. "I had nervousness," Walk said. "The Pirates had all those scary bats. I didn't know what was going to happen."[7]

In the first inning, Walk thought he should have been 0-2 on Parker, who ended up walking. "I didn't get the calls," he said.[8]

The next batter was Stargell, who hit 475 lifetime home runs, made seven All-Star teams, and was elected to the Hall of Fame on the first ballot in 1988. "I am very proud that the first major-league home run I gave up was to a guy like Willie Stargell,"

Walk said with a sense of humor he probably didn't feel at the time.[9]

Yep, Stargell ripped a 2-1 pitch out of the park and Walk trailed, 2–0, in his first inning in the majors. He lasted 2 2/3 innings and allowed five runs, though on only two hits as he walked five while striking out four. After Walk was lifted, the Phillies came back and won the game, 7–6, saving him from a defeat. Reed, the fifth Phillies pitcher of the game, was the beneficiary of a bottom-of-the-ninth rally.

Pitchers on a short leash after just being called up to the majors have been sent back to the minors in a hurry after such outings, but the Phillies did not pull the trigger. Things got better for both the team and for Walk, and he notched his first big-league win on June 6.

It was not as if that one was a thing of beauty, either. Walk allowed 10 hits and five earned runs in 5 2/3 innings, but the Phillies edged the Chicago Cubs, 6–5. Sometimes pitchers lose games they deserve to win and sometimes they win games they figure to lose. This game could easily have been a Walk loss, but when it was over, with a little help from his friends, his record was 1–0.

5

PETE ROSE

CHARLIE HUSTLE WILL always—first and foremost—be remembered as a Cincinnati Red. However, there will be an asterisk next to that in Philadelphia. Yes, Peter Edward Rose made his reputation while playing for his hometown team, but Phillies fans will always remember him fondly in connection with their breakthrough 1980 team.

Heck, he chose them! Rose was already a 16-year veteran with two rings when he became a free agent after the 1978 season. There was competitive bidding for his services, but the Phillies won out—even if they did not offer the most money over the longest term. Rose wanted to play with a winner, and in the late 1970s the Phillies were winners ... just not the top-of-the-heap winners. Rose, management felt, could be the missing piece. The last piece to making the team a World Series champ.

"To be honest with you, I took the smallest offer," Rose said recently. "Ewing Kauffman [owner of the Kansas City Royals] offered me an already-proven oil well. Augie Busch [St. Louis

Cardinals and Budweiser owner] offered me a beer distributorship. The Pittsburgh Pirates offered me race horses. Ted Turner [Atlanta Braves] offered me $1 million a year and $100,000 for life."[1]

Instead, Rose settled for ready access to Philadelphia's pretzels and cheesesteaks, and, oh, for a $3.2-million contract spread over four years. That was big money in baseball back then, though not in 2020 when some players are making $30 million a year … which could cover establishment of numerous soft pretzel carts and cheesesteak shops. Of course, Rose's deal would still be big money in the real world today.

By the late 1970s, Rose was appreciated as one of the best players in baseball, a superstar—not because he smacked the ball out of the yard, but because he was a genius at knocking out hits, scoring runs, getting on base, and his willingness to field any position and play it at an All-Star level. There was also the fact that he was a symbol of going all out 100 percent of the time. A player who, somewhat like a point guard in basketball, helped make the players around him better with his positive attitude in the clubhouse. There was not really anyone else like Rose in the sport with the same combined attributes—maybe not ever.

He was also approachable, cooperative with fans and the media … just a guy who enjoyed talking baseball almost as much as he loved playing it. The man didn't have to tell you he lived and breathed the game. He exuded that fact so thoroughly it was like an aroma surrounding him.

This was part of his all-around package right from the beginning of his major-league career in 1963 (when he won the National League Rookie of the Year Award as mainly a second baseman). Rose made things happen on the diamond that season, batting .273 with 13 stolen bases and 170 hits.

Rose did not take a lackadaisical approach to anything. While other players strolled to first base when they received a walk, Rose sprinted down the line. He ran out to his position in the field. Some other players considered him a show-off because he did that. His actions did not start a trend, but over time everyone realized this was merely Pete being Pete.

Rose's measurements were listed at 5-foot-11 and 192 pounds. He played a small man's game, but he was strong and up close appeared more muscular than he did from the seats.

It took a little time for Rose to fully mature on the field, but by his third season was an All-Star for the first of seventeen times, batted .312, and led the league in hits with 209—one of ten times during his 24-year playing career Rose would reach the 200-hit mark. He began showing his durability in 1965, too, when he played in all 162 games and had 757 plate appearances. That was one of six times Rose led all of baseball in plate appearances (and would lead the NL in 1978). To qualify for eligibility for a batting title, a player must have 502 plate appearances. Since Rose stayed healthy, it was never a close call for him. Rose was forty-five years of age before he played in fewer than 119 games in a season, except for the 1981 labor strike year when the season was cut short.

Rose was a 13-time .300 hitter and a three-time batting champion by the time he became a free agent, and had been a member of the celebrated Big Red Machine Cincinnati team that won World Series titles in 1975 and 1976, which has been acclaimed by some as one of the greatest teams in big-league history. As recently as 1976, Rose made $188,000 for a season. He was coming off a two-year, $375,000 deal when his contract expired. Rose should have been a break-the-bank type of player for the Reds, but they did not want to pay him big money. It was not in the organization's DNA—at least at the time.

"I didn't want to leave the Reds," Rose said.[2]

But he liked the Phillies, not only for the team's potential, but because of some of the top players on the roster. Men like Mike Schmidt, Larry Bowa, and Greg Luzinski, whom he respected on and off the field. "I'd go out to eat with those guys," Rose said. "We were all about the same age."[3]

Equally as important was what Phillies' management saw in him. There should have been no mysteries. "I walked in with two World Series rings and 3,000 hits," Rose said. "Pete Rose is what they saw twelve times a year (playing against him).[4]

Indeed, what was not to like? If there was one question about taking on Rose and making a long-term commitment to him, it was his age. For the 1979 season, Rose was going to be thirty-eight. Sudden slippage in performance is probably the biggest worry general managers have when negotiating contracts. But Rose was still playing like he was in his prime. In 1978, he played in 159 games, came to the plate 783 times, smashed 51 doubles, and batted .302—and he was still an All-Star. If there was risk in signing Rose, it was in no way apparent.

Both parties signed on the dotted line and, beginning in 1979, they were partners. As a demonstration that he was worth the money, Rose was very much Rose that year, the one that began with Danny Ozark in charge and ended with Dallas Green as manager. Rose batted .331 with 95 walks, led the NL in on-base percentage, and, yes, made the All-Star team—his first appearance for anyone but the Cincinnati Reds.

"I had a great year, but we didn't win that first year," Rose said.[5]

The team's overall outcome, however, was definitely not his fault. One day Rose was served with divorce papers leading up to a night game, and then played his heart out and hit well. Luzinzki, Rose said, asked him how he did it without being distracted. Rose said it was his job and responsibility not to let anything interfere with his concentration on the field, "whether I'm hitting .460 or .160. I'm not going to involve my teammates."[6]

Rose did involve his teammates in other ways. His style of play was an example, as well as his enthusiasm in the clubhouse before a game, which helped energize the other players. He came to play every day and enjoyed playing every day.

"Pete was the missing piece of the puzzle," said shortstop Larry Bowa years later. "Pete, there's no one like him. His hustle, his energy all rubbed off. Pete would say, 'It's fun to play.' That was huge."[7]

Rose's 1980 start mirrored that of the team, or there could have been some cause and effect. As April ended with the Phils at 6–9, Rose was hitting an uncharacteristic .226. He was the full-time regular at first base and played every day. It took dynamite to get Rose out of the lineup, and he was bound to heat up because … well, he had always hit.

However, May opened not so much differently than April had closed. Though they won the first two games of the season, they would not get back to .500 until winning the first three in May to get to 9–9, and taking the next two of three (both wins against the Braves) before they had a winning record after their May 6 victory, bringing them to 11–10 (their first time over .500 since April 19, when they were 4–3). Was that jump-starting a run? Not quite. On May 17, Christenson pushed his record to 3–0 and the Phillies went to bed at 15–13. It was the first time they were two games above break-even since the first two games of the season. At that point they more resembled the 1979 Phillies than the clubs that won National League East crowns for three years in a row before that.

Dallas Green was not the most patient man in the city, and when he saw something he did not like, he spoke up. Still, baseball is the long game, a season that when extending into the playoffs and World Series, lasts for six months. How soon do you begin to panic? Being 10 games under .500 in mid-May would provoke front office discussions. Being two games over might not be the fast start a team may have hoped for, but it is hardly damning or dooming. It helps if no other team in the division runs away and hides with a spectacular start. On May 17, the Phillies were in second place and only three games out of first, so no harm as of yet. A little more consistency might be nice. A little winning streak to flex a few muscles and show the rest of the league what this team was all about.

On that day, when the Phillies topped the Houston Astros, Rose had two hits. Over those first 17 days in May he would bump up his batting average 17 points to .243. He was getting there.

The Phillies seemed to be inching forward at the same pace. In 1980, the NL East included the Expos, Pirates, St. Louis Cardinals, New York Mets, and Chicago Cubs, in addition to the Phillies. The Pirates won the division, the pennant, and the World Series in 1979. The others had been also-rans behind the Phillies in those other late-1970s years, but the Cardinals and Expos had also finished ahead of the Phillies in '79, so it was no foregone conclusion around the league that Philadelphia could rebound and surpass them all.

Pittsburgh still had the power hitters of Willie Stargell and Dave Parker in their lineup that Bob Walk so respected. The Cardinals were anchored by .300 hitters Ted Simmons, George Hendrick, Keith Hernandez, and Garry Templeton, but had no true ace on the mound. That season their top winner was Pete Vuckovich with 12 wins and Bob Forsch with 11. They had added Jim Kaat, who went 8–7 after he parted with the Phillies, to the rotation. The Cardinals were projected to do much better than they did. From an 86-win season they declined to 74 despite their hitting prowess.

The team that was receiving extra attention, that for the first time in its history seemed to be a genuine pennant threat, was the Expos. Manager Dick Williams, who had led the Boston Red Sox to an improbable 1967 American League pennant and then skippered the Oakland Athletics to World Series championships (and was on his way to the Hall of Fame) was at the helm for the Canadian club.

Williams was blessed with some deadly weapons, including catcher Gary Carter and outfielder Andre Dawson, also both bound for the Hall of Fame. As is so often the case, the Expos could have used some more pitching, with starters Steve Rogers and Scott Sanderson both finishing 16–11, though twenty-one-year-old rookie Bill Gullickson proved to be a wise addition.

Over the course of the 1980 season, 145 players appeared in their first big-league games. Two of them—Harold Baines and Lee Smith—became Hall of Famers, both elected by the Veterans Committee in 2018. Every team dreams of unearthing a player who will reach the pinnacle of achievement, but those debuts are rare. There were some other good ones, including Fernando Valenzuela, who had a brief call-up with the Los

Angeles Dodgers, but would not launch "Fernandomania" until the 1981 season.

Of those on the list, six broke into the majors in Phillies uniforms that year. Outfielder Bob Dernier played in 10 games, catcher Ozzie Virgil played in one, pitcher Scott Munninghoff in four (going 0–0 and serving the only big-league action of his career), And lefty reliever Mark Davis got into two games at age nineteen. Davis had a 15-year major-league career and won the Cy Young Award by leading the National League in saves in 1989, but did so for the San Diego Padres. Then there was pitcher Marty Bystrom, whose first game was not until September. And, of course, Bob Walk, the biggest rookie contributor of the lot.

Green said he wanted to work young players into his lineup, but no rookie position players made an impact that year. At different times during the season, he was hurting for pitchers and two of the rookies he called upon, Bystrom and Walk, were difference makers.

Of course, Green was on the lookout for another Pete Rose, too. Unfortunately Pete Roses do not grow on trees—at least, not this kind of rose. Being thirty-nine was not much more of an obstacle for him than being thirty-eight.

* * *

On May 31, the Phillies overwhelmed the Chicago Cubs at Wrigley Field, 7–0. That day was pretty much the Steve Carlton show, as the lefty threw seven innings, allowed four hits, and struck out 11. At that point in the season, Carlton was 9–2 with a 1.84 earned run average, raising the question of how he had lost two games.

Perhaps noticed with just a little bit less fanfare, Rose had two hits in the game and celebrated Memorial Day with a .284 average. Since his sluggish beginning, Rose had increased his batting average by nearly 60 points. That was more like Pete.

The thing most identified with Rose, aside from the number of hits he piled up, like logs beside a fireplace for winter wood, was how he played in the field and on the basepaths, whether he was on a hot streak or in a slump. That was an offshoot of his built-in hustle gene—and it pretty much was in his genes.

Rose's father, Harry Francis Rose, was nicknamed "Pete." He and his wife, LaVerne, always encouraged Pete to compete in sports. The elder Rose coached his son and demanded the constant effort and hustle that were clearly passed on as a stern recommendation. He did not want a loafer in the house.

When Rose ran over Ray Fosse at home plate in the 1970 All-Star Game, it was a play that could be admired as going all out regardless of circumstances, but it infamously severely injured Fosse's shoulder and affected the rest of his career. Rose said he was not attempting to injure Fosse and his goal was to score the winning run for the National League, which he did. Some criticized Rose for going so hard in what was only an "exhibition" game. But Rose always played to win and this was hardly a spring training exhibition, it was *the* All-Star Game. Afterwards, he told sportswriters that was how his dad, Harry Francis, had taught him how to play the game.

The critics did not understand that Pete Rose was never going to ease up on a ballfield—nor did his managers want him to do so. In the autumn of 2018, reminiscing about his career with the Phillies and beyond, Rose gave this explanation for his style: "If you knew my dad, you'd know why I played the way I did."[8]

* * *

The 1975 World Series was an epic showdown between the Cincinnati Reds and Boston Red Sox. The sixth game is regarded as perhaps the finest World Series contest of all, but the Series would not be decided until Game Seven. The Reds outlasted the Red Sox, winning four games to three. If Boston had won that game and that Series, nobody would be discussing the Big Red Machine today.

It was 3–3 entering the ninth inning of Game Six, with the Reds at the plate. Cincinnati worked Jim Burton for two walks, a sacrifice, and a single for the 4–3 victory. Rose drew one of those walks, also adding two hits in the contest. But he believed his biggest contribution came earlier on the basepaths when he slid hard at Boston second baseman Denny Doyle.

"We won the World Series in 1975 because I broke up a double play," Rose said. "I knocked him [Doyle] on his ass and he threw it in the dugout."[9] That was one of two errors Doyle made in the deciding game.

Rose ruminated about many such plays during his career and the attitude he brought to such situations. "I've got to try to knock him on his ass," Rose said of any second baseman and his obligation to his team to try to prevent an out as typifying his game temperament and demeanor.[10]

That was no secret. Besides his consistently high average, when the Phillies entered the free-agent market in their bid for

Rose, that was part of what they were buying. They were after a take-no-prisoners approach on the field, and Rose provided it.

Philadelphia sports fans are renowned as difficult to please. There is the famous story about the time they booed Santa Claus at an Eagles game in 1968. The tale has solidified in legend, and it is true. At the request of the team, a fan dressed up as Santa Claus and was asked to cavort with the cheerleaders on the field at halftime of a December 15 game against the Minnesota Vikings. This was the last game of the season at Franklin Field, and the Eagles were on their way to concluding a 2–12 season with another loss. Eagles fans had had plenty of practice booing that year, and Santa was also on the receiving end of some snowballs thrown at him by dissatisfied spectators. Some may say they were just not in the Christmas spirit.

That is always the story told to summarize just how tough Philadelphia fans are to please. But Rose did not see things that way. "I really enjoyed Philadelphia," he said. "Here's the Philadelphia fan in my eyes: They want you to play hard and they want you to win."[11]

Which meant, basically, they agreed with Pete Rose about the important things in life.

6

DALLAS GREEN

HE WAS THE alpha male in the dugout and clubhouse, by title and by nature. Dallas Green was the leader of the wolfpack, and he had little tolerance for those not willing to follow. If his men let him down, if they showed a lack of fire, he would light one.

When the Phillies turned the team over to Green late in the 1979 season, asking him to replace Danny Ozark, they were making a multi-pronged statement. The front office indicated it was not happy with a team that was floundering in the lower reaches of the National League East after three straight seasons of playoff ball, and there was discontent with the play of a club that was flirting with .500. The insertion of Green, the farm system director, was a testament of faith in a man who had closely watched many of the Phillies' regulars on their way up. But it was also an admission the brass did not like the team's mood. They knew if the players were sloughing off at all, Green would deflate egos and kick butts.

Green, then forty-four, had been in baseball for decades, but this was his first shot at a big-league manager's job. He had been a major-league pitcher and a minor-league manager and a front office executive. He was now standing in the brightest spotlight of his career, and introduced himself with distinct candor when he got the job. Some players like to confide in managers about their personal lives. Some players want to be pals with the manager. Green was not that sort of guy. His demeanor did not encourage the notion he was going to be a player's close personal friend. He was not touchy-feely. What he wanted from a guy was 100 percent effort and production that justified his staying in the lineup, or on the roster.

Players were more likely to fear Green than buddy up to him, more likely to be reamed out by him than given a hug, or have an arm placed around a shoulder in encouragement.

Just as Phillies owner Ruly Carpenter, vice president Bill Giles, and general manager Paul Owens understood exactly what to expect from Pete Rose when they signed him as a free agent, they knew what placing Green at the helm of the team would be like. For others, who may not have known him so well since his leadership and administrative jobs played out in small markets or behind the scenes, Green told all what to expect.

"I express my thoughts," Green said. "I'm a screamer, a yeller and a cusser. I never hold back."[1]

If profanity offended you, cover your ears. If you didn't wish to be criticized after making an error or striking out, well, be perfect next time.

George Dallas Green was born on August 4, 1934, in Newport, Delaware. He spent most of his life, professionally and otherwise, living either in Philadelphia or within hailing distance of it, except for brief playing stints within a 100 miles of the community. Green's hometown was 35 miles from Philadelphia and he attended college at the University of Delaware, also pretty much right down the street. Green stood 6-foot-5 or 6-foot-6, depending on some listings. That was a good height for a pitcher in the 1950s, and his size emphasized the firmness of his verbal delivery during his managerial days.

The right-hander was twenty-five years old when he broke into the majors with the Phillies in 1960. During parts of eight seasons in the bigs, mostly in Philly (but also very briefly with the New York Mets and Washington Senators), Green's lifetime mark was 20–22 with a 4.26 earned run average. Green's best season was 1963, when he finished 7–5. He was also part of the 1964 club that collapsed with a late-season fade when the NL pennant was all but clinched. Green knew firsthand about the suffering Phillies fans had endured.

Green was finished with the playing field in 1967, but his baseball career was far from over. He managed a Phillies Class A team in Huron in 1968, and Pulaski in the Appalachian League in 1969. The following year, Green became assistant farm director, and became head of the club's farm system in 1972. That's what he was doing when the Phillies called upon him to manage the big club.

This was portrayed as an interim job, with Green evaluating personnel as he guided the team through its final 30 games of the 1979 season. It was not a job he really sought, nor the career path he wanted to follow. But there were signs right from the beginning that the Phillies' higher-ups thought Green's stay in the dugout might last a bit longer than 30 games.

"Dallas is going down on the field on an interim basis," Owens announced. "But don't rule him out for next year." Green countered by announcing his plans, saying, "Being a general manager is my goal."[2]

Ozark was a baseball lifer. Born in 1923, he was a minor-league hitter of note, cracking more than 200 homers. But even with those numbers, he never got the big-league call-up . He managed in the minors and his first major-league appearance was as a coach with the Los Angeles Dodgers in 1965. He spent eight seasons in that role under Hall of Fame manager Walt Alston.

The Phillies summoned him for the top rung in the dugout for the 1973 season, and he presided over the rebuilding of the last-place 1972 team, turning the Phillies into a perennial winner and playoff presence. Ozark had performed admirably, but something was lacking in 1979, even after Pete Rose was added to the team. Ozark was fired with a month remaining and with the team two games under .500. It was too late to think of making the playoffs, but Green did turn the team around in a short time and that kindled the desire for management to keep him in the job.

While the 1979 Phillies under Green did revive, there were still indicators in the dugout that turned him off. He felt there was a prima donna attitude despite there being several first-rate veterans around. He knew some level of a shake-up was necessary. "It's not going to be a country club," Green said. "It's going to be tough."[3]

Ozark was in his late fifties and a lot mellower than Green. His nurturing style had worked as young players were added to the roster during the 1970s, and those under him enjoyed playing for the man. They felt he treated them like mature adults.

"Ozark put out the lineup the first day of the season and left us alone," said catcher Bob Boone. "We policed ourselves."[4]

Everything was hunky dory for years—especially after two 101-win seasons (in 1977 and 1978). But when the team began failing in 1979, management suspected internal erosion and change was urgently needed. Used to the way Ozark managed his players, those in the clubhouse were shocked with the way Green would verbally beat them up. He had issued the warning that it was his style to let his anger, his emotions, run free. Over the years since, Boone has been blunt about what the players thought of Green.

"We hated him," Boone said in one interview. "He was driving us crazy." But Boone admitted the approach seemed to spark something in the group. "I don't know if it was a unique approach, but it was a relationship that worked."[5] At least in terms of results, if not necessarily in terms of cementing enduring friendships.

At another time, Boone said of the Green of 1980, "Being a manager later on, I know there are times you have to say something. You say, 'Do I want to play this angrily? Do I want to do this fatherly?' We needed to do something and he put it on the line. If he did it and we collapsed, you could blame him. But we went on a run, so it turned out good."[6]

Boone was correct. If the 1980 Phillies rebelled against Green's management style and fell apart, the experiment would have been judged a failure. Green would have been fired after the 1980 season, rather than feted. Management probably would have blown up the entire team if that was the case, shipping several veterans elsewhere and then starting from scratch. They would have lived the rest of their lives with the disappointment and belief that this group had peaked in 1978.

This was a risky strategy, and not just anyone could handle the role Green was handed and thrive. It was both a great opportunity and a perilous one. It was believed the Phillies were too casual in their approach at the ballpark, that these men of great talent were squandering it when they could have been emerging as heroes for all time in a city starved for success. Then Green emerged as the elephant in the room, too big to ignore, too powerful to challenge. In whatever manner Green ruled, he was going to rule, not as a benevolent king, but as the man players couldn't cross, and as the king who demanded obedience. If Green felt players became lackadaisical, his all-seeing eye meant they would be called out.

In his foreword to Green's 2013 autobiography, longtime Phillies beat writer for the *Philadelphia Inquirer* and ESPN national baseball writer Jayson Stark, as astute of a student of Green and the sport as there is, issued his impressions of the man who led the Phillies in 1980.

"He was the smartest man in the room," Stark wrote. "He was also the loudest voice in the room. Any room. He was larger than life. He was louder than life. And he had a message to deliver—which was pretty much every minute of every day—he had a way of getting his point across."[7]

Stark knew that firsthand. Not in 1980, but a season later, on August 12, 1981, when the journalist became the igniter of a Green rant that remains legendary in Philadelphia and wherever entertaining baseball stories are told. Baseball had been inflicted with a strike that had disrupted the year, ruining much of the feel-good mood of the baseball fan not only in Philadelphia, but all across the country. It had just ended and teams were engaging in what became known as a split season. The basic format of play had been turned upside down, and Green was hardly the only one who was grumpy.

Stark asked an innocent question, one he later said was intended as a joke. Green, who was never invited on *The Tonight Show* for his comedy routines, erupted. He seized on the notion advanced that maybe if a team had won the first half of the season (which Philadelphia had) it had no incentive to win during the second half. "(Bleep) you Jayson!" Green uttered with force, bringing silence to the room. Then Mt. Vesuvius continued its eruption. Even mildly irritated, Green had more than a passing acquaintance with curse words (as advertised by himself).

In part, Green frothed: "And no, we're not trying to lose the (bleeping) game. I'll answer the (bleep-bleeper) before you (bleeping) guys start on it. I'm (bleeping) sick and tired of some of the (bleeping) comments I see in this (bleeping) press. You (bleep-bleepers) think we're in this (bleeping) game for 25 (bleeping) years (and) don't have a nickel's worth of (bleeping) pride? The (bleep) we don't have it."[8]

Stark said he realized then—and that was repeated many times over the years—that Green's tirade was not really aimed at him and other members of the press (OK, maybe a little bit), but was really for the benefit of the players, who outside of the little circle in Green's office could hear every word in the clubhouse and were most certainly paying attention.

That was neither the first time, nor the last, Green mixed it up with the media, or launched into chandelier-shaking decibels to make a point. But it was worthy of a lifetime achievement award for artfully combining profanity, a not-so-secret message, and cleverly calling a misdirection play that scored a touchdown with the real intended audience. On the Dallas Green Greatest Hits album, this was the featured track.

There was never any doubt Green was the commanding officer, but even chief-of-staff generals are aided by lieutenants. Three of the 1980 coaches were holdovers from the 1979 team that had worked with Ozark. Billy DeMars, Herm Starrette, and Bobby Wine were the veterans. They were supplemented by Ruben Amaro, Lee Elia, and Mike Ryan in 1980.

Given that Green formulated his own domestic and foreign policy, for the coaches it may have been a little bit like being a White House aide under a certain president. There was no ambiguity about Green's policies.

William Lester DeMars was born on August 26, 1925 (and turned ninety-four in the summer of 2019), spending more than 50 years in professional baseball. When he was younger his nickname was "Billy The Kid." His playing career lasted from 1948 to 1951, and he first played for Philadelphia, though with the American League Athletics, and then with the St. Louis Browns. In limited play, DeMars batted .237 with 14 runs batted in. DeMars coached 13 years for the Phillies, then with the Montreal Expos and Cincinnati Reds. Pete Rose praised DeMars lavishly based on their time together in Philadelphia, and made him the Reds' hitting coach when Rose took over as manager later in the 1980s. DeMars also later spent many years back with the Phillies as a roving minor-league instructor.

First the property of the Brooklyn Dodgers, DeMars was seventeen for his first minor-league gig, but said he looked fourteen, so his youthful visage gave him his nickname. Much later, DeMars was pleased when the Phillies signed Rose. Even though

Pete was a big star, he continued to work hard on his batting and DeMars worked with him. That was how the two developed a relationship. Even before Rose was in the fold, DeMars said he rooted for Philadelphia to sign him.

"I knew Petey was the missing ingredient," DeMars said. "He was the thing we needed." He was convinced Rose's clubhouse presence was as important as his on-field play for the Phillies. "He wasn't afraid to jump on somebody in the clubhouse."[9]

Starrette, who joined the coaching staff in 1978, previously coached for the Atlanta Braves and San Francisco Giants, and had a short big-league career, going 1–1 in parts of three seasons for the Baltimore Orioles after a long minor-league apprenticeship.

When he was hired, Starrette, who died in 2017 at age eighty, said, "The Phillies have a sound pitching staff, some very good young pitchers. I'm just looking forward to working with them." Starrette had worked with Dick Ruthven and Ron Reed in Atlanta and general manager Paul Owens called him "a good, basic teacher. He's had lots of experience as a pitching coach on the minor-league level."[10]

Wine was family. Somehow he managed to stick in the majors for 12 years, most of them with the Phillies, while batting just .215 for his career. He was the ultimate good-field, no-hit guy. But Wine was savvy. He knew the game. His strong arm was respected at short, and he won a Gold Glove in 1963.

Soon after leaving the field, Wine resurfaced as a Phillies coach and held that job from 1972 to 1983. When Ozark was ousted, it was rumored Wine was going to replace him. Instead it was Green's turn, and Wine became the new manager's bench coach, the role he played during the 1980 World Series run. The biggest surprise is that Wine never became the Phillies' manager, which was his dream job. He was a company man who worked tirelessly in out-of-the-limelight roles. His parting from the Phillies was not sweet.

In 1983, the Phillies removed Pat Corrales as manager when the team was one game over .500. Again, there was much speculation Wine would take over. Instead, GM Paul Owens moved down from the front office. The Phillies won 90 games and the National League East and beat the Los Angeles Dodgers to reach the World Series again, although they lost to the Baltimore Orioles.

Team president Bill Giles, who had previously held the role as VP, approached Wine and said, "Thanks, genius." Yet the Phillies then cut loose their wise baseball man. It was Owens, in fact, who felt he was being undercut by Wine. "How come he was so smart when we won and I was so dumb when we lost?" Owens said.[11]

Never mind promoting Wine to manager after 1983, they ditched him altogether. When Owens and Giles told him they were going to let him go, he responded, "You're gonna what?"[12]

That has long been considered one of the most grievous acts of betrayed loyalty in Phillies history. Wine did manage the Atlanta Braves for part of the 1985 season, but all of that came much later. In 1980, Wine was a key advisor to Green on all baseball matters, and had more in-game bench experience than Green at the time.

Mike Ryan's on-field career resembled Wine's in that he was able to earn a big-league salary between 1964 and 1974 because he was an ace fielder. His career fielding percentage behind the plate was .991, and his playing career was split between the Boston Red Sox and Phillies, except for a final year with the Pittsburgh Pirates. Though he had a stellar fielding percentage, his lifetime batting average of .193 was one of the worst for a player with as much longevity since 1930.

Humorously, when the Red Sox were wooing Ryan, who was from the local suburb of Haverhill, the team arranged a meeting with legend Ted Williams. Williams, who some call the greatest hitter who ever lived, was having a rubdown in the clubhouse when the team brought in a tongue-tied Ryan. The men shook hands and then Williams startlingly asked, "Can you hit?" Ryan was caught off guard. Williams jumped in with the right answer. "F*ing right you can hit," said the Hall of Famer, whose lifetime average was 151 points higher than Ryan's. "Don't you forget it."[13]

Yet also like Wine, Ryan understood the sport and would serve as a Phillies coach for a decade-and-a-half, one of the longest runs in team history. Unlike Green, Ryan must have been capable of extraordinary diplomacy, as he coached under seven different managers.

Lee Elia had the same kind of career as Wine and Ryan, barely making a ripple as a player with the Chicago White Sox and Cubs (his lifetime average was .203). Elia had two stints as a Phillies coach in the 1980s, and managed the club in 1987 and '88. In between he managed the Cubs and, ironically, joined Green in the pantheon of outrageously issued manager rants, one that has also endured in lore.

On April 29, 1983, when the Cubs, who in those days were often guilty of slumping, were in a slump, fans at a day game in Wrigley Field booed the team and shouted insults.

Elia lost it in front of reporters in his postgame analysis. He actually matched Green for profanity, too.

"I'll tell you one f...ing thing," Elia growled. "I hope we get f---ing hotter than s... just to stuff it up them 3,000 f...ing people that show up every f...ing day. Because if they're real Chicago f...ing fans, they can kiss my f...ing ass.... What the f...am I supposed to do? Go out there and let my f...ing players be destroyed every day and be quiet about it? For the f...ing nickel-dime people that show up? The motherf... don't even work! That's why they're out at the f...ing game! They ought to go out and get a f...ing job and find out what it's like and earn a f...ing living. Eighty-five percent of the f...ing world is working. The other fifteen come out here."[14]

There was more, but like Green's speech, if either were going to be in *Bartlett's Quotations*, they would be heavily edited.

Ruben Amaro Sr., a native of Mexico, was a major-league infielder between 1958 and 1969. Batting .234 lifetime, he won a Gold Glove in 1964 and is a member of the Mexican Baseball Hall of Fame. Amaro's son Ruben Jr. also played big-league ball and eventually rose to become general manager of the Phillies. Ruben Sr. had a longstanding relationship with Green, scouting the Caribbean for him when Green supervised the farm system.

Green, the comparative novice manager, was placed in a tough position and about to unleash an approach that was bound to make himself unpopular. But he did surround himself with a very talented coaching staff. Some of those men later went on to manage their own teams, and most thrived as coaches in the long run.

A decade after Green molded and shaped the 1980 Phillies, he participated in a managers panel discussion with Earl Weaver, Dick Williams, and Gene Mauch. He was asked what a manager's greatest influence is on a team.

"The manager's job is to prepare the talent that he is given to play at the best of its ability," Green said. When asked if strategy is overrated, he said, "There is a strategy to having a game plan and being able to deal with the athletes, making them strive to achieve their goals, even though they may be somewhat rebellious."[15]

Strategy? It sounded more like a philosophy, and the very same one Green applied to the 1980 Phillies.

7

MIKE SCHMIDT

BY THE END of May, the Phillies were 23–18, looking much livelier than they had been to begin the season. Third baseman Mike Schmidt, the top slugger in the lineup, was an indispensable man for the Phils. This was Schmidt's team before Pete Rose showed up—he had been the go-to guy for the big hit. The club may have needed Rose's bat, and he definitely was a larger clubhouse presence than Schmidt, who, periodically did a Steve Carlton imitation by hiding in the trainer's room after a troublesome game to duck the press. He was not a regular companion of Carlton's out of sight, as it depended on the day. But the Phillies were not going to win anything in 1980 without Schmidt's bat wreaking havoc against opposing pitchers.

Schmidt blasted his 14th homer of the season in a 6–3 win over the Pittsburgh Pirates on May 28, giving Randy Lerch a win—his first of the season—in a game where Pete Rose was a mighty contributor as well. The Phils, mainly courtesy of Schmidt's two-run shot, led 3–0 after the home half of the first.

"I'm sure that helped him as a pitcher," Schmidt said. "But that ain't never enough against the Pirates. It was a fastball, inside."[1]

Rose, who went 3-for-5 with two runs scored and an RBI, was wielding such a bat it could have ignited his own fire. Between May 4 and May 28, he raised his average by 72 points. The night before, Rose said, he hit the ball hard four times, but fielders grabbed three of them.

"All's I can do is hit the ball," he said. "They've got the gloves. It's not that I haven't been hitting the ball hard. That's why I didn't let it bother me."[2] Actually, Rose's two doubles that night at the Vet gave him 625 for his career and moved him past Hank Aaron on the all-time list.

The funny thing was that Rose had sometimes been criticized because he knew *exactly* how many hits he had. But that was the big statistic, the record he was truly chasing. "I don't keep track of that," Rose said of moving ahead of Aaron in doubles. "I have an idea of the big ones, but not when you pass a guy for tenth, or eighth, or sixth. I don't worry about that."[3] In the long run, Rose retired with 746 doubles, second on the career list behind Tris Speaker.

Schmidt, meanwhile, was in his prime at thirty years old and on his way to becoming one of the most prolific home-run hitters in baseball history. Not Barry Bonds, Hank Aaron, or Babe Ruth level, but in the next tier. By the time Schmidt was finished, he had 548 homers (which was seventh-best upon his retirement). He complemented that power with the slickness afield of a shortstop, winning 10 Gold Glove Awards. To be so proficient in two so different disciplines made Schmidt a rarity in the sport. It was Ruth who was the best power hitter-pitcher in baseball annals. It is possible Schmidt was the best power hitter-fielder. Certainly, he was in the picture for consideration.

Schmidt was 6-foot-2 and 195 pounds, essentially possessing a near-perfect athletic build. Born on September 27, 1949, in Dayton, Ohio, he attended Ohio University and took the Bobcats to the College World Series. When Schmidt was named an All-American, it was as a shortstop. Although regarded as one of the best third basemen in big-league history, he played some second base and shortstop in the minors, too.

It was Rose, who was muscled, but could appear chunky, who looked at Schmidt and saw someone who had the kind of physique he would never have even if he signed up for one of those programs advertised on the back of comic books.

"To have his body, I'd trade him mine and my wife's and I'd throw in some cash," Rose said.[4]

When Schmidt was making his debut in the majors, the Phillies were terrible. In 1971, the season before making the club, they went 67–95. Schmidt was called up for a 13-game cameo in 1972, but did not have an opportunity to show much. Even so, the club went 59–97 that season. As desperate for help as the Phillies were after those seasons, they kept Schmidt with the big club going into the 1973 season. It may have been a year too soon. In 132 games he batted .196 while striking out 136 times. While he did hit 18 homers, of all the great players in major-league history, Schmidt probably had one of the worst single-season performances on his résumé.

But he was a different player the next year. Though he still struck out a lot (a major-league–leading 138 times), he also led baseball in homers with 36, while driving in 116 runs and batting .282. That was the Mike Schmidt who baseball would soon come to know. A veritable unknown before the 1974 season began, he was not listed on the All-Star ballot for the fans. To say his sudden rise was unexpected would be an understatement. A popular Philadelphia sports radio talk show host named Howard Eskin opined repeatedly on the air that it would be an injustice if Schmidt was left off the National League roster. Eskin campaigned as if Schmidt was running for the presidency, and the bang-the-drum-loudly effort produced 100,000 write-in votes. Schmidt did not win the starting position, but came in second. That was enough support and attention to catch the eye of New York Mets manager Yogi Berra, who would be at the helm for the NL All-Stars.

"The guy is having a fantastic year," Berra said. "And, besides, I don't want to get shot the next time I go to Philly."[5] That might only have happened if Berra had been dressed as Santa Claus.

When a player endures a season-long slump as Schmidt did in 1973, there is always a temptation to tinker with his batting stance. Since Schmidt already had a quirky stance, the degree of desire was even higher. But when the youngster emerged as a star that season (he was chosen for his first of 12 All-Star Games), he still had a style that would make purists squint and grimace. His unorthodox batting stance had him standing way back in the batter's box with his body half-turned sideways to the pitcher. When he stood in, he also shook his backside, as if reacting to music playing in his own head rather than just hunkering down for a pitch he liked. Once a batter demonstrates that he knows what he is doing with a form most comfortable, coaches and managers stay away and let him do his thing. Another point about Schmidt that would have scared most scouts away when he was still in high school was that, as a teenager, he had already had operations on both knees. He had raw talent, but he was not truly a prospect until college.

Schmidt assuredly did not overrate himself at this point of his career. Reflecting back, he said, "I was about the fourth or fifth best baseball player—a .250 hitter—and if you don't hit .400 in high school, nobody knows you're alive. I was always the kid with potential, but even that potential was jeopardized by a couple of major injuries in high school. I was also a late bloomer when it came to confidence and aggressiveness."[6]

After his 1973 breakthrough, Schmidt was viewed as a future superstar and greatly fulfilled those prophecies. Although he continued to whiff at Ruthian levels, Schmidt led all of baseball in home runs for three straight years starting with that 1974 campaign, then smacking 38 in both 1975 and 1976. He hit 38 once more in 1977, though was far behind George Foster of the Cincinnati Reds, who hit a whopping 52 dingers. Schmidt was also knocking in 100 runs per season, give or take, and making up for his strikeouts with roughly 100 walks per year.

This provided great satisfaction after that trying rookie season. The Phillies, who needed help at just about every position, traded third baseman Don Money to Milwaukee for two pitchers, clearing the way for Schmidt. Originally, there was some debate about whether or not he would be better served in the minors for one more year, with front office figures Dallas Green and Paul Owens leaning toward the minors and manager Danny Ozark wanting to take the gamble that beginning the season in the bigs would benefit Schmidt in the long run.

"Mike had proven he could hit Triple A pitching," Ozark said. "What was he going to prove down there?" Ozark raved about Schmidt's swing, making a fascinating comparison. "He had great hands, quick reactions, and his swing was like a Ben Hogan golf swing. The ball came off the bat like a rocket."[7]

Soon enough, Schmidt was launching long balls, yet that freshman year was disappointing. He was only twenty-three years old, with a lot of growing up still to do. He resisted some coaching and when his average sunk, Philly fans booed (no surprise there). He also had to deal with his teammates razzing on him as the rookie.

"All I wanted to do my first season was hit the ball out of sight," Schmidt said. He also made the mistake of soaking up the big-league nightlife after good games and off-days. "If I do good, I celebrate it by partying. If I do badly, I forget about it by partying. I'm young, I can handle it."[8]

All of those circumstances and choices contributed to the unsightly .196 batting average. But after that, Schmidt's work ethic became a thing to admire. As Ozark hoped, Schmidt did learn and quickly improved.

By the mid-1970s, Schmidt was winning the Gold Glove every year and was annually being selected for the NL All-Star team. In 1979, he clouted 45 homers, drove in 114 teammates, and scored 109 runs with 120 walks. Given all that offensive production, it was surprising his batting average was only .253. The main reason being that, with all those stellar numbers, he had just 137 hits in 675 plate appearances. It was somewhat of a weird combination all around.

Many sluggers of lesser all-around stature who compiled a large number of home runs during their career did not hit for high averages, either. Dave Kingman walloped 442 homers and batted .236. Darrell Evans swatted 414 homers and batted .248 lifetime. Schmidt was a superior player to them, but some guys seemed to have a unique ability to powder the ball. At the end of the day, hitting singles and doubles just wasn't his game.

Ruth was an interesting case himself. He smashed 714 career home runs, practically inventing that weapon. He also walked 2,062 times and struck out 1,330 times. Schmidt walked 1,507 times and struck out 1,883 times. The best sluggers tended to strike out frequently due to their aggressiveness at the plate, and tended to accumulate walks due to pitchers often nibbling the corners or choosing to pitch around them so as to avoid the damage they might cause with a big blow.

The Phillies' pursuit of Rose was a highly publicized matter. Schmidt said he understood when the organization sought out and signed the superstar hitter. It was clear what Rose brought to the table, both as a hitter and as someone who would be a vocal presence in the clubhouse.

"The team needed an emotional leader," Schmidt said, recalling that second baseman Dave Cash filled that role earlier in the 1970s. "We needed a guy we all respected, a guy who offered different perspective, someone from another team who was a blue-chip player. Great teams have leaders at the top of the order who understand how valuable getting on base is, and no one understands this better than Pete."[9]

It was a right-on observation. While they were both perennial All-Stars, Rose brought different talents to a team than Schmidt had. For instance, Rose was going to bat leadoff and Schmidt was the perfect cleanup hitter and would not get in the way of one another. In fact, they were going to complement and supplement one another.

* * *

The Phillies had a high opinion of themselves and they, along with their fans, felt they should be playing better as spring turned to summer during the 1980 season. Between the first day of the season and May 26, the Phillies were never in first place again. They inhabited that spot for a day, but it was well before they made their true pennant run.

Schmidt had been a home-run slugger for a number of years prior to the 1980 season, but was hitting them at an even faster rate than he did during his three-year top-of-the-heap stretch (though not at a much different rate than in 1979). He attributed this prowess to gaining more muscle mass during the off-season.

"I gained 12 pounds over the winter," Schmidt said in late May. "Only four were by eating. Hopefully, the other eight came from weight lifting. I tried to get a little stronger so that maybe as many as 15 of those fly balls to the warning track make it over the fence. What I'm talking about is those long fly balls that are caught."[10]

Since Schmidt hit 45 homers in 1979, that would have given him 60 for the season. At that time, the only players who had hit 60 in one season were Babe Ruth and Roger Maris. Schmidt would have garnered an enormous amount of attention and time in the spotlight if he had concluded his campaign with 60 homers. Of all the players in the game at that time, he would probably have been voted "most likely to succeed" at that challenge.

Randy Lerch gave the Phils their one-day perch in first. Lerch, a 6-foot-4, 190-pound, twenty-five-year-old lefty was young, but had status with the team entering the 1980 season, solidifying his place in the rotation. He had already been a 10-game winner twice and an 11-game winner in 1978, the latter season when he pitched the division clincher for the Phils, the winner in a 10–0 triumph over the Pirates. What made the win sweeter was that he also hit two home runs. The big-game win, combined with the prize it produced, probably represented the single-day highlight of Lerch's 11-year major-league career.

While Lerch floundered with his 0–6 start in 1980, Larry Christenson got hurt and both Bob Walk and Dan Larson had been called up from Oklahoma City. Lerch lost his starting role and was sent to the bullpen to fix his problems.

After some shaky early-career woes in Houston, Larson, a 6-foot, 170-pound right-hander who was a former No. 1 draft pick of the St. Louis Cardinals, had become Phillies property in 1978 when they swapped him for pitcher Dan Warthen. In two partial seasons totaling four games, Larson was 1–1 for Philadelphia. At twenty-four years of age in 1980, he got a little more work. While his 3.15 earned run average in 12 games was solid, his record was 0–5.

"I pitched well," Larson said, though apparently without much luck. "I threw two different types of fastballs, a curveball, slider and change-up. When I was effective, I was getting three or four pitches over a game, but not necessarily blowing the ball by anybody."[11]

Dallas Green gave Larson chances, but they were episodic. He never knew when he was going to be called on and could develop splinters from riding the bench. But Larson also recognized the 1980 season was a special one.

"There were sometimes I wouldn't pitch for 21 days," Larson said. "Other times, two weeks, 10 days, a week. [But] that was some of the best baseball I've ever seen."[12]

There was no reason to believe that Lerch would not be a major contributor in 1980, and that the late-May win was going to be a major highlight. But of all years, Lerch's season went haywire from the beginning. He finished 4–14 with a 5.16 earned run average, devolving into an afterthought as the year progressed. He watched with dismay as Walk and Larson took turns starting games, while he was trying to figure out what went wrong from the bullpen.

"Sure, I was ticked off," Lerch said. "I thought I should have started a couple of games even though I was 0–6. Maybe Green's psychology worked, but I wasn't very happy about it."[13]

As he had shown from the beginning, Green had zero tolerance for players who demonstrated what he considered a certain kind of negative attitude. Not only was Lerch being lit up early in games, but in Green's mind he didn't seem to be handling the situation well. If the youngster felt he was being sent to the corner as punishment, he was not far off in reading Green's thinking.

"After Randy lost his sixth game we thought it best to drop him out of the rotation," Green said after the loss. "We wanted him to go to the bullpen and think about his pitching. The thing I was concerned about most was his lack of enthusiasm for pitching and his lack of demeanor on the mound. I like aggressiveness and he was not showing it, especially when he got in trouble."[14]

Neither Lerch, nor the Phillies, could imagine the best seasons of his career were already behind him.

If there was a belief the team was about to catch fire after concluding May five games over .500, that proved incorrect. Play in June was just as uneven as it had been in April and May.

Indeed, on June 6, with a 25–21 mark, the Phillies dropped into third place in the division. They kept performing like an eight-cylinder car with just seven cylinders fully operational. Depending on the season, a teams can falter early, but recover. Other years they just dig too deep a hole to come back. That was a fear three months into the campaign.

There were a few guys Green never had to worry about that season—Schmidt, Steve Carlton, and Rose. Ten years later, when Green was participating in a managerial forum with other big-league bosses, he was asked, "Who was a player you greatly appreciated as a manager?" The first player he named was Mike Schmidt. Then he quickly added Carlton and Rose. And he put in a pitch for Phillies shortstop Larry Bowa, too.

The Phillies had quite a bit of fun in a June 14 game against the San Diego Padres, scoring seven runs in the first inning of a 9–6 victory at Veterans Stadium. Randy Jones, who not so many years prior had won a Cy Young Award, was in the midst of a depressing decline in 1980 when he finished 5–13. Jones allowed five runs on five hits by the first five Phillies batters without getting an out.

The game began with a Lonnie Smith single. Then Pete Rose singled. Schmidt then ripped his 19th home run, followed by Greg Luzinski and Bob Boone singling. Jones was yanked. Smith and Rose each collected four hits that day and Schmidt two, with two RBIs. Dick Ruthven wasn't in top form, but it didn't matter and he got the win. What could have mattered long term was his catching a spike on the ground, falling, and hitting his shoulder. That's when Green lifted him.

Oh, and Rose's outburst propelled him past Honus Wagner for fourth on the all-time hits list.

"I'm just happy to get the base hits," Rose said. "When you have in your mind you can be No. 1, you don't get excited about being fifth."[15]

Smith tried not to make too big a deal about his big night, but he admitted seeing more action was helpful.

"Every day I'm out there, I feel more comfortable," said Smith, who looked it. "The more you play, the better you're going to play."[16]

It was the type of output Green wanted to see more of, but the next day offered up a completely different kind of win. The Phillies beat the Padres, 3–1 (couldn't they play the Padres every day?), behind a Steve Carlton six-hitter over eight innings that featured 13 strikeouts. That gave him an 11–2 record with a 1.78 earned run average on the young season.

"I can't imagine him pitching any better," was catcher Bob Boone's postgame comment since Carlton, per usual, had nothing to say about his performance. Boone said Carlton's slider could have been registered as a deadly weapon. "It looks like a fastball coming in and it just explodes down. It's an unhittable pitch. It puts a hitter in checkmate."[17]

Tug McGraw came in to pitch the last inning, doing what he did best: shutting down foes in their last at-bats. It was McGraw's fifth save of the year.

Schmidt was 2-for-2 that day, adding one RBI and scoring two runs. The previous season, when he was being roundly celebrated as his eventual total of 45 home runs was piling up, he (and Dave Kingman, who was also hot), were frequently mentioned in the fun way the press jumped to early-season projects of who might be on a pace to hit more homers than Ruth or Maris. He did not think the 60-homer marks were in danger.

Schmidt also said bashing homers was not the No. 1 thing on his mind.

"In fact, it's pretty far down the list," he said. "If I look in the paper and I see where I'm leading the league in runs scored and runs batted in, I know I am helping my team. To me, that is more important than hitting home runs."[18]

Rose was a player who demonstrated the importance of many other baseball skills beyond hitting home runs. He was good for Schmidt individually, as well as for the Phillies as a team. In 1979, Rose's first season with the club, he held a confab with Schmidt where he boosted his ego by telling him he was a great athlete who could accomplish just about anything he wanted on the field.

"Pete instilled in me a new vitality I think was the turning point for me as far as the athletic part of my baseball career is concerned, " Schmidt said later. "Pete gave me a great new outlook on the game of baseball, a feeling of youth, a feeling that when you go onto the field, you should have fun playing the game."[19]

In 1980, although not old by the sport's standards at thirty, Schmidt did play as if he had sipped from the Fountain of Youth

Greg Luzinski hit his 15th home run of the season early in a 3–1 victory on June 14 against the San Diego Padres, and Schmidt just continued to bash away at National League pitchers, hitting his 20th later in the game. Carlton didn't really need any more help than that.

Those two wins gave the Phillies a 29–24 record, but they were really textbook lessons on how they could continue winning.

8

LARRY BOWA AND MANNY TRILLO

YEARS AFTER THE 1980 season, Dallas Green thought about his shortstop from that year and took note of some of the things he liked about Larry Bowa. By 1980, Bowa was a 10-year veteran, a five-time All-Star, and a two-time Gold Glove winner.

Bowa carried himself like a winner in general. He was feisty. He could be vocal, occasionally abrasive. He had tough-guy attributes that could be infectious with his teammates. Although not as purely talented, he had some traits in common with Pete Rose.

"I liked Larry Bowa's spirit," Green said. "He had great intensity and work habits. Here's a guy who had really limited ability. He had to beg to get signed. He made himself into a major-league baseball player and was one of the best at his position."[1]

Bowa was born on December 5, 1945, in Sacramento, California. He stood 5-foot-10, but weighed just 155 pounds during his playing days between 1970 and 1985—mostly with the Phillies (and with all of his finest years with the Phillies).

Given his limited size, it was no surprise Bowa hit just about one home run for each of his 16 years in the National League, barely shy of one per year (15, to be exact). If Bowa came up with the bases loaded, the opposing pitcher was not worried about the long ball. His specialty was advancing the runner. He batted .260 lifetime, which was not bad for a shortstop, but his biggest asset was his glove, which was important for a shortstop.

Growing up in a baseball family, Bowa was passionate about the sport. His mother, Mary, said his first acquaintance with a baseball came when he was eighteen months old, and it seemed he never let go of it. Bowa's father, Paul, was a minor-league infielder and manager. Larry Bowa, though, did not have immediate success in the game. He did not make his high school team, but found a home on the local junior college team, Sacramento City College. Bowa kept improving but, despite expectations, went undrafted. The Phillies checked him over as a possible free agent, but notoriously, Bowa, who had a temper, was thrown out of the game they were scouting. He got a break when he hooked on with a winter league team and got a $2,000 deal to sign with Philadelphia after all.

Bowa willed himself to the majors through persistent practice and a fiery personality, which seemed to draw attention his way. He was twenty-four when he made his debut with the Phillies in 1970. Bowa did not merely make cameos, but was an instant starter, playing in 145 games while hitting .250. He also stole 24 bases, the first of 13 times he stole at least 10, with a high of 39. In 1972, when Bowa won his first Gold Glove, he also led the National League in triples.

A mainstay in the lineup throughout the 1970s, Bowa was one of the veterans who played in nearly every game during the late-decade run that included the three consecutive East Division championships. That meant he was also one of the frustrated veterans aching to reach the next round of the playoffs and keep playing well into October.

"From top to bottom, from 1976 on, we could beat you a lot of ways," Bowa said. "We kept losing to the Dodgers. Our main objective [in 1980] was the World Series and we finally got there."[2]

While Bowa displayed many leadership qualities, he occasionally viewed sportswriters as the enemy. In 1978, he blew a fuse after some of the Philadelphia dailies wrote critical stories about his play, and he tried to get all writers removed from the clubhouse two hours before games. Bowa erupted at some of the writers, using obscenities in his speech. Things deteriorated and one sportswriter was struck in the face, the blow causing swelling. Bowa subsequently charged another sportswriter who was near the action.

Manager Danny Ozark was riled over the confrontation. After talking with Bowa, Ozark issued an apology to the press. "I don't believe it will ever happen again," Ozark said. "I'm sure he feels very distressed about the incident and I think he's man enough to face the facts."[3] There was a dispute over the "facts," however, with Bowa saying, "I did not touch anyone. I will be willing to swear in a courtroom on a million Bibles I didn't hit him."[4]

While Bowa could be somewhat volatile, this level of screaming and physical showdown was uncharacteristic, and he was usually cooperative with those asking questions. He was a wise analyst of the games, one reason he was able to stay in the sport for many years as a coach (including twice with the Phillies in stints lasting seven and three years, sixteen years apart) and as a manager of the San Diego Padres and the Phillies, too, between 2001 and 2004.

Actually, Bowa had had a blowup late in spring training in March 1980, as well. He let off steam at management when he discovered that despite his regular National League All-Star appearances, he was not getting paid as much as many other shortstops around the circuit. Bowa was making $300,000 a year, but learned that St. Louis' Garry Templeton's salary was $700,000 annually, and was infuriated that Bill Russell, Craig Reynolds, Davey Concepcion, Frank Taveras, and Tim Foli were all making more than he was.

"I couldn't believe it," he said. "I'm not saying I should be at the top, but I'm saying that I should be paid comparable. I don't think I'm worth $600,000 or $700,000, but I am the lowest-paid starting player on our team. I have been here ten years and been consistent. I was told all along if I hit .200 the way I play defense [and he was regularly way higher than that], I could forget about raising the average. I worked hard. I became a respectable hitter."[5] It wasn't that much later that Bowa was making $500,000 a year.

* * *

By the end of June, the Phillies had twice reached seven games over .500, but always seemed to slip back a couple of games and remained in second or third place in the competitive division. The fans were bugged by the lack of high-level consistency, but sometimes the players were, too. They had a strong belief that

1980 was their turn, and were 70 games into the season and yet to show such a spark.

"We were getting tired of how we were doing," Bowa said. "But we couldn't get over the hump. We kept thinking, 'Now is our time.'"[6]

In early July, winning a doubleheader against the St. Louis Cardinals, 2–1 and 8–1, behind excellently pitched games by Dick Ruthven and Bob Walk, the Phillies woke up in first place on Independence Day. They promptly lost two games to the Cardinals and fell back to second place. Those were the kind of maddening back-to-back results that caused sleepless nights for Green and his coaches.

In the first game of the doubleheader on July 3, Dick Ruthven allowed just four hits, but the Phillies batters only produced four hits, too. Bowa went 0-for-3 and was hitting .259. There was more support for Walk, who moved to 4–0 with a five-hitter in game two as the Phils belted out 16 hits. Bowa had one hit and two walks in that one.

On July 11, Walk beat the Cubs, 7–2, and after Kevin Saucier collected a victory the next day over the Pirates, the Phillies were nine games over .500 at 44–35, and led the division by one game. Saucier blew the save, but got the win in relief of Steve Carlton.

Saucier was a young left-hander who got into one game as a twenty-one-year-old in 1978, went 1–4 in 1979, but came through in the clutch several times during the 1980 run, finishing 7–3 with a 3.42 earned average. Green deployed him in relief 40 times, and he was one of the unheralded contributors of the season, his record outstanding even if he only tossed 50 innings.

Saucier was out of the majors by 1982, finishing with a 15–11 career record, due to complete loss of his control. His next career in baseball was as a scout. The hurler's departure from the game was sudden due to his inexplicable inability to put the ball over the plate. His depressing fate was somewhat like pitcher Rick Ankiel, who lost his control and ended up going down to the minors to rejuvenate his career as an outfielder.

"Sometimes I was afraid I was going to kill somebody," Saucier said. "It's really a lot of pressure on you when you're out there and you don't know where the ball is going to go. Everybody says, 'But what about the money?' People don't know what you go through. The money's good, but I wanted to keep my sanity."[7]

There are hundreds of players in the majors each season, and while every one of them has accomplished something special by finding a roster spot, they do not all thrive for years. For every Pete Rose, Larry Bowa, and Mike Schmidt, who become All-Stars and play for more than a decade, there are those like Saucier whose careers end when they are in their mid-twenties.

Bowa was one of the Phillies who believed the signing of Rose in 1979 was a special addition. He was not only one of the greatest hitters in history, but brought panache to the field. During Rose's first season, Bowa made a keen observation. Somehow, when Rose made a game-winning hit, it seemed to produce more excitement on the bench than if others did so. On August 27, when Rose collected an RBI in the bottom of the eighth for a 4–3 victory over the Dodgers, Bowa was just as happy as his teammates, but couldn't help but remark on Rose's ingrained enthusiasm and hustle that was locked into his image.

"See, it makes a difference when Rose does it," Bowa said. "You notice even the cool guys like Schmitty [Mike Schmidt] and Garry [Maddox] and a guy like the Bull [Greg Luzinski], who never says anything, were out there jumping up and down when Pete broke up that game. If I did something like that, then went out of my mind showing how much it meant to me, the guys would be hollering at me to key it down, cut out the grandstanding, asking me who I thought I was, Pete Rose?"[8]

Rose was not about to change his ways after seventeen years in the game, and Bowa wasn't asking him to do so. The addition of Rose, playing first base, to Bowa and Schmidt's longtime presence, helped provide the Phillies with a glittering infield. "His hustle rubbed off," Bowa said. "He always said it was fun to play."[9]

Another key addition after those division championship years was second baseman Manny Trillo. Trillo, who was from Venezuela, spent two years with the Oakland Athletics in the early 1970s and four more with the Chicago Cubs before joining the Phillies. He had one National League All-Star appearance on his résumé, but over the next few years hit and fielded better for the Phils than he had elsewhere in his career.

Trillo, who was twenty-nine in 1980, was acquired from Chicago along with Greg Gross (another invaluable figure) and Dave Rader, in a trade that sent Ted Sizemore, Jerry Martin, Barry Foote, Derek Botelho, and Henry Mack to the North Side of Chicago. Without that deal, the Phillies probably don't win the World Series.

Trillo was on his way to a career high .292 average that year, and won the Silver Slugger Award for his position. Trillo, who was a four-time All-Star during his 17-year career, was noted for his strong throwing arm. Ironically, he was first signed by the Phillies in 1968 when he was playing catcher. It was Dallas Green, who managed Trillo during his first season in the minors, who was responsible for converting him to an infielder. It took a decade for the two to reunite, but Green got Trillo back when he was in his prime.

The arrival of Trillo for 1979 spring training in Clearwater, Florida, was overshadowed by the arrival of Rose at the same time. The Rose deal was the talk of baseball. The Trillo trade had wait and see written all over it. Many baseball experts, though, viewed Trillo as an integral piece of the lineup before he showed up.

"Oh...what can I say," Trillo commented in accented English. "A lot of people have told me that, but the Phillies say they bring me here to play second base. That is what I will do. Rose, all that attention and everything, it don't bother me. We all know what he's done, the .300, all the hits, that hitting streak [hitting in 44-consecutive games for the Reds in 1978], he deserves it."[10]

Manager Danny Ozark was about to be surprised by the pop Trillo began showing in his bat since he was mainly acquired for his defense and to team with Bowa on the double play.

"Trillo is a glove man," Ozark said. "He really gives us some defense up the middle, where you want it. Now, we had to give up some good players to get him, but that's the way it works."[11] Yes it does, and Ozark was speaking before the ballots were in, but the results of the deal proved to be lopsided in favor of the Phillies.

Trillo's early season hitting was a revelation for the Phillies during the first segment of the 1980 season. The team was so up and down, and Trillo's consistency was sorely needed. By mid-

May, he was batting .371. In mid-June he was at .305. *Then* Trillo heated up in the summer and was back up to .322 by mid-August. At the beginning of September, Trillo was batting .319.

In the American League, Kansas City Royals third baseman George Brett, a future Hall of Famer, was turning in the best year of his 21-season career. He spent much of the year flirting with a .400 batting average, a level that had not been reached in the majors since Ted Williams hit .406 for the Boston Red Sox in 1941. Brett cooled off slightly to notch a .390 average, which won the AL batting crown. In early September, when Trillo was hitting .324, he laughed upon hearing Brett was so sizzling hot he could see the stitches on the ball as it approached the plate.

"Me, the only time I ever see the stitches is when I look at the ball before I throw it to first," Trillo said. "If I was hitting .400, I might see the spin on the ball, too."[12]

When he first reported to the Phillies, a team of championship caliber, Trillo compared what he expected to what he had lived with the Cubs, a team that in that era was a regular loser, always near the bottom of the standings.

"Let's put it this way," Trillo said, "in Chicago we were expected to win for half a season. Here, I'll be happy all year 'round. We know we're supposed to win."[13]

That was true, although the Phillies took their time about it in 1980. That may be remembered as a dream season, but the final results in part blotted out all the nerve-wracking days of the journey. It was curious how Trillo's hitting garnered so much attention, as he was still doing what he was hired to do: vacuum clean up everything hit his way in the field. His fielding percentage that season was .987, and Trillo made just 11 errors while handling 838 chances. He was even better a couple of seasons later when he set a second baseman's record of going 89 games (109 days) without an error, fielding 479 clean plays during the streak.

At the time, Rose said, "He's the best."[14] Rose's comment raised eyebrows a bit because he had played with Hall of Famer Joe Morgan in Cincinnati. Rose said Morgan was the best offensive second baseman, but Trillo had him beat in the field.

While Trillo was receiving all sorts of attention for what he was doing at the plate, Bowa continued doing what he had for years. He scooped up grounders, hit in the mid-.200s, and periodically threw in games where he tormented a pitcher with his hitting. One of those days was on August 15, when Larry Christenson teased the Mets in an 8–0 victory. Bowa went 3-for-5 that night, while also scoring a run.

Bowa once sought to duck out from under the commonly applied comment that he was a fiery player. He didn't like the word. "Fiery is a word to where you think he's crazy," Bowa said. The dictionary does not agree, although one definition is of a person who has a passionate, quick-tempered nature—and fiery is not an insult. "I'm well aware of what I do out there. I think intense is a better word than fiery."[15] Intense is a thesaurus synonym for fiery, so Bowa may be right about that.

Interestingly, while Bowa attempted to place a disclaimer on the use of fiery in connection with his name, there were many times the word *angry* was used in headlines and stories about him. Angry is not as complimentary. He even authored a book titled *Bleep*, which was an all-purpose word replacing profanities. Radio and television shows regularly bleep out words that slip from guests' mouths. By comparison, fiery isn't so bad.

And Bowa did use bleeps in his vocabulary when he got mad at people.

Bowa was also asked who was the fiercest competitor he ever played against, and he named Pete Rose with whom, of course, he also played with and saw on a daily basis. Bowa did not ask if he could name himself and one might wonder if another player of the era would have listed his name if given the same question.

During the same discussion, when Bowa tried to spike fiery as a personal description, he was asked directly to react to this: "Larry Bowa player?" He replied, "Plays hard for 27 outs, never quits, and would do anything to beat you."[16]

That sounds precisely like the words sportswriters and others in the game used for Larry Bowa.

9

THE OUTFIELD

WHAT WERE THE odds that Bake McBride would ever play major-league baseball? His was a remarkable story of achievement and survival for 11 seasons in the big leagues. And how many people would guess that his lifetime batting average was just shy of .300, at .299?

The three starting outfielders for the Philadelphia Phillies during the 1980 World Series run were McBride, the gazelle-like Garry Maddox, and the hulking Greg "Bull" Luzinski. It really was a first-rate combination. Add a pinch of Bob Dernier, George Vukovich, fill-ins and pinch-hitters deluxe Greg Gross and Del Unser, and a heavy dose of Lonnie Smith and this was a pretty special group that any team could win with. Compared to the All-Stars in the infield, these guys were probably underappreciated, but there were a lot of difference makers in this crew.

It may be that McBride was one of the unlikelier baseball success stories of his generation. Not only did he overcome obstacles to jump-start his career, it seemed as if, every step of the way, something interfered whenever he made progress. At times, McBride was a personal MASH unit. It was impossible to say he was a walking MASH unit because he wasn't always able to walk, never mind run.

McBride was born on February 3, 1949, in Fulton, Missouri. He had good genes, with his dad, Arnold, a former player for the Negro League Kansas City Monarchs. McBride was an excellent athlete, but although he played football and basketball and competed in track, there was just one problem: his high school did not have a baseball team. One might call that strike one to his career. After high school, McBride attended Westminster College, a small Missouri school where he played basketball, ran track, and finally had a baseball team to call his own. McBride sported a solid athletic build, standing 6-foot-2 and weighing 190 pounds, one appropriate for several sports.

A pitcher in college, McBride was a sprinter in track, and his speed attracted attention. To get any notice at all, he showed up at a St. Louis Cardinals tryout camp. His hurling did not interest the team, but his above average running ability did. The Cardinals, likely the only team that knew his name at the time, drafted McBride in the 37th round in 1970. Players taken so low are definitely longshots to reach the majors, and big-league teams usually do not have much invested in their progress. It is pretty much expected that such a low selection will flame out in rookie ball or Class A. Not McBride. He kept advancing through the farm system.

In 1973, McBride was brought to St. Louis for a look-see. In 40 games he batted .302, a performance that basically ensured his future. In 1974, as a full-timer for the Cardinals, McBride was the National League Rookie of the Year, a season highlighted by a .309 average and 30 stolen bases. A *Sporting News* headline suggested McBride was an 800-to-1 shot to stick in the majors. McBride didn't pretend, even then, that baseball had been his favorite sport and said it ranked behind basketball and track. "I didn't care to watch baseball on television," he said.[1]

McBride, who picked up the nickname "Shake n' Bake," was traded to the Phillies in 1977, and was a major component of the division winners and the World Series club.

In 1980, at age thirty-one, he was the team's regular right-fielder. As such, he had one of his finest years, batting .309 with 87 runs batted in, 13 stolen bases, and 10 triples as part of his 171 hits. He still had wheels. It was remarkable how McBride could perform at such a high level for 137 games because he was coping with lingering knee and foot problems. But then, McBride's physical misfortunes hounded him throughout much of his career. Hampered by an eye infection one season, he also played around two knee surgeries.

McBride was among the most soft-spoken of the Phillies on the 1980 team, and preferred to be left alone by sportswriters as one of the milder personalities on the club. He wanted to play and go home, not explain his stats. However, like several other players, McBride wondered if the Phils really appreciated his work and resented it on one occasion when manager Dallas Green criticized his baserunning, giving the impression he did not believe McBride ran hard. He charged right into Green's office and explained in a little more detail about the problems with one of his knees. They made peace.

While McBride said he got along with Green OK, for the most part, he later hinted he had liked playing for Danny Ozark better because Ozark treated him with great fondness.

"He [Green] ran the club with more discipline than Danny," McBride said, "and he knew from the way a guy was playing whether or not he needed a rest. He stayed on top of things like that. I can't say I had a better relationship with Green than I did with Danny Ozark, because Danny treated me like a son."[2]

Certainly, Green did not cultivate warm and fuzzy relationships with his players who were a generation younger. He would more likely be associated with the father who meted out punishment with the belt when he came home from work and was tipped off by his wife about a particular misdemeanor committed.

McBride said one flaw Green exhibited during the 1980 season was a lack of communication about why he made certain moves that affected a player's life in a major way.

"The only problem most of the guys had with Dallas centered around communications," McBride said. "If a guy wasn't starting, he wouldn't go to that guy and tell him why he wasn't starting. That's why he and Garry Maddox had their differences. Dallas wouldn't go to Garry and Garry wouldn't go to Dallas. It was a stand-off."[3]

Perhaps McBride is correct about how that lack of information poisoned the clubhouse at times, because there definitely were occasions when what he described was occurring.

For much of the summer, McBride hit very well. But to go out and play almost every day was sometimes an ordeal because of the feedback his knees gave him. For someone who had always been blessed with speed, it was frustrating to have his gift tampered with by injuries. At various times during the season, McBride had fluid drained from his knees, treatments that definitely slowed him down.

"In the beginning, I only had trouble with one knee," McBride said. "But now it's both and they are painful. This is something I am going to have to learn to deal with throughout my career. I don't see any way out of it."[4]

Yet while enduring these hassles, McBride was having his best season and one of the best among the regulars on the club. On July 29, the Phillies topped the Houston Astros, 9–6, in a night game at Veterans Stadium before 30,252 fans. McBride went 5-for-5 with three runs batted in and two runs scored, pushing his average to .312, though the Phillies were still drifting along at 51–46, just five games above .500 in third place and four games out of first. McBride said it was probably his best game ever, and that seemed to be a reasonable analysis.

Around the same time, McBride had a slightly off-kilter, but somewhat charming conversation with sportswriters. He urged them to come visit him even after games when he wasn't the star of the day. Most players would just as soon not go into detail about how they went 0-for-5, so this was an out-of-the-box request.

"I liked to be treated the same every day," McBride said, advertising himself as a creature of habit. "When I have a good game like going 5-for-5 or making a game-winning catch, I know you guys want to talk to me. But most of the other times I am ignored. Just because I go hitless, or make an error, doesn't mean we cannot be friends. Just stop by the locker and say hello or something. But don't just stroll past my locker and act like I don't even exist."[5]

That was certainly a welcome-mat gesture, but McBride did have to make allowances for reporters on tight deadlines after night games without resenting them.

Although McBride was a top-notch fielder, it was center fielder Garry Maddox who was more likely to make a game-saving catch. The 6-foot-3, 175-pound Maddox seemed to be equipped with radar that allowed him to get the necessary jump on fly balls and track their destination, whether they were going to land in front of him or over his head. Maddox, who batted .285 lifetime, won eight Gold Gloves between 1975 and 1982. He played center almost like a goalie, preventing objects struck by opponents from getting past him.

Maddox rivaled McBride for being the least chatty player in the Phils clubhouse. He carried a big glove and let it do the talking for him. Maddox had been an American soldier during the Vietnam War, and that was not a topic he wanted to discuss.

"It has been the one part of me that I have kept private because it brings back memories, some of them too painful and sad for me to deal with," Maddox said. "I've spent a lot of time trying to block those things out of my mind."[6]

This hardly made Maddox unique among those who served in Vietnam and returned either physically or mentally scarred and sought to pick up their interrupted lives in everyday American society. It wasn't until somewhat later, after he had experienced unexplained stomach pains for a while, that he became concerned about possible exposure to Agent Orange. "Right or wrong, all kinds of things run through my mind. I know the wind blows. I know there's a chance I was exposed. And yes, like thousands of other guys, I'm concerned. But I don't want people worrying about me. My life has been blessed."[7]

Just because Maddox was a prominent baseball player did not exempt him from the risks that others faced, and the Agent Orange issue did affect many returning American veterans in serious and unhealthy ways. Although he spoke in limited fashion, Maddox did believe he had the forum to bring awareness to the issue.

Maddox was not the happiest camper in the spring of 1980. He felt underpaid, and was in the process of negotiating a long-term deal, even as he was bugged about what kind of atmosphere the Phillies would have under the Green administration. Green knew it, too. He understood that Maddox had had a special rapport with Ozark. While he was not going to change his demeanor for Maddox, he understood when the player was standoffish.

"Garry sincerely loved playing for Danny Ozark," Green said, "and he had a rough time understanding my gruffness and my approach. But I was not a grudge holder. I let them know when they did something wrong, but I didn't hold grudges. I played the guys that performed."[8]

A close observer of the Green-Maddox dynamic was outfielder and pinch-hitter Del Unser. But he, like most of the Phillies, were fans of Maddox, even if there were tense times.

"Garry wasn't a rah-rah guy," Unser said. "He was quiet and sullen sometimes and that just wasn't Dallas' way. Dallas wanted players that were extroverted and showed emotion."[9]

Not everyone could be Pete Rose or Larry Bowa, so despite the success there were times Maddox was quite uncomfortable. That was particularly true in the spring, when he wondered where he stood with the organization. The debate over how much money he was worth—and how long was long in a long-term contract—reverberated while exhibition games were being played. Instead of spending his time in Clearwater dedicated to preparing for the upcoming season, he was steeling himself for a trade.

Maddox told his agent he wanted to stay in Philadelphia. The negotiations sounded somewhat like congressional budget deliberations, with both sides moving up and down in their demands. Then, only days after the regular season began, a lucrative deal was announced. Maddox signed a six-year contract with a no-trade provision covering the first four years, with $4 million of the salary guaranteed. It was now clear Maddox wasn't going anywhere.

"Had the negotiations remained stalemated," said general manager Paul Owens, "I would have explored all avenues to move him. We consider him the best centerfielder in baseball, but we did not want to lose him as a free agent."[10]

That would have been too high a price to part with Maddox, though his departure would have left a big hole in center with a resulting unknown that could have seriously impacted the Phillies' pennant hopes.

Maddox was to be paid $675,000 for the 1980 season, a munificent sum in that era. His overall contract was valuable enough to occasion this headline in *The Sporting News*: "Phillies Give Maddox Combination to Vault."

Maddox was no selfish ballplayer. The year before he signed the big deal, he was already deeply invested in the community as a high-profile athlete who gave back. Maddox, Mike Schmidt, and Larry Bowa all helped with fundraising for the Philadelphia Child Guidance Clinic. Some of the children were learning disabled, some were hyperactive, as well as children dealing with other ailments. The clinic itself had financial difficulties, and the trio of Phillies helped raise money through a bowling tournament, a golf event, and a disco dance.

Initially, Maddox said, he showed up at the clinic to play basketball with some of the kids, show a team highlight film, and visit in passing. Then he had a revelation. "But I realized I owed the community something," he said. "I realized this was a chance for me to do something for the people who support me, who support the ballclub." [11]

As Maddox negotiated his new contract, as always selling his strength—as Owens put it—as the best center fielder in the game, he had one notable stain on his fielding record: no player fields 1.000. No player is perfect. Over the course of history, mistakes made in the World Series and playoffs become magnified, especially if a team loses the Series because of it. These things happen, like Bill Buckner of the Boston Red Sox allowing a ground ball to roll through his legs in the 1986 World Series against the New York Mets. Fred Snodgrass of the New York Giants dropping a ball that led to the Red Sox winning the 1912 World Series. Brooklyn Dodgers catcher Mickey Owen dropping a third strike that cost his team against the New York Yankees in the 1941 World Series.

So Maddox's reaction was understandable after he dropped a Dusty Baker fly ball in the 10th inning of the deciding game of the 1978 National League Championship Series against the Los Angeles Dodgers.

"I'll probably be reminded of this the rest of my life," said Maddox, who was shedding some tears at his locker after the game. "I faced adversity before and I'll come back. Nothing distracted me. I just messed it up. It was a routine fly ball. I should have caught it."[12]

Maddox's mea culpa showed character. He faced the situation head on when he could have ducked the press. He handled the circumstances with class, as emotionally devastated as he was. Interestingly, the error did not stick to Maddox's reputation as firmly as might be expected, or his standing as a first-class fielder for that matter. Nothing could erase the moment, but Maddox could only hope that one day he would be in a similar situation and be celebrated for a game-saving catch in a big playoff game.

Whatever the odds, George Vukovich the outfielder, was one of two Vukoviches on the Phillies in 1980, the other being backup third baseman John, but they were not related. George was a rookie that year who appeared in a deceptive 78 games (deceptive because he amassed only 64 plate appearances). He batted just .224 in those chances with zero home runs and eight runs batted in. In 1981, although George Vukovich played in just 20 regular-season games, he wielded a reliable bat, hitting .385.

Bob Dernier was a twenty-three-year-old rookie for the Phillies in 1980, but a rare fill-in who was soaking up the atmosphere more than anything else, though he was considered a solid future prospect. Dernier got into 10 games and hit .571, something to normally get excited about, though he only came up to bat eight times.

There wasn't much room for guys like George Vukovich and Dernier in the Phils outfield that season. The three regulars were solid, and Lonnie Smith was penciled in as the fourth guy. Del Unser and Greg Gross were always available and they were cool, calm guys off the bench who were staple pinch-hitters; men who were clutch under pressure.

The third starter in 1980 was Greg Luzinski. Luzinski was the strong man of the team, and had been a Phillie since 1970. He seemed to be imbedded in the DNA of the franchise, but was still only twenty-nine after his decade in Philadelphia. It was no mystery why Luzinski received his nickname "Bull," as it fit someone who measured 6-foot-1 and 220 pounds.

Luzinski also had the power of a bull. In the 1970s, he posted seasons where he hit 29, 34, 21, 39, and 35 home runs, while driving in 120 runs in 1975 and 130 in 1977. He also hit .300 four times and was a four-time All-Star. During his 15-year big-league career, Luzinski stroked 307 homers and knocked in 1,128 runs—most for the Phillies (811), but some for the Chicago White Sox later in his career (317). In 1973, Luzinski made only two errors all season for a fielding percentage of .993.

By 1980, the only problem with Luzinski was his relationship with the tough-to-please Philadelphia fans, as his batting average had been cratering. Luzinski put up big power numbers in 1978, smacking 35 homers and collecting 101 RBIs while also walking 100 times. But his average plummeted 44 points from the previous season to .265. His track record and other contributions gave him a pass. OK, an off year in terms of average.

However, Luzinski never hit for a high average again. In 1979, he fell to .252, with 18 homers and 81 runs batted in. His weight jumped to 240 pounds—too much—and he experimented with replacing his contact lenses with glasses. Players in prolonged slumps become desperate and seek remedies—sometimes simple and other times complex. By June 1979, those heartfelt supporters in Veterans Stadium had blurted out their first boos at a guy they had long adored. Suddenly, there were critics of his weight. It was really all about wondering what the heck was wrong with a guy who always hit. The timing of Luzinski's slump coincided with the team's decline, which not long later resulted in the replacement of Ozark with Green in the dugout.

"It was the worst I have ever been through," Luzinski said. "What made it even worse was the fact that the team was not winning. I knew they were looking at me for some big hits and I was not producing. I was not seeing the ball well."[13]

From favorite son to possibly expendable player, Luzinski's status with the club was altered, and there were trade rumors he was headed somewhere else prior to the 1980 season. When the team headed north, though, Luzinski was still property of the Philadelphia Phillies. Then he hit a three-run homer in the first inning of Opening Day. It was a nice pick-me-up.

Green had issued a prediction that Luzinski would be more like his old self once the 1980 campaign began, and he reminded sportswriters of that comment after the first game.

"I told you I'd bet my house that Bull would have a helluva year," Green said. "The first payment's down and I couldn't be happier for him."[14]

Luzinski responded in kind, making nice with Green, someone he knew was not going to be going by past performance, but by immediate performance.

"There's no question he's in my corner," Luzinski said. "It's great to have him on your side and know he's behind you."[15]

Things would not remain hunky dory between Luzinski and Green throughout the 1980 season. Luzinski never could raise his average to his old levels, and his inconsistency was perturbing. While the Phillies were experiencing their greatest season in history, Luzinski was not enjoying his greatest personal season. He finished with a .228 batting average—unthinkable for the former All-Star. While Luzinski did contribute 19 home runs and 56 RBIs, he also spent many games sidelined with a knee injury from July 28 to August 24, playing in 106 of the 162 regular-season games.

Worse for Luzinski, Larry Bowa, Pete Rose, and Mike Schmidt—in the middle of the season and in the middle of the pennant race—they were mentioned in disturbing fashion in the July 8 edition of the *Trenton Times*. The paper reported that players had illegally obtained amphetamines from the club's Reading, Pennsylvania, minor-league team doctor Patrick Mazza. The situation created a tempest, but by the fall—about a month after the World Series—the Pennsylvania Department of Justice cleared the players, and it was Mazza and two other men left facing charges in the case.

The Phillies players did not cooperate in the inquiry, and the Pennsylvania agency statement read, "There is no evidence indicating any participation by the players in the illegal conduct."[16] In this modern era where social media is so prevalent, it is difficult to imagine the short lifespan of this issue and how quickly it disappeared.

A beneficiary of opportunity when Luzinski was hurt and slumping was the young Lonnie Smith. Smith played in 17 games in both 1978 and 1979, sample sizes too small for a full evaluation. He was twenty-four entering the 1980 season, technically still a rookie. He also believed Green, more than Ozark, recognized what he could bring to the team because of his familiarity with the young player through his previous job as farm director.

"We had a new manager who I knew better than Mr. Ozark," Smith said. "Before, I wasn't sure I was ready myself. I felt like a boy against men. I felt like a lemon on an apple tree. [In 1980], I felt like I was ready. Pete Rose was telling me I was."[17]

Smith got into 100 games that season and hit a stunning .339. He was no power hitter, but was a disruptive force on the base-paths with 33 steals. Some thought Smith was the fastest man on the Phillies, but he didn't make the claim. Maybe, he said, if not for Bake McBride. If they had been in a 100-meter match race, Smith thinks McBride might have taken him.

"I think Bake could have out-run me," Smith said.[18]

Luzinski suffered through a terrible September, batting .175. The good news for Luzinski in a trying campaign, though, was getting back to good health in time for the playoffs, and he said he wasn't worried about how he would do. He had more seasoning than Smith or any alternative for left field, and he got the call to play. Luzinski became one of the team's darlings of the postseason, cranking out big hits once again with the style that had made him famous, salvaging some satisfaction.

"I have never felt better than I did the first half," Luzinski said. "The second half was a different story, something I want to forget."[19]

But while the epilogue could not completely make up for the frustrations of the long regular season, it was worth the wait.

10

DEL AND GREG

DEL UNSER AND Greg Gross are not the same person with two different names, but are often paired together in Philadelphia Phillies' fans memories. Reason being that, during the 1980 season, they could have been described as Mr. Clutch 1 and Mr. Clutch 2.

If the fundamental core of the lineup listed Mike Schmidt, Pete Rose, Larry Bowa, Garry Maddox, Bake McBride, Greg Luzinski, Manny Trillo, and Bob Boone ahead of them, the car still wouldn't have gotten too far down the road if they were not aboard to make mechanical repairs, fix things in an emergency, and taking turns behind the wheel.

Championship teams almost always have players like Unser and Gross, the do-it-all helpmates who are turned to when the manager needs a replacement for an injured player or when the chief strategist senses opportunity that can best be seized by a savvy veteran who won't get rattled.

Unser only retired from baseball in 2017 after more than 50 years in the sport. He was around the game so long that when he broke into the majors in 1968 after his minor-league apprenticeship, it was with the Washington Senators. No, he was not a teammate of Walter Johnson's, but the last time the Senators represented the District of Columbia was 1971. During a 15-year playing career, Unser was twice a Phillie—for a couple of seasons in the early 1970s—and again for the final four years of his career, encompassing the World Series run. After 1982, Unser spent the rest of his professional life as a major- and minor-league coach, a farm system director, and a scout.

Unlike many other ex-ballplayers, Unser didn't become an automobile salesman, sell insurance, or run his own small business. He stuck with the game that captured his heart as a youth. A year-plus into retirement, Unser wryly said, "It was a good industry. It was recession-proof."[1]

A left-handed hitter and thrower, the 6-foot-1, 180-pound Unser was born on December 9, 1944, in Decatur, Illinois. His father, Al, was a longtime professional ballplayer. Most of the elder Unser's career was spent in the minors, but he was in the majors between 1942 and 1945 with the Detroit Tigers and Cincinnati Reds. For Del Unser, baseball was like going into the family business. Unser the son took at least one piece of advice from his father that stuck in his brain.

"Dad always told me, 'When you put on a uniform, you hustle,'" he said.[2]

Unser was never an All-Star, but always handy to deploy in the outfield. He never hit for a high average, but his periodic power snuck up on pitchers. Five times he reached double figures in home runs, but mostly, as a line-drive hitter, hit balls off walls—not over them. Unser had sufficient speed to twice steal 10 or more bases, and once led the American League in triples with 8.

Philadelphia picked up Unser in 1972 in a trade that sent Roger Freed and Oscar Gamble to the Cleveland Indians. In 1974, the end of his first stretch with the Phillies, he was traded to the New York Mets in a multi-player deal that brought reliever Tug McGraw to Philadelphia (as well as Don Hahn and Dave Schneck). Unser played for the Mets and then the Expos before the Phillies brought him back as a free agent in 1979, though at thirty-four years of age and with no expectation of being a full-time starter.

With his second go-around with the Phillies, Unser burnished his reputation as a dependable pinch-hitter. Pinch-hitting is always a challenge. Typically, the substitute hitter has been sitting around the dugout for several innings before getting the manager's call. Sometimes it is literally true that he is cold, depending on the weather. But his muscles are definitely not warmed up and he has had no at-bats to work out any kinks. The job requires laser focus and an ability to quickly get ready for what is often a critical moment in the game.

During the 1979 season, Unser set a still-existing record by hitting home runs in three straight pinch-hitting opportunities. Between June 30 and July 10, when called out of the dugout, Unser smacked three straight pinch-hit home runs. Numerous players had belted two straight in pinch-hitting opportunities, but none has ever matched Unser.

The first occasion occurred at Busch Stadium in St. Louis on June 30, a day when the Phillies beat the Cardinals, 6–4. Filling in for Manny Trillo, Unser slammed the ball to right field off reliever George Fazier. There were two outs with Garry Maddox on base and the shot tied the game, sending it into extra innings. The Phillies won in the 10th after Greg Gross led off with a pinch single and scored and the team added one more run.

On July 5, the Phillies took on the New York Mets at home in Veterans Stadium, and although Philadelphia lost this one, 3–2, Dallas Green put Unser in to pinch-hit for Larry Bowa and Unser homered again, driving in both of Philadelphia's runs in that game.

There were more than 30,000 fans in attendance on July 10 when they faced the San Diego Padres. Entering the bottom of the ninth inning, the Padres led 5–1. The Phillies rallied, scoring five in the home half, and the big blow was Unser's three-run shot. That hit gave him the pinch-hitting record of bashing three straight homers. Unser knocked the ball over the center-field wall on Hall of Famer Rollie Fingers's first pitch.

When Unser recorded the achievement some twenty-two players had pinch-hit two homers in a row, thirteen in the National League and nine in the American League. He pushed them all out of the way.

"I wasn't really looking for something to hit out," Unser said. "I was just trying not to guess and just look for something good. I try not to think in pinch-hit situations. My problem in hitting comes from thinking too much."[3]

It was during the 1980 season that Unser provided insight into his mental approach to pinch-hitting. "The whole idea of pinch-hitting is to leave the bench swinging and get something that you can hit," he said.[4]

During the 1980 season, Unser got into 96 games, but it wasn't as if when he played he got to the plate for four turns. In all, he only had 123 plate appearances and didn't even hit a single home run. He batted .264 in sporadic late-game fielding replacement work at first base in relief of Pete Rose, or as a pinch-hitter, of course.

"He's there when you need him," said Phillies coach Bobby Wine, summing up Unser's value. "He's not one of those guys who get teed off if he isn't playing and he always keeps himself in shape. No matter what the situation is or when you call on him, he's always ready to go."[5]

By that point in his career, Unser understood his role as a backup counted on for his readiness. In his last season with Montreal in 1978, he played in 130 games but never got into 100 in any one season again. Not that he felt with the Phillies' stacked lineup he should be playing regularly ahead of anyone else.

"I didn't play very much every day after I got traded from Montreal," Unser said. "There were younger guys and I was just looking to get a few swings."[6]

As things worked out, when the pennant race was hot late in the season, outfielder Garry Maddox was injured and Unser started six straight games.

The fact was, the pennant race was dragging on. For a team that felt it was the class of the division, the Phillies weren't playing that way. They were actually living down to the expectations of the prognosticators who said that, after their three-year run and one-year slump, they were no longer factors for the playoffs. The belief was there, but the results were not—at least not on a daily basis.

After their last game at the end of July, when they defeated the Houston Astros, 6–4 (a game in which both Unser and Gross appeared, though in minor roles), they were pretty much right where they had been at the end of May and June (five games over .500 in both instances). The victory on July 30 left Philadelphia at 52–46, six games over .500—hardly a championship pace. They were in third place in the division. It was as if their season was mirroring so many of their fans who made their traditional pilgrimages to the nearby Jersey Shore—all of them running in sand, making little progress.

One guy who could not be blamed for anything resembling mediocrity was Silent Steve. Lefty Carlton was blowing everybody away just about every time he took the mound. On August 7, the Phillies moved seven games above .500 with a 3–2 win over the Cardinals. That day, with nearly two months remaining in the regular season, Carlton had won his 17th game. He pitched 8 2/3 innings (Tug McGraw closed it out), giving up six hits, two runs (only one of them earned), with a low-for-him four strikeouts. That made Carlton 17–6 on the season with a 2.23 earned run average. No other starting pitcher in the league could match him.

Dallas Green's wish list might well have included the acquisition of another Carlton (or, being more realistic, just another hurler of 15-game-win capability), but no one was coming in via trade. Nor did Carlton's win putting the Phils seven games over the break-even mark signal a fresh beginning where they would ignite and put distance between themselves and the other teams.

They were still in third place and instead of moving forward, went backwards, dropping back to five over before at last going on a winning spree in the middle of August. On August 16, Bob Walk took the win over the Mets, 11–6, and the club then took a doubleheader from New York the following day, with victories credited to Carlton and Randy Lerch. After a day off, Dick Ruthven got the win on August 19 over San Diego, and the Phillies were at 63–53—10 games over .500. They were running to daylight … or so they thought.

Unser was 2-for-2 in the Walk win, and Gross sneaked into that game, too. Only Gross got into the Ruthven victory, a late-inning left-field replacement for Lonnie Smith. This was frequently how Green used Unser and Gross that season. They did not start often, but appeared in the box score often with 0-for-0 lines as they had only played in the field. If they weren't pinch-hitting as part of a take-advantage-of-the-moment situation, they might relieve a regular in the field the way McGraw would relieve a starter from the bullpen.

It was that kind of life for Gross with the Phillies. A left-handed hitter and thrower, Gross broke into the majors with the Houston Astros in 1973 at the age of twenty, though showing up in just 14 games. Once upon a time, Gross was a full-time starter, playing in 156 games and coming to the plate 676 times. For three years, 1974 through 1976, he played consistently and batted .314, .294, and .286 for the Astros. In 1977, he hit .322 for the Chicago Cubs in 115 games.

Two years later, Gross came to the Phillies in the Manny Trillo trade. His role began shrinking to that of a platoon player in the outfield, at first base, and as a pinch-hitter, but he batted .333 in limited action. One thing Gross, a contact hitter, never did was hit home runs. In 17 years in the bigs, he knocked just seven career home runs. Maybe that was because he distributed just 160 pounds over his 5-foot-10 frame.

"I know I'm not a center fielder, so I'm limited to right or left," Gross said when he joined the Phillies. "At least I know my role here. I'll be ready in case someone gets hurt. I'll be a pinch-hitter. I'll be ready as a late-inning defensive replacement, if they need one."[7]

Gross made those comments before any of that played out, but it all came true and accurately described what he did for the 1979 and 1980 Phillies. The "if" scenario of an injury occurred when Greg Luzinski pulled a muscle in the summer of 1979, and for a time Gross played every day. "I've got all the patience in the world," Gross said, "and when I get a chance to help out it gives me a good feeling."[8]

Although Gross had some of the same issues with the Cubs in terms of being stuck behind other players in management's eyes, when he joined the Phillies he sensed things would be better, if only because he was joining a winner.

"In spring training, I sort of had that feeling when I first got over there in '79," Gross said. "I had been with the Cubs in the same division." It took a year longer for the Phillies to prove they were winners after the off-year of 1979, but Gross appreciated the difference being with a contending club. "It was my first experience being in a pennant race and I was just enjoying it."[9]

Every player wants to be in the lineup every day, and there is always a bit of built-in frustration not having a permanent position. You practice, you warm up ... and then you sit. In essence, when a player has that role, he is being told every game when he doesn't start that he is not good enough. It's hard on the ego, and not every player can cope with such a reality.

Ironically, given how much eventual success he had with the job, Gross said initially he was not a very good pinch-hitter. In the long run, it was important for his psyche that he knew the Phillies needed him for that role.

"In my situation," Gross said, "it was the most fortunate thing for me. I didn't have that much success when I first started doing it. When I got to Philadelphia, they had an All-Star at every position. It was more adjusting to that. Playing time just wasn't there. But every manager there found a way to get me some at-bats. The guys on the team knew the importance of having someone to spell them. It fell into place. "I was with a team that needed what I did. I was a line-drive hitter. I didn't have to hit home runs. I didn't have to change what I did. I think that was one of the reasons I was in Philadelphia."[10]

Gross, like his teammates, could not fathom how this team was plodding through the summer, not running away from the rest of the division. He was personally not hitting that well, especially compared to some of his other big-league years, and the team just did not click for the long stretches of time needed to take over first place and put a death grip on the division. For what turned out to be the most memorable season in team history, there were no free rides, and it took a generous share of struggles to reach the destination. Many times players on championship teams say they revel in the journey. This was a journey where flat tires had to be replaced, gas tanks were emptied, and potholes interrupted the smooth highway.

"It had been a tough year most of the way," Gross said. "It was frustrating because we all felt we had a better team than we were showing, and personally, I was not contributing."[11]

A selective hitter who walked often given the infrequent number of his at-bats, Gross hit .302 and .322 in his early thirties for the Phillies beyond 1980. When he did eventually leave Philadelphia, he held the franchise's all-time record with 117 pinch hits—and he still owns it.

Near the end of the movie *The Natural*, the Robert Redford character says his goal in the game was for people to view him walking down the street later in life and say, "There goes the greatest hitter who ever lived." In real life, Ted Williams said something similar. No one goes into the majors hoping for a legacy that reads, "There goes the greatest pinch-hitter who ever lived." Yet sometimes people sum up Gross's career as a player who was merely a great pinch-hitter.

"I hear that," he said. "That was my game. It was what I did."[12]

11

BASEBALL LIFERS

IF ONE LOOKS closely at the seasonal individual stats of the Philadelphia Phillies for the 1980 season, the name Tim McCarver pops up. McCarver, best known for his youthful years with the St. Louis Cardinals and subsequent lengthy broadcast career, appeared in six games and came to the plate seven times, batting .200.

Where the position played is listed, it reads first baseman. This was the last of McCarver's days as a big-league player and up until those moments, brief as they were with what would become a championship club, he was primarily—and almost always—a catcher. A good one, too, with a lifetime .271 batting average and 21 years in the majors with two All-Star appearances.

McCarver served two tours of duty with the Phillies, the first from 1970 into 1972 and the second from 1975 to 1980. He had a close bond with Steve Carlton, and that was an important thing for the Phillies: McCarver was often Carlton's interpreter to the press.

When McCarver, who was born on October 16, 1941, in Memphis, Tennessee, rejoined the Phillies for his second stint with the club, many seemed to think it had a rejuvenating effect on Lefty. McCarver certainly did not see the difference between the current Carlton and the earlier Carlton when Danny Ozark reunited the pair as a battery.

"The same hopping fastball, a snappy curve, and the knack of getting better as he went along," McCarver said.[1]

The days of McCarver and his old knees catching 130 games a season were long gone. With the Phillies he played 47 (after being released by the Boston Red Sox), 90, 93, 90, and 79 games before the short group of games in '80. McCarver was a trusted partner of Carlton's, but he was now thirty-eight, and for most catchers that is a long way from prime years.

It was surprising McCarver dressed at all in 1980. He had announced his retirement in September 1979 as the season was drawing to a close. In his final planned game, he caught Carlton, who pitched a shutout over the Montreal Expos. McCarver already had a deal in place to begin his broadcasting career once the campaign concluded.

"Sure, I am thinking about what this means," McCarver said. "You can't be a part of something for so many years and not think about the last day."[2]

McCarver was a cerebral player, which served him well. He ended up remaining in broadcasting longer than he spent on the field, and was eventually inducted into the National Baseball Hall of Fame for his work in the booth as opposed to on the field. McCarver was behind the microphone for 23 World Series calls and 20 All-Star Games. He was awarded the Ford Frick Award, and won three Emmy Awards.

McCarver might have preferred catching for the Phillies forever, but in May 1979 he was pushed aside, losing his monopoly hold over Carlton's games. It was on Ozark's say-so, as he felt using Bob Boone gave the team a better chance to win.

The entire McCarver-Carlton partnership was initiated by the lefty, who had said he did not like the way Boone called a game. But the days when Carlton insisted his catcher had to be McCarver had passed. When Boone began catching Carlton again that season, things appeared to go smoothly ... at least in Boone's mind.

"Although he didn't talk, I think Steve concentrated on throwing the pitches I called," Boone said after a game against San Diego. "He shook me off just once."³

Like so many catchers—McCarver included—Boone brought more than the basic tools to the field. The best catchers are take-charge players who exert their personality to steady pitchers in trouble, position fielders, call out the number of outs, etc. Most of the time, they are valued more for their glove than their bat.

Boone was born on November 19, 1947, in San Diego, California. Drafted in 1969, he did not reach the majors until he was twenty-four, in 1972. He was a staple behind the plate for the Phillies through 1981, but played for the Angels and Kansas City Royals for years longer, 19 seasons in the majors. Boone was an All-Star with the Phillies three times, and won two Gold Gloves during that stint. He was chosen for another All-Star team with the Angels and went on to win five more Gold Gloves. A lifetime .254 hitter, Boone hit as many as 10 home runs only three times, all early in his career for Philadelphia. He fought off retirement until he was forty-two.

Boone, who attended Stanford, was a participant in the Alaska Baseball League in the 1960s, when the league was new. He raised two major-league players as well, in Aaron and Bret, who both played in the summer league in Alaska as well. While hundreds of ballplayers who went on to the big leagues passed through Alaska, the Boone family may be the most accomplished as a group. Going back in pro ball a little further, Boone's dad, Ray, or Ike, also played in the majors.

Interestingly, Boone nearly gave up baseball while attending Stanford. He had an alternative career in mind: going to medical school and becoming a doctor. That was his road not taken. For that matter, he thought he was going to be a third baseman when he signed with the Phillies. Instead, he became one of the most active catchers in history, appearing in 2,225 games behind the plate (ranked third all time).

In the 1990s and early 2000s, Bob Boone managed the Kansas City Royals and then the Cincinnati Reds. As the 2019 season began, Boone was still in the bigs, yet in a different capacity. At seventy-one, he was vice president of player development and assistant general manager for the Washington Nationals.

When the 1980 season began, Boone felt the Phillies were a special outfit. He had been with the team when it won those three straight East division titles, as well as when it slumped in 1979. After that disappointing year, he said, like others, that the feeling in Clearwater going into '80 was a good one. "We had the best team in our division," Boone was sure. "You kind of played it one at a time, but in the past we had jumped out and won 100 games."[4]

Because of those playoff losses that left the Phillies short a World Series berth, Boone said the team, which had so many veterans, had a very hungry approach. It was felt, more than spoken, in spring training, but maintained right through the playoffs. "We were going to win or die trying," Boone said.[5]

The real question for the club as summer passed its midway point and the season stretched into August, was if they were indeed going to die again, just as they had the previous year, whether Dallas Green's managerial philosophy was going to lift the team to a championship or destroy morale.

"All I was trying to do was wake them up and win a championship," Green said. "There was no secret agenda."[6]

In 1980, Boone was thirty-two years old. He felt the ticking clock of an aging catcher, too, though he made sure to keep himself in top shape. He knew the history of catchers' lifespans. They more or less tracked the descriptions that followed Bush pilots, as in there are no old, bold pilots. Boone actually played another decade, a monument to longevity playing behind the plate. Later, with the Angels, Boone remained in the clubhouse after games lifting weights and going through kung fu exercises, a routine he had imported from the Phillies and had begun in 1976. Boone said that the combination of the up-to-an-hour reps in the workouts, even after games, did physically hurt, but made him push through the pain.

"It's an attitude. The kung fu helps because you reach a level beyond pain, beyond exhaustion, and you always know you can do more," he said. "I tell myself it's only pain. Can I play, or can't I play? It's just pain. I can play."[7]

But back in 1980, less the threat to his body than to the composition of the team, he felt the clock ticking on this bunch of his fellow teammates. They did not wish to go into an unknown future feeling their window for success had closed. Management not only kept the core of those three-time division champs together, but had spent more funds to beef it up. Front office individuals also subscribed to the win-now mentality. If this team didn't win in 1980, it was probably going to be the end of them as a group.

The problem for Boone that year was a sudden struggle to hit. He played in 141 games, went to the plate 535 times, but his average was .229 (the lowest of his career) and had an on-base percentage under .300 (.299) for the first times since 1974. That was uncharacteristic for him and, as the team floundered inconsistently, that was a sore spot. Boone was irritated with himself, but Dallas Green was irritated with everyone.

On August 10, the Phillies were on the road, playing a doubleheader against the Pittsburgh Pirates at Three Rivers Stadium. The Phillies were barely treading water in the National League East, in third place and six games out of first. Backup catcher Keith Moreland and outfielder Greg Gross each stroked two hits out of the eight the Phillies managed in a 7–1 defeat. Demonstrating how the Phillies had not yet caught fire, they were only three games over .500 in June, July, and August combined.

Green was so upset at his team's performance that the steam was almost literally seeping from his head and through his baseball cap. He didn't want to wait until the end of the day—even until the end of the second game. He wanted to tell the players what he thought of them immediately, before they escaped the clubhouse to try again in game two.

When it came to Green's Greatest Hits, this only ranked second. There was no ambiguity of the targets this time. In fact, the traveling writers were locked out of the clubhouse, in a hallway, waiting to obtain some quick quotes about what transpired in the first game.

Ray Didinger, the esteemed sports columnist for the *Philadelphia Daily News*, was one of the writers on the scene. In part, he wrote, "Dallas Green stalked into the clubhouse and opened up on his players, spraying them with a machine-gun burst of anger." Green's voice, he said, was "echoing through the Allegheny Mountains."[8] By that, Didinger meant, everyone on the other side of the door could hear Green clearly as the decibel level reached by his voice challenged the loudest of rock and roll, or a jet plane engine.

Green peppered his tirade/rant/pep talk—however one might characterize it—with many of his favorite words that come under the heading of those you cannot say on television. In his Oscar-nominated performance, Green said, "This (bleeping) game isn't easy. It's tough, especially when you have injuries. But you guys [have] your (bleeping) heads down. You've gotta stop being so (bleeping) cool. Get that through your (bleeping) heads. If you don't, you'll get so (bleeping) buried, it ain't gonna be funny.

"Get the (bleep) off your asses, and just be the way you can be because you're a good (bleeping) baseball team. But you're not now and you can't look in the mirror and tell me you are. You tell me you can do it, but you (bleeping) give up. If you don't want to (bleeping) play, get the (bleep) in that manager's office and (bleeping) tell me because I don't want to (bleeping) play you."[9]

So there. Didinger salted an already salty speech with commentary, noting it was Green's "longest and surely his loudest thrust at what remains of his team's conscience."[10]

The skewering did not pay instant dividends, either. The players did not have much time to chew on the rip job, think it over, or do anything but shrink from it. The second game of the doubleheader beckoned, and they did not play much better, this time losing, 4–1. It would conclude a four-game sweep by the Pirates, bringing their season record to 55–52.

"The Phillies did not win one for the Griper," Didinger continued, "but then, who really expected them to?"[11] The Phils' recent track record at Three Rivers had been abysmal, as Didinger put it. When taking the field there, they were "like butterflies waiting to be pinned."[12]

Actually, emotions were so raw that after the second loss, after Green ordered reliever Ron Reed to intentionally walk Willie Stargell when he did not want to do so (although it led to Bill Madlock hitting into an inning-ending double play), they were practically spitting words at one another on the mound … and nearly came to blows in the locker room afterward.

Though not helping against the Pirates, the Phils went on to win eight of their next nine contests, including the game when they beat the San Diego Padres to go to 10 games above .500 on August 19. Boone excelled in that 7–4 victory over the Padres, going 2-for-2—both doubles—and scoring two runs while also walking twice.

Did the Phillies have liftoff at last? Well, not really. They went 2–5 over the next several games, followed that with a three-game winning streak, and then lost the last two games of the month. But the division as a whole had been erratic all season. so on August 30 the Phils were just 68–60, but were only a half-game out of first place in the East.

* * *

September is the month of the season where the horses turn for the final stretch. Many teams are eliminated from the race by then. They are no-hopers, already making their offseason plans. Things could have gone either way for the Phillies at that moment. They could have folded the tents with the result being the roster would have almost surely been blown up, or could discover the consistency they had been searching for over five months.

Green's oratory lives on in Philadelphia lore, but not nearly as well remembered is the September 1 tongue-lashing delivered to the players by general manager Paul Owens. He was equally as fed up as Green, and finally decided to descend from on high in the front office to the clubhouse for a stern talking-to.

The Phillies were in San Francisco for a three-game series against the Giants to start the month. Owens was more subtle than Green had been in Pittsburgh. When he closed the door to the clubhouse to ream the players, there were no sportswriters around, and his voice did not shake the walls. But his message was pretty clear, as it was relayed to writers from players later. If there was any profanity in Owens's tongue-lashing from the principal, it was left out of the translation.

"He said we played the last five months for somebody else, and now he wants us to play the last month for him and [owner] Ruly Carpenter," Pete Rose said. "They're the ones that put this team together. They're the ones that stuck with this team over the winter."[13]

Whereas Green spoke generally, including all the players in the room, Owens got personal, criticizing shortstop Larry Bowa and center fielder Garry Maddox for not playing up to standard. Bowa was ordinarily an explosive personality and one might assume he did not take this attention well. Yet when he spoke about the incident, he was calm and conciliatory. There really was no arguing with the record.

"The Pope's the general manager," Bowa said, invoking Owens's nickname, "and he has every right to come down here and say what he said. He jumped on Garry and me. We have not been playing well."[14]

For the most part, except for third baseman Mike Schmidt, pitcher Steve Carlton, and outfielder Lonnie Smith, all of whom were putting together career years, few players on the roster were exempt from front-office disappointment.

One other guy, another deep thinker on the game in that room—like a McCarver and Boone but without their skill sets, who was never one to rock the boat—was utility man John Vukovich. To some degree, it was miraculous that Vukovich still inhabited a locker during these contending times. He was thirty-two at the time. A savvy baseball man, yes, but one who was hardly used. In 1980, Vukovich appeared in 49 games, went to the plate just 66 times, and batted .161.

Somehow, Vukovich survived 10 years in the majors with a lifetime batting average of the same .161, and never got into more than 74 games in any season. He was not a power hitter, with six total homers over his entire career. Nor was he a valuable pinch-hitter. Del Unser or Greg Gross were going to be called upon before he was. But Vukovich was not only a decent man, he was a smart one with a good spirit, and could be deployed as a defensive replacement at one of several positions.

A onetime Phillies first-round draft pick with a good glove and an excellent arm, he never blossomed at the plate but provided a special quality in the clubhouse. His style in the field was so spectacular when he was first called up at twenty-two in 1970, the first impression he made diving for catches had many raving about him. "We called him the Brooks Robinson of our farm system," said then-Phillies manager Frank Lucchesi.[15]

There was a recognition Vukovich was a natural leader, which is pretty difficult to demonstrate when you are the weakest hitter on the team. In 1980, Schmidt missed 11 games at third with a pulled muscle and Vukovich filled in. The team won seven of those contests.

"All of us, including myself, realize we have to have Schmitty in the lineup to win the division," Vukovich said while filling in. "I know I am not going to take his spot, but if I can minimize the loss as much as possible while he is out, I have done my job."[16]

During his decade-long playing career, Vukovich had two stints with the Phillies covering seven seasons. He promptly went into coaching with the Chicago Cubs upon retiring in 1981, but then returned to the Philadelphia fold and became the longest-serving coach in club history, from 1988 to 2004, including spending a short time as interim manager (going 5–4 in 1988).

Vukovich just missed out on holding a key role with the Big Red Machine Reds in 1975. He started the season in Cincinnati, but was displaced at third base when George Foster's bat bloomed and Cincy moved Pete Rose into his slot.

And then there they were, Vukovich and Rose, together again for the Phillies during the tumultuous, aggravating, dramatic 1980 season, chasing the same goal down the stretch of the National League season.

12

PENNANT RACE

BASICALLY, **NO ONE** in Philadelphia outside of the Phillies front office had heard of Marty Bystrom before September. Not the man in the street, nor any baseball fan.

When September began, the race was on for real. The Phillies were out of time. If they wanted to regain the National League East crown, they had to take every game seriously. To make it a September to remember in order to make October into something special, they had to start winning more often than every-so-often. And with a three-team tie at the top of the East—between the Pittsburgh Pirates, Montreal Expos, and Phillies—there was no room for error.

As Labor Day passed, Bystrom, a 6-foot-5 right-hander, was twenty-one years old. His twenty-second birthday beckoned on September 7. He had spent the summer in Oklahoma City, and had not overpowered hitters in AAA. He made himself into a prospect, someone whom management would look at in Clearwater in the spring of 1981 based on his 6–5 record and 3.66 earned run average.

It seemed that was Bystrom's ceiling of the moment. However, two years earlier, when he was in Class-A ball for the Phillies' Peninsula team in the Carolina League, he demonstrated his promise in two ways. That year he went 15–7, with one of the victories being a perfect game. The masterpiece required just 89 pitches and took ninety minutes to complete. His father, Franklin, happened to be present, arriving on the day of the game. Bystrom also was aware he was perfect as the game wound its way into the late innings. "I kept saying to myself when I came into the dugout, 'I know I can do it,'" Bystrom recounted later.[1]

Even if the game was played in the lower minors, that was a lifetime item for the résumé.

Baseball has long allowed for expanded rosters in September, the last month of the regular season. Teams that are buried in the standings tend to bring up more players than teams fighting for a pennant. The losers want to test their young guys in a major league-environment. The contenders, however, don't have much playing time to offer because they are concentrating on weightier issues.

But the Phillies took a flyer. Bystrom made his big-league debut on his birthday. The Phils were busy losing, 6–0, to the Los Angeles Dodgers when he entered the game as the fifth Philadelphia pitcher used. He threw one inning and his line in the box score was otherwise all zeros. No hits and no runs were allowed.

A few days later, on September 10, when the Phillies were in New York to face the Mets, Bystrom was assigned the start. He pitched a complete-game shutout, allowing five hits with five strikeouts, giving him his first career victory. That also made the Phillies 75–63.

Only the day before, the Phillies outlasted the Pittsburgh Pirates, 5–4, in 14 innings at Veterans Stadium. This was one of those non-stop strategy games. It seemed as if everyone in the dugout played, including rookie Jay Loviglio, who made his major-league debut on September 2.

Nineteen Phillies got into the game, including Loviglio and Bob Dernier as pinch-runners and George Vukovich, Del Unser, Bake McBride, and Keith Moreland as pinch-hitters. Three pitchers appeared in relief of Steve Carlton: Dickie Noles, Ron Reed, and Warren Brusstar. The Phillies scored the winning run when Garry Maddox doubled, moved to third on a Larry Bowa ground out, and crossed the plate when Bob Boone executed a sacrifice bunt.

Brusstar, who pitched one inning, picked up the victory. That made him 2–0, but it was a big deal at that point in the season because after being a key reliever in 1977 and 1978, he was plagued by injuries. This late-season performance signaled he was healthy again when the team needed him most.

"I was hurt and missed the first half of the season," said Brusstar, who was a career relief pitcher in 340 appearances spread over nine big-league seasons. He was frustrated not to be part of the early games, especially because he sensed all along that the Phillies were going to emerge as a special team in 1980. "I was very excited. It was a matter of time when we felt we were going to win."[2]

It really took until September for the club to jell, and while Mike Schmidt was the best player in the National League that season—always a good start for success—they did not come together until the number of players helping out expanded.

"That is what it takes," Brusstar said. "It takes 25 to 28 to 30 guys. It takes everybody to contribute."[3]

Before September, who knew Marty Bystrom would be one of them? Before May, who knew Bob Walk would be one of them?

"Bob Walk and Marty Bystrom, without those guys doing what they did, we don't get there," said Greg Gross.[4]

On September 13, Steve Carlton, who had been in his own zone all season, won his 22nd game on the year. Carlton beat the St. Louis Cardinals, 2–1, pitching another complete game with five strikeouts. His earned run average was at 2.29. In a season of angst, nobody wasted a single thought all year worrying about Carlton. He was as untouchable by opponents as anyone could guarantee.

A day later, the Phillies topped the Cardinals again. Bystrom went seven innings this time and was 2–0 when the final out was recorded. He was three appearances into his big-league career and had yet to allow a run. However, getting to the conclusion of this one was a bit of an adventure. Philadelphia won, 8–4, but Sparky Lyle was a shaky closer, giving up four runs over the final two innings.

Lyle, who won 99 games and saved 238 during a 16-year career, earning a Cy Young Award with the New York Yankees as a reliever, was an insurance acquisition on that very day, even if it was too late to add him to the postseason roster—if the Phillies even qualified. Lyle was swapped from the Texas Rangers for a player to be named later. The player sent over turned out to be Kevin Saucier, though happily for him, not until mid-November, so he was still part of the Phillies' glory before exiting. Lyle was thirty-five and threw 14 innings in 10

(Left to right) Phillies Mike Schmidt, Larry Bowa, Manny Trillo, and Pete Rose in a hokey spring training pose in Clearwater, Florida, leading up to the 1979 season.

Steve Carlton, a.k.a. "Lefty," was the dominating pitcher in the National League during the 1980 season, on his way to 329 victories and a place in the National Baseball Hall of Fame.

Pete Rose, who joined the Phillies as a free agent in 1979 after his lengthy career with the Cincinnati Reds, became the catalyst propelling Philadelphia to the first World Series title in franchise history.

Greg "The Bull" Luzinski, long a Phillie fan favorite, felt he had something to prove in 1980 after having an off-year the season before, and delivered several big hits during the championship run.

Manager Dallas Green was promoted from farm director by the team's higher-ups to mold the existing talent into a championship team with his my-way-or-the-highway outlook.

When manager Dallas Green had a strong opinion on a matter he would not hold back, even if he was addressing an umpire.

Shortstop Larry Bowa was a scrappy player, great with the glove, and someone who regularly hit for a higher average than people expected.

Center fielder Garry Maddox was not the most talkative of players among the Phillies, but was such an excellent fielder that he was called "The Secretary of Defense."

Outfielder Garry Maddox was renowned for his fielding, but was a very reliable hitter as well.

Pete Rose was in his late thirties, but still ran the bases with determination and abandon. Here he sent San Diego Padres shortstop Ozzie Smith flying during a June game at Veterans Stadium.

Outfielder Bake McBride overcame balky knees to hit .309 and drive in 87 runs during the 1980 season, here being carried off the field by teammates after catching the final out of the NLCS, sending the Phillies to the World Series.

Pete Rose and Greg Luzinski welcome Bake McBride at home plate after his three-run homer in the first game of the World Series versus Kansas City.

No one was better at the plate in the National League during the 1980 season than Phillies' third baseman Mike Schmidt, who led the league with 48 home runs and 121 RBIs, on his way to winning the Most Valuable Player Award.

A Phillies mob scene after winning Game Five of the World Series over the Kansas City Royals.

The crowning moment when the Phillies topped the Royals to capture Game Six and the World Series title came when reliever Tug McGraw struck out Willie Wilson with the bases loaded and leapt into the air.

Mike Schmidt is mobbed by his Philadelphia teammates after the last out was recorded, clinching the Phillies' first World Series Championship in team history, on October 21, 1980.

The city of Philadelphia threw a grand parade for the Phillies the day after they won the title at Veterans Stadium, and Pete Rose enjoyed his time spent with the trophy on a float.

games for the Phils in the last two weeks of the regular season, his ERA ending up 1.93 after the shaky start. Maybe he was just jet lagged.

Lyle barely had time to pull off some of his patented practical jokes, such as putting goldfish in the water cooler, sitting naked on birthday cakes waiting to be delivered to teammates, or sending pizzas to the opposing team's bullpen. Given the circumstances at this point in the season, the Phillies—and manager Dallas Green in particular—may not have viewed him as a laugh riot.

It wasn't as if Tug McGraw lost Green's confidence or his closer job down the stretch with the arrival of Lyle, either. During the season's final days, McGraw won five games in September and October—and that was after giving up just two earned runs in July and August.

It was in the middle of September that McGraw said aloud that the Phillies were likely to run through October.

"I think with the talent and the experience we have, we are in an excellent position to win it this year," he said. "It's going to go down to the wire, but we're going to be on top."[5]

By the end of the regular season, McGraw was 5–4 with a 1.46 earned run average and 20 saves. But he also thought back to the beginning of the season, when Green posted signs all over the place reading, "We, Not I." It did seem a little bit too rah-rah for the returning players. "All the veterans rolled their eyes at this one," McGraw said. "But Dallas knew he had to do something to shake us up. Dallas, who once described the 1980 team as 25 different players who couldn't stand each other, did what he had to. A lot of guys didn't take well to Dallas, but hey, it worked."[6]

Bystrom moved to 3–0 as the Phillies beat the Chicago Cubs, 7–3, on September 20. He only lasted 5 1/3 innings that time and finally allowed his first three major-league runs. That raised his ERA all the way up to 1.21. The Bystrom Effect was still in play.

Five days later, with Bystrom now taking a regular turn in the pitching rotation, he beat the New York Mets, 2–1, this time going 6 2/3 innings. On September 30, Bystrom went seven innings, gave up two runs, and Philadelphia crushed the Cubs, 14–2. The Bystrom mini miracle was complete. From nowhere to instant stardom, the phenom completed a 5–0 regular season with a ridiculous 1.50 earned run average. Bystrom was the elixir the club needed. A superhero riding to the rescue to save the day in the waning hours of the pennant race.

Walk was never better than on October 2, when he won his 11th regular-season game over the Cubs, going seven innings and giving up just one run.

One of the most thankless jobs in baseball back in 1980, before the closer gained much more stature, was the middle reliever. He was unlikely to pick up a win or a save, and was often merely a mop-up man to get to the end of the game in blowouts. The starting pitcher was preeminent by far, with the closer getting a tip of the cap.

One of those mostly unheralded guys during that season was right-hander Dickie Noles, who was listed as standing 6-foot-2, but weighed only 160 pounds. He was just twenty-three, and his future was wide open. However, Noles took the mound for parts of 48 games. While his record was just 1–4 with six saves, he threw a critical 81 1/3 innings, bridging the gap from the starter to McGraw.

To some degree, the 1980 season was the highlight of Noles's 11 years in the majors, including some key work during the World Series. After the 1981 season, he moved eight times until finally concluding his career with the Phillies once again in 1990.

Noles was new to relieving in 1980, after going 3–4 in 14 starts the previous season. He was a somewhat cocky player, and had a "There's no way they're going to beat me" mentality coming out of the pen. "I like the way Dickie comes at hitters," Green said of why he chose Noles for the role, which paid off heavily late in the season.[7]

Like many young pitchers at the beginning of their careers, Nole was all about staying in the big leagues, whether it was as a starter or reliever. "I don't mind switching to relief," he said. "I'll do anything to pitch in the majors. I've never relieved this much, but I'm willing to give it my best."[8]

No one could read the future in September of 1980—not even as it spilled into October—with doubt in the air over whether the Phillies could claim the division title, never mind what was in store for Noles. His erratic career, bouncing from team to team, was not only attributable to a lack of consistency, but also a drinking problem. His off-field issues led him to being arrested and sent to jail for a drunken confrontation with a Cincinnati police officer in 1983. He pleaded no contest to assaulting the officer, and was only given a 16-day sentence.

Noles recognized he was harming himself, including when the Phillies sent him to the minors in 1981. "Maybe some of the things I did hurt me," Noles said. "I'm a free spirit and I've done some wild stuff and I'm trying to key down a bit. You never know when your last pitch will be. I've got all the rest of my life to party."[9]

However, in a foreshadowing comment in 1982, when Noles was asked if his parents thought they raised a Frankenstein, he replied, "My mother reads all the crap and says once in a while, 'Is it true you're doing all that...are you the bad guy they say you are?' But my dad played ball. He just laughs it off. If I did half the things people say I did, I'd be in prison."[10]

As evidenced by his Cincinnati fiasco, Noles was not yet ready to stick to his tone-down-the-partying pledge and *could* have been in prison. He began drinking in junior high school and had difficulty shaking the habit. The details of the big fight in Cincinnati included him being tossed out of two bars, kicking and injuring a bouncer, and battling three police officers.

Noles was living so recklessly, drinking so much, that those who knew him didn't even think there was anything very unusual about the incident. "Everybody thought it was just another night in my life," Noles said, five years later, when he was trying to again resurrect his career during another trip to the Triple-A minors.[11]

The dustup in Cincinnati occurred on April 9, 1983, and it would be the last time Noles drank an alcoholic beverage. He sinned no more from then on, and preached against drinking. He had realized he was an alcoholic and that when he was drunk he lost control of the real Dick Noles.

While the team on the field was built around veterans, Noles, Walk, and Bystrom were youngsters on the mound who supplemented Carlton's brilliance when they were called upon by Green.

There wasn't much room in the field for a young player because it was a loaded, set lineup, in theory. But Lonnie Smith found his time. Surrounded by stars and top-notch veterans,

Smith had to scrap for playing time. At twenty-four, after two very brief summonses to Philadelphia in 1978 and 1979, he hungered for more playing time. His startling batting average of .339 with an on-base percentage of just under .400 made him valuable when inserted into the lineup.

"We had guys who could come off the bench and fill in," Smith said of that season. He also said being around Garry Maddox, "The Secretary of Defense," allowed him to absorb important pointers on playing in the outfield. "I just wanted to play as much as I could. It was a new experience for me."[12]

While Smith knew Dallas Green from his time in the minors, this was a different Dallas Green running the Phillies. He was gruff and could bruise feelings, but Smith was not bothered. "We knew he was a steadfast, hard-nosed, kick-ass person," Smith said. "He was fair, though. We would have meetings and we would get blessed out."[13]

What a polite way of summing up Green's tirades. The big one, of course, was his August blast between the games of the doubleheader against the Pirates when it seemed as if everything was slipping away. Yet McGraw felt that August 10 explosion was effective.

"It was our worst stretch of the season," McGraw said, "putting us in third place, six games out. Our season was sort of on the line. Dallas just yelled at everybody. He just got in everybody's face, called everyone out, challenging our character. As a player, I had been in lots of meetings, but most of them were BS. This one was real. It was like a slap in the face. It was so rough that reliever Ron Reed had to be restrained from going after Dallas then and there. What Dallas was saying went right to the core."[14]

That was followed a few weeks later by Paul Owens's extra-curricular visit to the clubhouse to echo Green, if not quite as loudly.

"Well, they were right," McGraw said. "We went 21–7 down the stretch and we won by one run an amazing 14 times."[15]

The Pittsburgh Pirates spent most of April, all of May, and a chunk of June in first place in the National League East. After fading to third for a little while, they surged again in July, leading the division through August 1. They dropped back again and then took over first again from August 10 (after that infamous doubleheader with the Phillies) through September 2.

Although the Pirates still had future Hall of Famer Willie Stargell, he was now forty years old. While he did hit 11 home runs, he only appeared in 67 games. Mike Easler had the team's highest average at .338. Dave Parker was doing his thing, batting .295 with 17 homers and 79 runs batted in. Pittsburgh also had Bill Madlock at third and some dangerous hitters off the bench, like Bill Robinson, Manny Sanguillen, and Lee Lacy, who hit .335 in 109 games.

Jim Bibby was the ace on the mound, finishing 19–6. But Bert Blyleven had an off-year at 8–13 and John Candelaria could muster only an 11–14 record. Rick Rhoden came through at 7–5, while Kent Tekulve was 8–12 with 21 saves.

But the Pirates began to sputter in September just as the Phillies heated up. Pittsburgh glided to the side of the road and, after controlling the division for much of the summer, finished just 83–79 and in third place. A four-game losing streak and a later-in-the-month six-game losing streak removed them from contention. The Pirates ended up eight games out of first.

That left the Montreal Expos for the Phillies to hunt down. During those first couple of days of September, just as the Pirates were about to go into freefall, the Expos reared up and tied them for first. Between September 5 and September 24, Montreal controlled the East.

This was a very good hitting Montreal club, with Hall of Famer Gary Carter catching, Hall of Famer Andre Dawson batting .308, and Ellis Valentine batting .315. Left fielder Ron LeFlore hit just .257, yet stole 97 bases. Second baseman Rodney Scott stole an additional 63 bases. The Expos could definitely generate runs. The pitching staff, led by Steve Rogers and Scott Sanderson, needed more depth, but the Expos, unlike the Pirates, were not going away.

On September 22, the Phillies beat the St. Louis Cardinals in 10 innings, 3–2, for Steve Carlton's 23rd victory of the year. McGraw got the save, Mike Schmidt hit his 42nd home run, and Larry Bowa cranked out three hits. The triumph moved Philadelphia into first place by a half game for the first time since September 5.

That lasted all of one day, as the Cardinals beat the Phillies, 6–3, on September 23. As the final days of the month ticked off, it went back and forth between the Phillies and Expos. Near the end of September, the Expos took two out of three from the Phillies in Philadelphia to move back into first.

There were two series remaining on the Phillies' schedule. They had four games at home against the Chicago Cubs before completing the regular season with the Expos in Canada. The Cubs were about 30 games under .500 and, as usual at the time, not in the mix for the playoffs.

PHILLIES 1980!

Between September 29 and October 2, the Phillies swept the Cubs, winning 6–5, 14–2, 5–0, and 4–2. They were now 19 games above .500 at 89–70, steamrolling teams at the tail end of the season. After the Cubs had been disposed of, Philadelphia and Montreal were tied for the division after the Expos thoroughly shredded the Cardinals in three straight games. The last of the regular-season drama would play out in Canada.

"We went to Montreal in a flat-out tie," said Phillies pitcher Warren Brusstar. "It was very intense."[16]

There were more than 57,000 in attendance at Olympic Stadium, the venue used for the opening ceremonies of the 1976 Summer Olympics. On October 3, Dick Ruthven started for the Phillies against Scott Sanderson, and it was a pitchers' duel. Schmidt drove in both runs for the winners in the 2–1 victory, and Rose had two hits. Lyle relieved Ruthven, who won his 17th game of the season, for 1 1/3 innings, and McGraw threw two innings to finish things off.

The Phillies were now in clinching territory. Nearly 51,000 fans showed up for the second game of the series, which featured a bit more hitting. If the Expos won, the race would come down to the final game of the season. If the Phillies won, it was over, and their incredible, rocky, colorful, ulcer-inducing journey would culminate with a division title and more baseball to come.

Larry Christenson started and pitched well against Montreal's Steve Rogers, who lasted seven innings. Christenson yielded to Reed, who gave way to Lyle, who turned the ball over to McGraw, as what was a 4–4 game after nine innings went into extras. On it went, into the 11th inning, when the Phillies, who had amassed 17 hits but left a boxcar load of runners on base, pushed across two runs.

Rose led off the 11th with a single and after a popout by McBride, Schmidt belted the game-winning home run. It was his 48th of the season, and lifted his RBI total to 121. He led the NL in both categories, and were both Schmidt's career highs.

McGraw hurled three innings of relief, allowing just one hit. That ended the division race, although there was one last game to play. Most of the normal starters rested and the backups filled many of the slots. The Expos won, 8–7, and Brusstar took the loss. The Phillies ended the season at 91–71, taking the East by a full game.

The results were a relief, they were satisfactory, but winning the division took an amazing amount of effort. And the real season—the playoffs—was just ahead.

13

THE REST OF BASEBALL

THE PHILLIES FINISHED one game ahead of the Montreal Expos in the National League East, going 91–71 while the Expos finished 90–72. The Pirates slipped to 83–79 and the division's other three teams were never a factor. The St. Louis Cardinals finished 74–88, the New York Mets were 67–95, and the Chicago Cubs were worse than that, at 64–98.

There was no wild-card playoff spot the way there is now, as only teams winning their division title advanced, meaning the playoffs began with the Championship Series.

Philadelphia was slated to meet the winner of the NL West, but it was not clear who that would be. It came down to the Houston Astros and Los Angeles Dodgers. Entering the last weekend of regular-season play, the Astros had a three-game lead. No sweat, right? Just one win would wrap it up.

Behind them, the Cincinnati Reds finished 89–73—close, but not close enough. The Atlanta Braves were 81–80, the San Francisco Giants 75–86, and the San Diego Padres 73–89.

Their bags were packed and they were leaving on a jet plane for the winter.

There was no mystery about the matchup in the ALCS. The Kansas City Royals romped in the AL West with their 97–65 record, 14 games ahead of the 83–79 Oakland Athletics. Trailing them were the Minnesota Twins (77–84), Texas Rangers (76–85), Chicago White Sox (70–90), California Angels (65–95), and Seattle Mariners (59–103).

There was impressive strength in the American League East. The New York Yankees prevailed with a 103–59 record, but the Baltimore Orioles chased them home with a 100–62 mark, one of the rare teams with 100 victories that did not make the play-offs. The Milwaukee Brewers were 17 games out of first with an 86–76 record, with the Detroit Tigers (84–78), Boston Red Sox (83–77), Cleveland Indians (79–81), and Toronto Blue Jays (67–95) bringing up the rear.

The Yankees were coming off a 1979, fourth-place division finish. Their so-so record of 89–71 was marred by the death of All-Star catcher Thurman Munson in a plane crash on August 2. The scarred Yankees regrouped from their mourning during the 1980 season.

At thirty-seven, lefty Tommy John, the man for whom the medical procedure to repair arm injuries was named, was the ace of the staff with a 22–9 record. Southpaw Ron Guidry went 17–10 and lefty Rudy May surprised everyone by finishing 15–5 with a league-leading 2.46 earned run average. Hall of Fame reliever Goose Gossage was a terror coming out of the bullpen, compiling a 6–2 record with 33 saves and a 2.27 ERA in 64 appearances.

Hall of Fame right fielder Reggie Jackson put together a hitting season that was right up there with his other top years. Jackson smacked 41 home runs, drove in 111 runs, and batted .300. He was not surrounded by a large number of All-Stars, but the Yankees regularly fielded a lineup dotted with above-average players. Bob Watson batted .307 at first base, Rick Cerone was the catcher, Willie Randolph staked a flag at second, and Graig Nettles and his vacuum cleaner glove held down third. Lou Piniella, always a solid outfielder, played left before his more accomplished managerial career.

Manager Dick Howser found playing time for Bobby Murcer and Oscar Gamble, either in the outfield or as pinch-hitters. This was a Yankees team seemingly better than the sum of its parts. It took a little while for the Yankees to find their footing, as April more resembled the season prior. They came out of the month 9–9, but much like the Phillies' division, no one got off to a fast start in the AL East and were just one game out of first.

May was livelier, as the Yanks won their first six games of the month and moved into first, where they remained for the rest of the season.

The Orioles kept the Yankees in their sights, much like a captain of the bridge watching through binoculars as he sought to pursue another ship, but having that ship always stay just out of range while maintaining just a little bit more speed.

New York was not oblivious to the challenge, but was playing so well it allowed Baltimore little hope of catching up. The Yanks won their first eight games of September, lost one, then won seven more in a row.

Baltimore might have liked some head-to-head games down the stretch, but the teams did not play each other even once in

September or October. Beating a team face-to-face offers bigger gulps of gain, but the last time during the 1980 season the Yankees and Orioles met were for five games in mid-August (Baltimore made not a smidgeon of progress, losing three of them).

Baltimore's Hall of Fame manager, Earl Weaver, loved the long ball and his teams lived by the home run. The best slugger on the club was Hall of Famer Eddie Murray. The switch-hitting first baseman belted 32 home runs, knocked in 116 runs, and batted .300. Outfielder Ken Singleton swatted 24 homers and collected 104 RBIs while hitting .304. Doug DeCinces hit 16 homers, Terry Crowley hit 12, and Gary Roenicke hit 10. Backup catcher Dan Graham also hit 10 homers, as did Benny Ayala, who did so in 76 plate appearances, Weaver's kind of guy.

The other trademark of Weaver's best Baltimore clubs was superior starting pitching, and this bunch had it in abundance. Jim Palmer, who at thirty-four was starting to fade, still won 16 games. Mike Flanagan did, too. Scott McGregor went 20–8. But one of the major stories of the summer was Steve Stone.

The 5-foot-10, 175-pound righty was thirty-two years old, a decade into an 11-year big-league career. He had never approached the type of results he produced in 1980, finishing 25–7 in the season of a lifetime, winning the American League Cy Young Award. It was a spectacular outlier of a season, as Stone had battled through frequent injuries and always believed he was a better pitcher than some of his records showed. He rededicated his mental approach and was a new man in 1980.

"All my life, because of my size, people have been telling me what I couldn't do," Stone said. "They said I was too small and not durable enough." After proving people wrong in 1980, Stone heard undercurrents of doubt that he would not have another good year in 1981. "Now those same people are saying I won't have a good year this year. That kind of thing is reiterated by people who've never achieved a great deal themselves."[1]

Alas for Stone, he was injured again that next season and retired without having much chance to take another run at a memorable season. He then embarked on a decades-long broadcasting career.

The Yankees needed the best record in baseball to fend off Baltimore just to win the division and earn the chance to meet Kansas City. The Royals were founded as an expansion team after the Athletics continued their move westward, from Philadelphia to KC to Oakland, where they still reside. The Royals' first year in business was 1969. After two extreme losing seasons, the Royals started playing as if they belonged. By its third season, 1971, the team won 85 games. Two years later they won 88.

By 1976, Kansas City was the class of the division, winning the crown for three straight seasons while hitting 102 victories in 1977. All three years the Royals advanced to the American League Championship Series, and all three years they lost (3–2, 3–2, and 3–1). The opponent each time was the Yankees, and by 1980 the Royals were sick of that unhappy situation. This time manager Jim Frey and his lineup seemed not only hungry to eliminate the Yanks in a triple revenge match, but seemed equipped to do so as well.

Kansas City had multiple weapons. Left fielder Willie Wilson batted .326 and stole 79 bases, utility man John Wathan batted .305, designated hitter Hal McRae batted .297, outfielder Clint Hurdle hit .294, first baseman Willie Aikens .278, and short-stop U. L. Washington .273. In addition, superb fielder Frank White (who would win eight Gold Gloves for his career) was an institution at second base, and although he didn't have his finest season, Amos Otis held down a slot in the outfield.

The Royals had six pitchers who won at least 10 games, starting with Dennis Leonard (20–11), Larry Gura (18–10), Paul Splittorff (14–11), Rich Gale (13–9), and Renie Martin (10–10). Oh yeah, and there was also closer Dan Quisenberry, who won 12 games and saved 33 with his submarine-style delivery. Quisenberry also led the American League in jokes.

"I've seen the future and it's much like the present, only longer," was a Quiz staple.[2]

And then there was third baseman George Brett who, like Stone, was one of the major storylines of the season. Brett was twenty-seven in 1980, at the peak of his powers, and after midseason was already a five-time All-Star.

While Brett was born in West Virginia, he grew up and went to high school in California. Showing the fallibility of the amateur baseball draft, Brett was not taken until the second round by the Royals in 1971. Brett imprinted himself on the national consciousness during the 1980 season when he made a bid to finish with a .400 average.

Hitting .400 is one of those near-mythical achievements of the modern era. In baseball's early days, especially during the Deadball Era, the finest hitters did record .400 averages. In 1894, when much about the game was different, outfielder Hugh Duffy hit .440, the highest official batting average ever recorded.

In 1901, the first year of the American League, Napoleon Lajoie, regarded as pretty much the sport's first superstar, batted .426 for the still-standing twentieth century–plus record. The great Ty Cobb batted at least .400 three times, including a .420 year in 1911. The esteemed Rogers Hornsby, whose lifetime average of .358 is second all-time to Cobb's .367, also put together three .400 seasons, including a high of .424 in 1924 for the St. Louis Cardinals. George Sisler twice hit .400 for the St. Louis Browns in the 1920s, reaching .420 in 1922.

When New York Giants first baseman Bill Terry batted .401 in 1930, no one would have surmised that was the last time anybody would ever hit .400 in National League play. Ninety years later, only Tony Gwynn for the San Diego Padres has come close. Gwynn, who won eight batting titles, batted .394 in 1994, a strike-shortened season. He appeared in 110 games when a labor dispute shut down the season on August 14.

It was in 1941, 11 years after Terry, that Ted Williams of the Boston Red Sox became the last man to hit .400 during a season in Major League Baseball. By rallying with six hits in a double-header on the last day of the season, Williams finished with a .406 average, the highest since 1924.

But Brett was going for it. Rather remarkably, the slugger got off to a fairly slow start for such a challenge. He batted just .259 in April, but came alive with a .329 May. He sizzled at the beginning of June, hitting .472 before missing a month of play due to injury. He batted .494 in the 21 games he played in July, and kick-started a 30-game hitting streak by mid-month. After dropping below .400 briefly and marginally in the 29th game of the consecutive games streak, he paused at .401. Brett clubbed two doubles and two singles in an 8–3 win at home over Toronto and the Kansas City fans went wild.

"It was just electric, standing on second base and seeing the crowd react like that," Brett said.[3]

Brett understood he was in magical territory and as the season turned for home, he was going to be in an increasingly brighter spotlight.

"I think the longer I'm up there, the more it's going to mount," he said, "and the longer the hitting streak goes on, the more it's going to mount. I'm sure it's going to be tough."[4]

He was right about the increased attention. Newspapers and broadcasters around the country began regularly asking the question, "Can George Brett hit .400?" The *Milwaukee Journal* even did a poll of famous players and baseball figures.

Hank Aaron, the Milwaukee hometown hero from his Braves days, and one of the greatest players of all time, said, "I think he has an excellent chance. He can't afford to have any bad days. But I really don't think George Brett has to worry about slumps."[5]

The *Journal* reached Bill Terry, too, who at the time, along with Ted Williams, was the only other living .400 hitter.

"He's a strong fellow," Terry said. "He's a fine ballplayer and a good hustler and that's what I like to see in a ballplayer. But it's hard going. You get anxious to get a hit and then it gets tough to get hits. He can't let that happen."[6]

Williams chimed in, too.

"He's a helluva hitter with a lot going for him," Williams said. "He's strong and he's a gutty guy. I hope he makes it."[7]

Brett was just about as hot in August and, as September began with five weeks of play remaining in the regular season, his average was .403. But then he had to sit out with another physical problem, tendinitis in his right wrist, and slowed down. He finished the season with a .390 average and a chase that energized baseball fans everywhere. Despite playing in only 117 games, Brett still hit 24 home runs and drove in 118 runs, averaging more than one RBI per game. He was named the American League's Most Valuable Player.

The same as any other team starting the season in April, the Royals' goal was to win the World Series. The roadblock, as it had been three times previously, was the New York Yankees. The Royals wouldn't have had it any other way. They had come close to upending New York before. This time they unleashed all of their guns right away, pummeling the Yankees in the first game of the American League Championship Series.

The Yankees, behind Ron Guidry, jumped to a 2–0 lead, but that was all Kansas City starter Larry Gura allowed. The Royals had three, two-run innings and won, 7–2. Brett added a home run to the onslaught.

There was no gap between games and the Royals, who had the home-field advantage, kept the Kansas City fans roaring with a 3–2 victory. They scored all of their runs in the third inning, and starter Dennis Leonard made them stand up with assistance from Quisenberry out of the bullpen. Rudy May took the loss for New York. Brett made a game-saving throw to the plate to catch Willie Randolph after outfielder Willie Wilson overthrew the cutoff man.

The teams headed to New York and didn't even have a day off before the third game. Frank White and Brett homered, and KC totaled 12 hits in the 4–2 elimination of the Yankees. The result was very meaningful besides the obvious reward of capturing the AL pennant and moving on to the World Series. It was the despised Yankees which Kansas City defeated to do so.

"They had beaten us each time they played us," said Royals designated hitter Hal McRae, speaking of all those previous ALCS losses to the Yankees. "We had won our division several years. Beating the Yankees, that was a big one. Everybody hates the Yankees. They always had more resources to get players. We really went at it. Everyone was gunning for the Yankees. We always felt we could beat them. We wanted to reach the next step [the World Series]. We felt we could win it all. We were not satisfied just being there."[8]

∗ ∗ ∗

Besides the drama of the National League pennant races and the American League East race, Stone's was a feel-good story during the season, Brett's was a pure excitement story sweeping the nation, but there was also a third storyline that gripped the nation. Unfortunately, it was not a happy one.

The significance of the development may well have affected the outcome of the National League Championship Series and whether or not the Phillies made it past the first round of the playoffs into the World Series, never mind win it.

During the first half of the 1980 season, J. R. Richard—not Nolan Ryan—was the No. 1 starter for the Houston Astros. Ryan ultimately won 324 games, became the all-time strikeout leader and threw a record seven no-hitters while being elected to the Hall of Fame on the strength of his blistering fastball, but went just 11–10 that season.

Richard, the 6-foot-8 flamethrower, who had twice struck out 300 men in a season himself, was off to a 10–4 start with a 1.90 earned run average.

"I was setting them up and knocking them down," Richard said. "I just felt as if I couldn't lose."[9]

The big right-hander was called on to start the July 8 All-Star Game at Dodger Stadium in Los Angeles. He was thrilled by the opportunity and pitched two innings, allowing one run while striking out two.

"By 1980, I was a big star in Houston," Richard said. "I got recognized all of the time." To him, being the All-Star starting pitcher in his first All-Star game "meant I was in the best company in the game."[10]

Soon after the All-Star break, Richard began experiencing strange feelings in his pitching arm. He was worried, visited a doctor, but received no firm diagnosis. Even more perplexing, he could still throw 100 mph. Later in July, Richard went on the disabled list.

He was on the field at the Astrodome doing a workout trying to right himself while the team was on the road, but suddenly "I felt a high-pitched tone ringing in my left ear. And then I threw a couple more pitches and became nauseated." He lost his equilibrium and tumbled to the ground.[11]

Richard was rushed to a hospital by ambulance and underwent emergency surgery where doctors discovered a blood clot and subsequently informed him he'd suffered three strokes. An in-his-prime, thirty-year-old professional athlete KO'd by a stroke? It was inexplicable for Richard, the Astros organization, and all of baseball.

Lost for the rest of the season, Richard later attempted a comeback, but would never regain his previous form.

"If you had told me that my appearance in the All-Star Game was going to be the next-to-last game I ever pitched in the big leagues, I would not have believed you," Richard said years later.[12]

Yet the Astros persevered for the rest of the regular season without their ace. The rotation then consisted of Ryan, Joe Niekro, Ken Forsch, and Vern Ruhle. Niekro, who like his Hall of Fame brother, Phil, relied on a knuckleball as his chief weapon, winning 20 games. Forsch and Ruhle won 12 apiece, and Ryan 11. Even though Richard was no longer with the club, his 10 victories were important. Combined, they carried the Astros into the season-ending series against the hopeful, but underdog, Los Angeles Dodgers. Just win one out of three and the Astros would move on to play the Phillies. That seemingly simply task, however, proved to be the equivalent of climbing to the summit of Mt. Everest.

Del Unser said the Phillies didn't care if they played Houston or LA. "It was getting to the big show in the end," he said. "That was the whole thing in a nutshell."[13]

The Astros were three games ahead of the Dodgers with three to play on October 3. The pitching matchup was Forsch versus Hall of Famer Don Sutton. Forsch pitched a complete game, allowing three runs—only two of them earned. However, he was on the losing side. Sutton also pitched well, going seven innings and surrendering two runs. He was relieved for the last two innings by Fernando Valenzuela, just nineteen at the time. He was a late call-up and pitched solely in relief in 10 games before his stupendous, "Fernandomania" 1981 season took the country by storm. Valenzuela got the win, his second and last of this abbreviated series of 1980 appearances.

As if there wasn't enough suspense, the Dodgers won the game in the bottom of the ninth on a Joe Ferguson home run. Houston's lead in the standings was now down to two games with two to play. Los Angeles had zero margin for error.

Ryan pitched very well the following day, going seven innings while striking out nine Dodgers and allowing just two runs. But he didn't win, either. Jerry Reuss won his 18th of the season for LA, permitting just one run while striking out seven and allowing seven singles. Reuss, who won 220 games in his career, was nicknamed "Rolls Reuss" and proved to be a top-of-the-line model in this outing.

"When I woke up this morning I knew it would be a one-run game," Reuss said.[14]

Reuss handcuffed Houston so the Astros could mount no late charge. He retired 11 of the last 13 batters he faced.

"He just kept after them," said Dodgers manager Tommy Lasorda. "He was aggressive. He didn't let anything rattle him."[15]

One more and done, the Astros hoped, on the last Sunday of the regular season. They could still escape with the West crown by pulling out the 162nd game of the season. Ruhle, who had replaced Richard in the four-man rotation, started for Houston, while Burt Hooton was tabbed for the Dodgers. But this was the equivalent of a playoff game, so the managers were poised with quick hooks if either starter seemed at all wobbly. As it so happened, both did, yet for different reasons.

Houston scored two quick runs in the top of the second, and Lasorda lifted Hooton after an inning-plus and allowing the runs while yielding three hits and a walk. Lasorda rushed to the bullpen for Bobby Castillo, who went the next four innings.

Meanwhile, although Ruhle was throwing well, he was also throwing painfully. The righty had cut the index finger on his pitching hand on a hook a couple of days earlier. It took two stitches to close the wound, but they ripped open two innings into the game. Manager Bill Virdon removed him for Joaquin Andujar, who gave up one run in 2 1/3 innings.

Lasorda and Virdon played chess, swapping out pieces for pitchers and pinch-hitters. Houston led, 3–0, into the fifth inning when Los Angeles finally got a run on the board. The

Dodgers added another in the bottom of the seventh, so it was 3–2 with LA batting in the home half of the eighth. How it got that way came with an assist from Manny Mota the previous inning. While the Phillies possessed Unser and Greg Gross, two extraordinary pinch-hitters, at that moment Mota owned the all-time record for most pinch-hits. The former record holder was catcher Smoky Burgess.

When he cracked the record, Mota bought himself a gold chain necklace with the No. 145. When he drove in Pedro Guerrero with a key run against the Astros as a forty-two-year-old, which was number 150, he joked about replacement jewelry.

"I've got to change the number now," Mota said.[16] He could have done so right then, as that would be the final pinch-hit for the Dominican, who posted a .304 batting average and then coached for the Dodgers for thirty-four years.

The Dodgers had won 23 games in their last at-bat in 1980, often doing so in the ninth inning. But they did not wait this time, eliminating the need for a last-minute rally. Third baseman Ron Cey hit a two-run homer in the eighth, his 28th of the season, off Frank LaCorte as the Dodgers prevailed, 4–3.

It wasn't as if Cey, whose nickname was "Penguin," offered any deep analysis of the deciding swing afterward. Limping around the trainer's room, it did not appear he would have been capable of beating out a bunt, so he might as well settle for the long ball.

"I was simply trying to get a pitch to hit," Cey said.[17] He found one, sending the National League season into overtime. The clock had run out, but now the teams were tied, both with 92–70 records. The situation demanded a 163rd game.

While most teams would be demoralized after watching a three-game lead evaporate, the Astros were down but did not talk as if they believed they were out. "It was a great series," Virdon said. "We just haven't won one."[18]

Second baseman Joe Morgan, who had been a linchpin of the Cincinnati Reds' Big Red Machine teams and later was elected to the Hall of Fame, was back with the Astros for this one year at thirty-six, playing for the team he broke in with seventeen years earlier. He did not sound at all panicked as the Astros prepared to engage in the fifth playoff in National League history.

"It would be different if we came in here and they beat up on us," Morgan said. "They just got more breaks than us."[19]

In addition to timely hitting, Houston would not be opposed to stumbling into a little bit of good luck.

Houston opened with its winningest pitcher, Joe Niekro, which was a good bet. The Dodgers started Dave Goltz, though that did not work out as well. Niekro pitched a complete-game six-hitter, permitting just one unearned run. The Astros pounced on Goltz, scoring early and often, and then roughed up his mound successors. Houston won the biggest regular-season game in the team's history to date, 7–1.

"I was confident," Niekro said. "I was very relaxed. After the first two innings, I found I had a good knuckleball."[20] When a knuckleball specialist says that, it's time for batters to be afraid.

This was the first pennant in Astros history, and champagne was the beverage of choice in the clubhouse. Virdon tried to smoke a victory cigar, but it got wet.

Someone asked Ryan what this felt like after being a member of the New York Mets when they won their first pennant (and World Series). He had also been part of the Angels when that California team won a division title.

"I enjoyed all of them," said Ryan, who had a champagne hair wash going. "I don't see any difference. They're different individuals, different uniforms, but I'm just as wet."[21]

That was an afternoon game, and there was no break between the conclusion of this playoff encounter and the first game of the World Series in Philadelphia, scheduled to open on October 7, the next night. The Astros were swiftly leaving LA.

"It's going to be an enjoyable flight," Ruhle said.[22]

Virdon had just survived four days of very stressful baseball, which nearly exposed his very good pitching staff still missing J. R. Richard, yet he had to ready a team for an even bigger series beginning less than 24 hours later. He knew the World Series beckoned, but wanted to digest this hard-fought win and celebrate it, if only for a few hours.

Still, he took a brief time out to think about the Phillies, waiting nearly 3,000 miles away.

"They've got good power," Virdon said of Philadelphia, where he might get a nap later the next day. "They're tough to contain in Philadelphia. But this is a new ballgame."[23]

He was happy to be able to say that instead of trying to explain how the Astros lost four-straight games and had to slink into the offseason. Instead, Houston was looking forward to the biggest games in franchise history.[24]

"We're not going to get much rest," Virdon said, "but nobody cares right now."[25]

14

NATIONAL LEAGUE CHAMPIONSHIP SERIES: VAMP TILL READY

ON OCTOBER 6, the day after the Phillies completed the regular season after ousting the Montreal Expos, the *Philadelphia Daily News* figured out a way to say a lot in few words. Front-page headline writers were concise, if screaming loudly in their own way. "Phantastic!" read the summary of the result, the capital "P" in the design of the Phillies' team insignia.

A spot representing the National League in the World Series was at stake when the Philadelphia Phillies and Houston Astros had finally negotiated their way through mazes of obstacles to outlast stiff competition and claim division titles. Each won their division by one game in the standings.

The Phillies had not won an NL pennant since 1950, and had never won a World Series crown. The Astros had never won a pennant. Both teams had known frequent recent heartbreak by thrice losing in the championship series. Someone had to survive and establish a milestone for their franchise.

Vern Ruhle had inherited more responsibility after J. R. Richard was lost for the season with his blood clot and strokes. Ruhle became a frontline starter in the rotation, an upgrade from spot starter. He definitely gave some thought to the Phillies within minutes after the Astros outlasted the Dodgers. He thought positive thoughts.

"Our right-handed pitching should neutralize their power," said the optimistic Ruhle. "If we keep it in the ballpark, we should be alright."[1]

The Astros had endured an exhausting last-weekend series to edge out the Los Angeles Dodgers. The Phillies had willed themselves past the Montreal Expos after a stirring September.

The Phillies won 91 of their 162 games. The Astros won 92 of their 163 games, one more than originally scheduled because of the playoff with the Dodgers. There had been enormous pressure on both teams during the closing days of the season. It is often said that playoff pressure is a different animal. A ratcheted-up version of normal play. But these teams had been pressure-cooked for weeks.

It was not as if there was a long time before the series began, unlike the National Football League playoffs when teams always had a week to get ready for their next game. This seemed more like a case of *What's the hurry?* The Phillies had it better. They were at home and had wrapped up the regular season on time on a Sunday. The Astros' season spilled into Monday, and then they had to fly across the country from Los Angeles. It almost seemed unfair.

One intriguing aspect of the series was the composition of the Phillies roster. Marty Bystrom, so important with his 5–0 record in September, had been called up from the minors on

September 1, even if he did not make his debut until September 7. Bystrom was so good, he was named National League Pitcher of the Month. Yet it was not 100 percent clear at first if Major League Baseball was going to approve him being part of the team during the playoffs.

Commissioner Bowie Kuhn and National League president Chub Feeney huddled and, in their confab, talked about Nino Espinosa, who had really gone down with bursitis in his shoulder and was not just being pushed aside as a ploy by the Phillies to use the hot Bystrom. They ruled in favor of adding Bystrom after two days of deliberations, which is not long to render a decision by Supreme Court standards, but seemed an eternity to the Phillies and Bystrom.

"I didn't think it looked very good yesterday," Bystrom said on October 7, on the first day of the playoffs. "I thought I was supposed to find out at the workout. Then they told me there was no point in hanging around waiting and to just come back tomorrow. I really didn't know what they were thinking. I didn't really know what was going to happen. Sometimes I felt good. Sometimes I felt bad."[2]

Bystrom reported to Veterans Stadium ready to play, though without knowing if he was going to be allowed to put on a uniform. Then he got the word he was on the roster. It was a thrill when he stepped out onto the field, a pinch-me moment for a player who five weeks earlier was in the minors.

"Here I am, my first year up, only been here 30 days, and here I am in the playoffs," Bystrom said, even if he underestimated the progress of the calendar. "It's a thrill, I'll tell you, because you don't get this chance very often."[3]

Bystrom probably didn't understand just how that sounded. He was surrounded by teammates, some of whom had spent a decade to get to this point in any season, and representing a team that hadn't had this chance in three decades.

The teams were not complete strangers, even if they played in different geographical divisions of the NL. They met for four series during the regular season. The Phillies won all of them, though there was not a single blowout in the 12 games. The teams played three times in mid-May, with Philadelphia winning, 3–0 and 4–2, while losing, 3–0, with Nolan Ryan the dominant presence that game. Less than a week later, they faced off for three more games, this time Philadelphia winning all of them, 3–0, 5–4, and 6–2. Steve Carlton won the shutout game.

After that, the clubs took a vacation from one another for a while before resuming combat with a three-game series from July 15 to July 17. Houston won the opener, 3–2, then Philadelphia won the next two, 4–2 and 2–1. Carlton won the close one at the end. Similarly, before the end of the month, the teams battled again for three games. Again, the Astros took the first game, 3–2, before the Phillies came right back and won, 9–6 and 6–4. The clubs would not face each other again until the NLCS.

At least Ruhle was offering his analysis from experience. But if it meant anything, the Phillies took the regular-season series, 9–3. The main thing that proved was the Phillies found a way to win against Astros pitching, even if their hitters rarely torched them.

The Astros, who overcame their challenges to move on to the playoffs, were constructed in the mold of their laid-back, but at least semi-strict manager Bill Virdon. Virdon was a slick field-ing center fielder who played in the majors between 1955 and 1968 for the St. Louis Cardinals and Pittsburgh Pirates, with a lifetime batting average of .267.

Virdon won the NL Rookie of the Year with St. Louis and a World Series title with the Pirates, as well as one Gold Glove. He was twice Manager of the Year, including in 1980 for his work with the Astros. He would end up just shy of winning 1,000 games as a manager with the Pirates, Astros, Yankees, and Expos.

He was a conservative leader in that he didn't approve of long hair and preferred facial hair to be limited to a trimmed mustache. He also had a rule banning alcohol on team flights.

"The only times I've been embarrassed by being in baseball," Virdon said, "as a player, coach or manager, involved players with time on their hands and the availability of alcohol. If any of them say anything to me about the rule, I tell 'em if they can't go without a drink for two or three hours, I'll get them a psychiatrist because they need help."[4]

That said, Virdon did not mind the champagne drenching one bit after the Astros held off the Dodgers. Still, it was not difficult to envision him as the anti-Dallas Green. Green had verbally lashed his team to its East Division crown. Virdon did not yell. He may have cajoled, but he did so earnestly. Of course, Green and Virdon would not play an out on the field, but the contrast was vivid.

"Houston or Los Angeles, it didn't matter," said Phillies pitcher Warren Brusstar when the opponent was determined. "You play whoever you play. Any time you open up at home, that's good. Thinking back, I had really never played well in Houston."[5]

Despite their recent success, the Astros were still a new team. It wasn't so long before, when they were an expansion team, that they were playing with a different moniker: the Colt .45s. While that original name hearkened back to the Old West, it only lasted three seasons. In reality, the Astros were named after a product, not an historical theme. Playing inside the first domed stadium in American professional sports, their ballpark was named the Astrodome and the artificial surface was AstroTurf.

Ryan, who figured to carry the weight of the pitching staff on his shoulders in the series, had not quite been around as long as the team, even if he did go back to the 1960s.

"Houston used to be considered a joke," he recalled. "You look around this clubhouse, you think about this season, what all we've been through. You know one thing. Houston isn't a joke in baseball anymore."[6]

Inarguably, the Astros were in a position to do something special. They had an opportunity to write a little bit of history for a young franchise. The Astros were not seen as a favorite to capture the NL West when the season began, but as the year wore on, fans seemed to get spoiled. Whenever any little thing went wrong, Virdon seemed to be the brunt of fan critiques. Yet his demeanor never seemed to vary, remaining unruffled throughout.

"I wish we could win every day," Virdon said. "But no matter how hard you try to not let any games get away, some of them do."[7] That actually sounded like a line for an instructional manual for children who didn't know a thing about baseball.

The Astros finished 89–73 in 1979 after taking a brief run at the division title when no one expected that to happen. They somehow finished 16 games over .500 while scoring just one more run than they allowed. Houston was in first place as late as September 9, but placed second, just a game and a half behind the Cincinnati Reds.

"This team is more mature," Virdon said of his 1980 club. "This is a lot better club."[8]

Funny thing is, the Phillies thought the same way; better as in ahead of the 1976-77-78 division winners, not the 1979 fizzle sticks who disappointed all year long, not only in October.

"In the past, when we got to the playoffs, I don't think we really understood what we'd done, or what we'd accomplished," said reliever Tug McGraw. "But this year I sense a different feeling, a feeling for the magnitude of the situation. I think this team understands the magnitude of what it's done. It's more enthusiastic. It's got a better sense of pride. Mentally, we are fine-tuned now. Physically, we're healthy."[9]

After six months of taking a browbeating from Green, of being reminded daily that they were responsible for being the best that they could be, and after walking through fire to outlast Pittsburgh and Montreal, the Phillies should have been prepared to take on the Murderers' Row 1927 Yankees. If they showed any signs of slippage, Green would verbally assault them all over again.

By then, of course, his messages should have been imprinted on the players' foreheads. And they did give him what he was looking for in the season-ending series against Montreal, when they were indeed facing considerable pressure and came through to put themselves into this series with Houston.

"I think we have a better feel as a team than the other groups that went into the playoffs," Green said. "I see much more intensity, much more desire." Green said he felt "much more at ease with this team than I have been all year.

"I'm not saying those other teams didn't care, or that they didn't go hard after it. I just think that in our hearts this team knows now what it is going to take to win."[10]

Whether it is true or not, if a team reaches the brink of playoff success and falls short repeatedly, as both the Phillies and Astros had done, there are always cynics in the crowd who fire off nasty comments suggesting their team has choked.

Pete Rose had been brought to Philadelphia because he was a winner and expected to help the Phillies to the promised land. The Phils were on the cusp of that achievement. Rose was elsewhere in the National League when the Phillies won their three division championships, but he didn't see a team that folded, only one that got beat by a better team or circumstances.

"This team never choked in the playoffs, regardless of what people think," Rose said. "They could have beat us very easy that one year [in the 1976 playoffs when he was with the Reds]. And they just didn't get the breaks against the Dodgers."[11]

Perhaps some veterans would rather have faced the Dodgers in 1980 because they felt they owed them for those playoff losses in the 1970s, but Greg Gross hadn't been there for that. "For me, personally, no," Gross said. "I was just thrilled to death to be in the playoffs."[12]

Outfielder Lonnie Smith, still officially a rookie, didn't care who the opponent was, either. "I just wanted to play," he said. "It was a new experience for me."[13]

As these playoffs began against Houston, the Phillies had two significant advantages—Mike Schmidt, who had been the best everyday player in the NL that season, and Steve Carlton, who had been the best pitcher in the NL that season.

Carlton finished 24–9, the most wins in the National League. He started a league-high 38 games, recorded a 2.34 earned run average, hurled a league-leading 304 innings, and was tops in strikeouts with 286. Carlton failed, however, to lead the league in words spoken in public. But when it came to pitching, he was not only the Phillies' staff ace, he was the ace of the entire league. Later, when trophies were given out, Carlton won the league's Cy Young Award. There was no other candidate to consider.

Even as a teammate, Carlton's day in, day out work was stunning to watch for months on end.

"Every time out," shortstop Larry Bowa said of how impressive Carlton was in 1980, "when he was pitching, we felt if we got two runs we had a good chance to win. His vibes were that he was going to win every game."[14]

However, Rose was one player who could not identify with Carlton's reclusive act. Much more of a natural in give-and-take conversation, Rose was a thoughtful interview no matter the outcome. He did not make excuses if something went awry, standing at his locker and facing the inquisitors.

"He was consistent," Rose said of Carlton's retreat to the trainer's room, "which was his prerogative. I thought as a member of the team you've got a job to do and that included talking to the press. All you have to do if you're a player is answer the (bleep) question. I did it. Some guys didn't respect the press.

"All you have to do is say, 'Yeah, I made the error. I can't bring it back. I wish I could.'"[15]

That 1980 regular season was not one of Rose's finest, but it was good enough. He played in all 162 games, led the National League in doubles with 42, drove in 64 runs, but batted just .282, which was low for him. But at thirty-nine, he still stole 12 bases.

The man whose greatness helped define the season was Mike Schmidt. His .286 season was very different than Rose's. Coincidentally, he also stole 12 bases, but also led the league with 48 home runs and 121 runs batted in. In a sense, this was Schmidt's Carl Yastrzemski year. In 1967, Yaz was the Mr. Indispensable of the Boston Red Sox in their Impossible Dream, pennant-winning year. When the Red Sox needed a clutch hit, Yaz was at the plate and made it happen. Schmidt was a magnet for big moments in 1980. It was the season that helped propel him into the Hall of Fame and recognition in some quarters as the greatest Phillie to ever put on the uniform—and perhaps the best third baseman of all time.

"One of the things that has evolved for me over the years is a drive," Schmidt said later in his career, "maybe a drive to succeed, but more like a drive to well … to keep driving, a drive to learn how to face this game."[16]

Schmidt was always viewed as a heavy thinker. This revealed an intense desire to push himself, to never falter, to always keep plugging and not be satisfied with his achievements. He gave some thought to what his baseball life would have been like if he was more relaxed, someone who just allowed himself to approach the plate more freely and actually, more empty-minded, one might say.

"If I were able to go out on the field with a real carefree attitude, if I was a player who doesn't have the same kind of pressure and salary and expectations, then I might love all this and never want to leave it. But I'm just not made that way. I take failure too hard. It's funny. It is almost a Catch-22 kind of thing. I take failure too seriously because I feel I know too much about why I fail. If I didn't think too much, if I didn't study things the way I do, if I didn't care, if I didn't have this need to succeed, then maybe things would be easier for me."[17]

Of course, then he wouldn't be Mike Schmidt, and Mike Schmidt knew it.

As the Phillies-Astros series dawned, Philadelphia was looking for the 48-home run Mike Schmidt. An introspective Schmidt was forced to confront why the Phillies had not been able to go beyond the NLCS before.

"I don't know if our character was lacking then, or not," he said. "It seems to me we just had some fluke blow that got us in every important game we had to play in. I think we've had our fill now of all the crazy freak breaks one team could have happen to it."[18]

This time around, the Phillies seemed poised to make their own breaks.

15

NATIONAL LEAGUE CHAMPIONSHIP SERIES: GAMES ONE AND TWO IN PHILADELPHIA

UNLIKE MANY OF the younger members of the Phillies, Pete Rose had not only been to the playoffs before, but had played for teams that won in the playoffs before. Now, after the long regular season, it was time to play for keeps against the Houston Astros.

"I'm ready," Rose said. "I feel great and I'm swinging good right now. This team has so many things going for them right now, it's scary. Our pitching is just the way we want it. The best pitcher in the league will be going for us against Houston with five days' rest. That's one plus. And we have the right guys swinging the bat right now—[Mike] Schmidt, [Bake] McBride and myself."[1]

The best three-out-of-five Houston series opened at Veterans Stadium on the night of October 7 before 65,277 full-throated fans. Steve Carlton, as Rose said, was the starting pitcher for Philadelphia, while Ken Forsch took the mound for the Astros.

Neither pitcher looked vulnerable early. Carlton was Carlton, Lefty in charge of whatever action was taking place at home plate. Righty Forsch, who finished the season with a 12–13 record, was no novice. He had been in the majors for 10 years and ultimately would retire with a 114–113 record. Basically, he was a .500 pitcher throughout his career, always reliable, while mixing in two All-Star seasons.

Carlton gave up a walk to outfielder Cesar Cedeno in the top of the first but was in no danger. Forsch gave up a single to McBride, but was never threatened. In the second, Carlton allowed singles to Gary Woods and Forsch, but nobody advanced beyond second base. In the bottom of the second, Larry Bowa and Bob Boone singled with two outs, but Carlton struck out to end the inning.

The Astros made Carlton look human in the third inning, scoring the first run of the game on singles by Jose Cruz, Cedeno, and Woods. Rose led off the bottom of the inning with a single, but when he tried to steal second base he was thrown out by Houston catcher Luis Pujols and the Phillies got nothing out of it.

The game stayed that way through five and a half, 1–0 Houston with Carlton and Forsch handling all other batting challenges. Rose, as he had been for his entire career, was the catalyst for jump-starting the offense for his team. He was again the leadoff man in the Phillies' home half of the sixth, swatting a single. Three batters later, with two outs, the Bull, Greg

Luzinski, stepped into the batter's box and propelled the ball out of the park. Two-run homer.

Much of the 1980 campaign had been a struggle for Luzinski, and Philadelphia fans had booed him at times. He had quickly gone from a loved figure at the park to one viewed with doubt, and even treated shabbily at times.

His approach to the opener of the playoff series, even before smacking a decisive home run, was to give the impression he was making a fresh start. As excited as Phillies fans had been when the team clinched the division, and as loud as they would be in Veterans Stadium, Luzinski thought they needed some prodding when the game began. So he took off his cap and twirled it. Fans always love to see their guys show emotion and are suckers for any physical signs of it.

"I was trying to get the crowd revved up," Luzinski said. "They seemed to be sitting on their hands. I wanted to get 'em psyched."[2]

Luzinski's blast gave the Phillies a 2–1 lead, but the Astros immediately threatened to tie it in the seventh. Forsch knocked out his second single of the game, but with Rafael Landestoy at the plate the pitcher was picked off first. Forsch had reached Carlton in the batter's box, but Carlton got him back on the bases. Enos Cabell singled later in the inning, but no harm was done.

In the bottom of the seventh, Garry Maddox singled and Bowa sacrificed him to second with a bunt. With two outs, Greg Gross came on to pinch-hit for Carlton, ending his night after throwing seven complete. He gave up seven hits and just one run. Maddox stole third as Gross worked the count to 2-1 on Forsch. Gross lashed a single to left, scoring Maddox with an insurance run.

Tug McGraw came out of the bullpen to pitch the eighth in place of Carlton. Close game, big stakes, this is what McGraw lived for and circumstances he thrived in. McGraw still had belief left in his system from his days with the Mets, and retired Houston in order.

The ninth was a little bit more complicated. The game was close enough that Astros manager Bill Virdon felt a comeback was within reach, and strategized accordingly. McGraw provided the Astros with optimism when he walked the leadoff batter, Luis Pujols. Virdon threw Dave Bergman out there to pinch-run for Pujols, and sent Terry Puhl to the plate pinch-hitting for Craig Reynolds. Puhl flied out to left.

Then Jeffrey Leonard pinch-hit for Forsch, but McGraw got him on a swinging strikeout. Rafael Landestoy's routine ground out to second ended the game. Forsch pitched well enough to win many games, going the distance while surrendering the three runs on eight hits. It was Luzinski who beat Forsch.

"The fastball was the right pitch," Forsch said. "I just wish I would have gotten it up a little more. I went 3-2 on him earlier in the game, too. Threw him a slider and he popped it up. You keep in a pattern, they'll figure it out. And I didn't want to hang anything."[3]

Instead, Luzinski hung the loss on Forsch. By the ninth, Luzinski was back on the bench, Del Unser replacing him in the field. Still, he clearly stroked the most significant hit of the game. As it so happened, surprisingly, Luzinski's homer was to be the only one in the series.

"I couldn't even tell you what kind of pitch it was," Luzinski said, "'cause it was 3-2 and I was just trying to pick up the ball. I knew that with two out Pete [Rose] would be running, and I figured if I could just drive one in the gap, he'd score, and we'd at least tie it."[4]

Smiting the key blow had to be a vindication for Luzinski. He had not been a major contributor in September when the standings were bunched, and there was some speculation manager Dallas Green might not even start him in the playoff opener, instead inserting Lonnie Smith and his .339 batting average into the lineup.

The manner in which the Phillies won, 3–1, hardly intimidated the Astros. The score was close, Philadelphia never put together a big inning, and Carlton was not as sharp as he usually was.

"I had the feeling that tonight was one of his off-nights," Woods said.[5]

This not being the NCAA basketball championships, a single loss in the playoffs did not send the Astros back to Houston for the offseason. The teams were scheduled to line up and do it all over again less than 24 hours after the first one ended. The mood in the Houston clubhouse was more or less, "What, us worry?"

"They didn't dominate us," said veteran Joe Morgan. "A break here or there and we could have won."[6] The future Hall of Famer did not even get into the first game because of a balky knee.

Morgan referred back to the Astros' recent suspenseful series against the Dodgers when his team fought back and won. Just because Houston was down 1–0 didn't mean the series was over by a long shot. One thing the Astros did have going for them in Game Two was starting Nolan Ryan (against Dick Ruthven).

Ryan, who came closest to pitching forever as any major leaguer, was hardly fazed by the situation.

"I always go out there with the intention of shutting out my opponent and the loss in Game One doesn't really change my attitude or how I'm going to pitch the game," Ryan said.[7] Since Ryan tossed 61 shutouts in regular-season play during his illustrious career, there was no reason for him to think otherwise.

"Any time I have a good game, I have to have a good fastball and a good curve, get my breaking ball over," Ryan said. "Look, we win one game here and we're in good shape."[8]

That was definitely true. The series could last only five games and after the first two in Philadelphia, all the remaining games would be played in Houston if it went the distance. An untimely loss in Philadelphia might turn the rest of the series into a tightrope walk, depending on how much home-field advantage made a difference.

Veterans Stadium opened in 1971, and was expressly designed to be versatile enough to be the home grounds for both the Phillies and the NFL's Philadelphia Eagles. Architecturally, it was lumped with Cincinnati's Riverfront Stadium and Pittsburgh's Three Rivers Stadium as being of the "cookie cutter" variety. What sounded like a good idea five decades ago was roundly derided in later years for being a park devoid of personality. Since then, most stadiums of that ilk have been dynamited, and the cities they inhabited have built two new ones—one for baseball and one for football.

Even worse than aesthetics, the Vet was allowed to deteriorate. Only weeks before the Phillies moved into Citizens Bank Park in 2004, Veterans Stadium was destroyed in a big bang that lasted just 62 seconds, or shorter than some ovations for Mike Schmidt in 1980. But that was later.

The Astrodome was drastically different. It was an enclosed park where baseball was played indoors and the field was not made out of grass, but artificial turf. The world's first multi-sport, domed stadium opened in 1965, and was the team's home park from 1965 through 1999. Built at a cost of $35 million, the Astrodome was so far ahead of its time, so innovative, that people called it "The Eighth Wonder of the World." This may have been a small step forward for mankind—especially from a sports perspective—but eventually things calmed down and it was looked at more as a place to play ball than on any lists competing for attention with the Great Pyramid of Giza or the Hanging Gardens of Babylon. The Dome just had better press agents.

While baseball as a whole seems less affected by home-field advantage than football, basketball, or hockey, this was one case where the environments were so different it could matter. At the least, teams had to play defense differently given the hard bounces ground balls took on AstroTurf and how neither sun nor clouds would affect circling under fly balls. Of course, a major difference was weather, as there was no weather in the climate-controlled Astrodome.

"I'd rather have more games at home," said Gross.[9] Alas, major-league schedule makers did not consult him.

Given the 3–2 imbalance in geography and scheduling, it behooved the Phillies to leave Philadelphia with two wins before tackling the Astros in the Dome. For one good reason: the Astros were 55–26 at home during the 1980 regular season.

* * *

Game Two unfolded slowly, and concluded in a rush. Ryan lived up to his credentials the way Carlton had lived up to his. Both regarded as great pitchers, both were very good to begin the series, but not overpowering. Carlton was good enough to win, as was Ryan, though he was out of the game by the time Game Two was decided. Ryan threw 6 1/3 innings, giving up eight hits and two runs while striking out six. Ruthven went seven innings, permitted just three hits, but also walked five. He also gave up just two runs.

The Astros scratched out the game's first run in the top of the third. With one out, Ruthven walked Craig Reynolds. A Ryan bunt resulted in a sacrifice with Reynolds taking second. Terry Puhl then singled to left, scoring Reynolds for a 1–0 Houston lead.

Philadelphia's retaliation came in the bottom of the fourth, as Schmidt cracked a leadoff double and Luzinski promptly followed with a double of his own. When Schmidt crossed the plate, the game was tied. Manny Trillo sent Luzinski to third on a sacrifice. Next up was Maddox, who singled in Luzinski for a 2–1 Phillies lead.

It took until the top of the seventh for the Astros to knot the score. Ruthven put himself in a bad spot by walking Ryan, who scored on a subsequent double by Puhl.

After scoring in the top of the eighth, Houston sent Dave Smith to the mound in the bottom of the inning. Luzinski came through yet again, this time with a leadoff single. Green then had Lonnie Smith pinch-run for Luzinski at first base. Following a pattern, Trillo laid down another sacrifice bunt to move Lonnie Smith to second. The improved speed on the basepaths paid off when Maddox singled to center and Smith came all of the way around with the tying run to make it a 3–3 game. Dave Smith ended the inning by getting pinch-hitter Del Unser to fly out.

McGraw, who allowed one run in the eighth, his first earned run in 16 games, had come and gone in batting and pitching changes, so Green waved in Ron Reed to pitch the top of the ninth. Reed avoided trouble and the Phillies tried to pull the game out in the bottom of the inning before embarking for Houston. There was a huge difference between being up two games to none and being tied 1–1 for the Phillies, with Philadelphia in their rearview mirror—possibly for the season.

Frank LaCorte was on the mound for the Astros when Rose stepped in. He flied out. McBride energized the crowd (again of more than 65,000) with a single to right field. Rally time, yes? Schmidt singled to center, but McBride had to stop at second. Lonnie Smith came through with a third straight single (on a 12-pitch at-bat), but it wasn't placed well enough in right to send McBride home.

Not everyone was certain the ball was going to land safely, and the Phillies could not afford a baserunning gaffe that would kill a hopeful inning. McBride said later he was sure the ball was going to fall in, and so took off as if he was competing in a 100-meter dash. Then he saw third-base coach Lee Elia waving at him to put on the brakes. Not without difficulty, since he was going all out, McBride screeched to a halt and did not proceed to the plate.

Bowa wondered how McBride even made it back to third base, rather than barreling into Houston catcher Alan Ashby.

"He said he was running on the pitch," Bowa said. "If you're going that far, you might as well keep going because it's a double play anyway (if the ball had been caught). That hurt. That gave them new life. If Bake kept running, he's safe."[10]

The decision to hold McBride resulted in some second guessing—by Elia himself.

"I screwed it up," Elia said. "The ball's caught, he wouldn't have a chance to get back, anyway. I should've taken the chance and sent him. But I held him up momentarily and when I tried to get him to go again, it was too late. It was a reflex action thing. My hands just went up. What can I tell you, fellas? It kills me as much as it kills the guys on this ball club."[11]

If McBride runs, he likely scores and there is no Houston extra-inning explosion. Instead, the bases were loaded with just one out (still a great spot to be in), and opportunity stared the next batter in the face. It was Trillo, who would become the Most Valuable Player in this NLCS, but not because of his work at the plate this time up. Trillo struck out, setting off a big sign of deflation which rippled through the Veterans Stadium stands. Maddox came up, hit a foul popup caught by first baseman Art Howe and the rally was over. Next stop, extra innings.

There had been three lead changes with only six total runs scored. This turned out to be foreshadowing for the suspense that kept building throughout this series, one that many people have termed the best ever of league championship series.

The Astros promptly pounced on Reed in the top of the 10th, as Puhl led off with a single and then advanced to second on an Enos Cabell sacrifice. Morgan was intentionally walked and Virdon put in Landestoy as a pinch-runner. Cruz singled, scoring Puhl, and then Landestoy scored on a fielder's choice. Green removed Reed and replaced him with Kevin Saucier. Bergman, the first man he faced, bashed a triple. Rally, yes.

Houston put up a four spot in the 10th, a crooked number blinking in the Phillies' faces when they came to bat in the bottom of the inning, trying to produce a salvage operation. Rally, yes? Rally, not quite. Bowa singled, Bob Boone walked, and Rose scored Bowa on a ground out. But that was it. The Phillies mustered a run, but lost, 7–4. The series was tied.

Suddenly the ambassador of cool, Dallas Green downplayed the task lying ahead.

"We were in the same position [must-win] in Montreal," Green said, "and we didn't do too bad up there. I don't feel too bad about it. We've played in the Dome before, you know. It's not like we're going down there cold. We were 9–3 against these guys for the year, so we had to beat them down there somewhere along the line. It doesn't bother us going on the road."[12]

Coping remarkably well with the missed opportunity, Schmidt said he wasn't worried going to Houston for an extended stay.

"No big deal," he said. "We're the best road team in baseball."[13]

False bravado, or unwavering confidence? Schmidt seemed pretty calm about things. Maybe not all of the Phillies did, however, and definitely not the ficklest of fans.

Relief pitcher Warren Brusstar was not an active party in the game. He was situated in the bullpen in case Green wanted him on the phone. While the Phillies were not scoring in the ninth and the Astros were scoring in the 10th, he heard plenty of nasty comments from disappointed fans.

After the game, Green told reporters that there was nothing he saw that meant the Phillies should be particularly nervous about the rest of the series against Houston. Clearly, the fans felt differently. "You're choking again," Brusstar said was one of the shouts he heard. "You can't win the big ones," was another. "We did lose a heartbreaker."[14]

Summing up the game, the 1–1 status, and in retrospect what was on the agenda in Houston, Brusstar said this was some play-off series.

"It was very intense," he said.[15]

It's a funny thing, but that word is tricky to truly define. The dictionary says intense is "existing or occurring in a high or extreme degree; acute, strong or vehement, as sensations, feelings or emotions." Somewhere in there is a reading on what Brusstar meant. It was intense in Philadelphia, and it certainly was intense in Houston.

16

NATIONAL LEAGUE CHAMPIONSHIP SERIES: GAMES THREE AND FOUR IN HOUSTON

THERE WAS ONLY one day of rest between the second game of the National League Championship Series in Philadelphia and the third game in Houston. Jump on a plane, head west, and suit up.

In a five-game series with teams deadlocked, 1–1, the third game can be pivotal. To survive the series, the loser must win two in a row after that. The old cliché is to take them one game at a time, but the spotlight was definitely magnified on this contest.

Game Three was a classic. Larry Christenson, back at full strength, was the starter for the Phillies. Joe Niekro got the nod from Bill Virdon to start for Houston in a Friday afternoon game at the Astrodome, back when day games were regular occurrences—if only rarely seen now—in the Championship Series.

The Astrodome was known more for being pitcher-friendly than hitting-conducive, and if it hadn't been before this game, it certainly ensured that reputation. This was assuredly a day for pitchers, as sluggers need not apply.

Niekro, who spent 22 years in the majors throwing for the Chicago Cubs, San Diego Padres, Detroit Tigers, Atlanta Braves, New York Yankees, and Minnesota Twins, as well as Houston, was, like his brother Phil, one of the rare long-term masters of the knuckleball. Joe Niekro's finest years in a 221-victory career came with Houston, including 1980. In truth, knuckleball pitchers do not boast that they have truly mastered the pitch, as even the best of them periodically needs to pull into the shop for tune-ups when the weapon deserts them.

This day versus Philadelphia, however, Niekro had not a bit of trouble communicating with his knuckler. It did everything he asked of it, and the result was a continuous, afternoon-long baffling of the Phillies.

As the visitors now, the Phillies had first at-bats before the Astrodome crowd of 44,443. First up was Pete Rose, who struck out swinging. Bake McBride then flew out to left. Mike Schmidt solved the knuckler equation well enough to stroke a single to center field. If the Phillies had known what struggles they were in for, they would have celebrated Schmidt's hit more vigorously. Schmidt then stole second, but died there when Greg Luzinski grounded out.

Terry Puhl, who was having a fine series, immediately doubled off Christenson to create worry. Just like that, the Astros had a man in scoring position. He went to third on an Enos Cabell ground out to stand 90 feet away from a run. Christenson did nothing to tone down the fans with a walk to Joe Morgan, but

Jose Cruz hit into a double play. So it was 0–0 after one, yet nobody could have anticipated it was going to stay that way for a long time.

Manny Trillo began the second for the Phillies the same way Puhl started the first for the Astros, with a double. But he never budged from second when Niekro got the next three Phillies out.

After Christenson breezed through the second, the Phillies got Niekro into some trouble in the top of the third. Rose and McBride each singled and Rose ran to third on the second safety. Houston catcher Luis Pujols couldn't hold on to a pitch and was charged with a passed ball that sent McBride to second, but the ball wasn't so far out of control that Rose could score.

When Schmidt connected, driving the ball to third, Rose made a dash for home but was thrown out by Cabell on a fielder's choice. McBride went to third, but was stranded when Luzinski flied out. There was action on the bases for Houston in the home half of the third, too, with a walk and an error, but no one made it around to score. It was still scoreless despite what seemed like a fair amount of chances for each side.

Garry Maddox made sure the bases were not lonely in the top of the fourth by cracking a single, but the Phillies didn't come close to scoring. The Astros did more threatening in the bottom of the fourth, making Christenson work hard to escape damage. Jose Cruz got the building rocking with a one-out triple and before Christenson got the side out he mixed in an intentional walk. It was enough for the Phillies players in the dugout to fret, but the results were the same: No runs scored.

Niekro and Christenson were even sharper in the fifth, posting 1-2-3 innings in both halves. Still no progress made on the scoreboard. Christenson played with fire again in the bottom of the sixth, allowing a leadoff single to Cabell, who collected two hits in the game, followed by an intentional walk to Cruz. Those guys didn't get anywhere, though.

Cesar Cedeno hit into a double play to conclude the inning, bad enough for him, but in hurtling past first base he tripped and dislocated his right ankle. He promptly underwent surgery, knocking him out for the rest of the season, however long it was going to last. He was actually transported to the same hospital where J. R. Richard was initially treated.

That was it for Christenson. Dallas Green pulled him after a worthy start, as the right-hander pitched shutout ball for six innings while giving up three hits, but also four walks. The hour was getting late, the at-bats were running short, yet nobody could push across a single run. That situation would spotlight any solo run scored by either side.

In contrast to what would happen these days, Virdon did not seem at all interested in yanking Niekro in the midst of his ongoing shutout. It was a different era of big-league ball when managers still had faith in their starting pitchers to not only stay awake later than 10 p.m., but believed they still had juice in their arms for longer than two-thirds of a scheduled game. Niekro pushed onward, and as has been known to occur when a knuckleball is cooking, the Phillies could do little to make noise.

It was three up, three down in Philadelphia's seventh, one of the outs recorded by George Vukovich pinch-hitting for Christenson. Dickie Noles came on in relief for the Phils in the seventh. The game was starting to reach a point where things like shuffling players, pitchers in relief, pinch-hitters taking a fresh look at Niekro, became appealing ideas for Green.

Yet Niekro remained one step ahead of whatever Philadelphia could throw at him through the eighth inning. Three up, three down in that inning, too, with Rose, McBride, and Schmidt hitting a couple of infield grounders and a fly ball.

In the bottom of the eighth, as the suspense increased, Noles appeared a bit vulnerable. Puhl hit safely once again, leading off with a single. Cabell sacrificed him to second and Green went to the bullpen a second time, bringing on Tug McGraw after Noles threw 1 1/3 innings.

McGraw's job was to douse flames. This was no conflagration, but merely a brush fire. However, it would only take one hit for things to get out of hand. McGraw stranded Puhl on second, getting two outs wrapped around an intentional walk.

In the top of the ninth, Niekro managed to get into trouble without allowing a hit or having a man reach on an error. He retired the first two batters before Maddox was hit by a pitch and stole second. Niekro replied by intentionally walking Larry Bowa. Although the force play set up did not come to pass, Bob Boone's lineout ended this Phillies challenge.

Houston had last licks. The Phillies had to hold to go into extra innings. McGraw did well, eliminating Denny Walling, Luis Pujols, and Craig Reynolds without a baserunner. On to extras in a scoreless tie.

McGraw, of all people, led off the 10th by reaching on an error, but none of the Phillies' real hitters could advance him. Only a Cabell single interrupted the outs for Houston, himself making the third one when he was caught stealing.

Virdon finally decided that Niekro had done enough. After 10 innings of shutout ball, while allowing just six Philadelphia hits, he exited in favor of Dave Smith. Smith was a twenty-five-year-old rookie that year, going 7–5 with a 1.93 earned run average with 10 saves in 102 2/3 innings. By that point in the season, he had earned Virdon's trust.

"He wasn't going to let us lose," said Astros president Tal Smith of Niekro's effort sometime later.[1]

Niekro had pitched an absolute gem. He had played for other teams before winning 20 games in a season for the Astros twice, but had never before appeared in a playoff game or World Series. This was his moment to shine, and he seized it.

"I've waited fourteen years to pitch a game like that," Niekro said. "If I was gonna get beat, it was going to be with my best pitch—my knuckleball. I made a few mistakes here and there, but I got away with them. Why? You know why. We're playing in the Dome."[2]

With Niekro out of the game, the Phillies pressured Smith in the top of the 11th. With two outs, Maddox ripped a double and Bowa was the beneficiary of an intentional walk to again set up a force play in the infield. And again, the strategy was not needed. Del Unser, pinch-hitting for Boone, struck out to end the inning.

The Phillies immediately faced an *uh oh* moment in the bottom half of the 11th when Joe Morgan touched McGraw for a leadoff triple. Still another intentional walk followed, again to Jose Cruz. But that didn't matter. Denny Walling hit a fly ball to left that was deep enough to score Rafael Landestoy, who was pinch running for Morgan. That was the winning run, the Astros sweating out a 1–0 victory at home. Above all, the three-hour and 22-minute effort provided Houston with that coveted 2–1 series lead. That was an even bigger *uh oh* moment for the Phillies.

While it was of secondary import to the Phillies at that moment, it was on this day the Kansas Royals eliminated the New York Yankees. So the American League nominee for the World Series was settled, and would be waiting in the wings for its future opponent.

"This has gotta turn around sooner or later," Schmidt said. "We've gotta break loose and score three, four, five runs [in an inning]. We can't keep [having] bad luck."[3]

Inability to push runs across or bad luck, whatever the Phillies' affliction was, it had to be remedied in a hurry.

There was plenty of frustration to go around over being behind in the series. It was no fault of Christenson the Phillies lost Game Three, but he believed the team should have not only taken this one, but Game Two in Philadelphia as well. "We should have won both games, hands down," he said.[4]

Woulda, shoulda, coulda would not be acceptable if the Phillies did not win Game Four.

Philadelphia players who had lived through three other National League Championship Series defeats before were not in the mood to contemplate a fourth time falling short of the World Series. They also knew how their hometown fans would take it, too.

"For a team that had lost in the NLCS three times before, we were desperate," McGraw said. "I think we would have been tarred and feathered and run out of town on a rail if we didn't bring back a pennant this time."[5]

Cesar Cedeno, who hit .309 that season and won five Gold Gloves during his stay in Houston, must have been of a desperate mindset when he communicated with the Astros clubhouse after being taken to the hospital. Before being operated on, he sent the message "Keep it going for me. I'll see you in the Series."[6] It was a nice thought, but there was no chance Cedeno was going to do more than see his teammates at the Series in street clothes, if they advanced.

As for the Phillies, it was a pretty good time to win a game. They had won enough of them in the regular season, but to stick around the postseason any longer, it was time to hit the ball or turn the luck, as Schmidt mentioned. Any methods were welcome.

Game Four was another afternoon contest at the Dome, in front of 44,952 fans thirsty for Phillies blood. They wanted to see a reverse Dracula—a stake in the heart of the other guys, not the vampire fellow. In fact, they might as well have been wondering what kind of stake it might take to put Phillies starter Steve Carlton out of commission. Vern Ruhle was the starter of choice for Houston.

Once again, for quite some time, it was all about the pitchers. The first three Phillies went out in order, as did the Astros. Bake McBride collected a single in the second and Art Howe put up a double in the bottom of the second, but nobody scored. Generally, someone would get on base, yes, but neither Carlton nor Ruhle yielded easily.

In the bottom of the fourth, McBride and Manny Trillo each singled, but Ruhle still squirmed free. Not Carlton this time, though. An Enos Cabell double led to a sacrifice fly and a 1–0 Astros lead, the same score by which they had won a day earlier.

In the home half of the fifth, Luis Pujols's triple shook things up early in the inning and he scored on a single produced by Landestoy, making the score 2–0. Compared to the previous game, it seemed a rout was on.

NLCS: GAMES THREE AND FOUR IN HOUSTON

Green lifted Carlton rather early, as he pitched only 5 1/3 innings, giving up those two runs, and was replaced by Noles. It wasn't the runs (two) or the hits allowed (four) that was Carlton's undoing, but rather the five walks.

In search of that good fortune Schmidt wished for, the Phils did get a break on a close call in the sixth just after Noles came in, when Gary Woods was called out for tagging up from third too soon. Pujols flied out to right, the ball was thrown back in to Noles, who threw to Schmidt at third. The Phillies won the appeal that Woods had left too early on an attempted tag, ending the inning.

Third-base coach Lee Elia, who took the blame for halting a McBride try for home in Game Two, was in a frenzy protesting what he saw. "I was jumping and hollering and some of the guys had to calm me down," Elia said of his dugout actions. "They reminded me that the ball had to go back to the pitcher and be put in play before we could throw to third and make the out."[7]

Noles, who threw the next 1 1/3 innings, seemed to be increasingly gaining Green's trust. He hadn't surrendered a hit (though he walked two) when Green still replaced him in the seventh with Kevin Saucier, who walked Terry Puhl and was immediately yanked in favor of Ron Reed. Reed would get the last out of the inning on a ground out by Denny Walling.

Soon after, in the visitors' half of the eighth, Gross pinch-hit for Reed and singled and Lonnie Smith, who started in place of Luzinski, followed with a single of his own. Then Rose made it three in a row, sending Gross home and breaking the Phillies' lengthy scoring drought. Virdon decided he was not going to count on the same type of heroics from Ruhle as he received from Niekro, so in came Dave Smith. Only this time he left his magic behind in the bullpen. Schmidt singled and Lonnie Smith scored, tying up the game at two apiece. Dave Smith was done, but the Phillies weren't. After newly entered reliever Joe Sambito struck out McBride, Trillo sent the fourth pitch of the at-bat to right field, scoring Rose on the sacrifice fly. But the too-late throw to the plate was relayed back to first base and caught Trillo by surprise for the inning's last out. Even so, it was now 3–0, Philadelphia.

Time was running out after the Astros had gone down readily in the eighth, with Warren Brusstar going 1-2-3 on two fly balls and a line drive. The Phillies did not add to their lead in the ninth. Green kept Brusstar on the mound, but a Landestoy walk and a sacrifice pushed him to second. The increasingly annoying Terry Puhl then singled, and Landestoy came all the way around to score to the game, 3–3. Again, it was on to extra innings.

"I blew the save," Brusstar said, describing how he worried that he had put the Phillies in an untenable position." I knew, 'I can't walk him.'" But he did. Cabell was next up. "I jammed him and he hit a little fly ball to Bake. Puhl ran right by me. He didn't tag up."[8] So the fly ball out to McBride and the throw back to the infield doubling up Puhl got Brusstar out of the inning and pushed the teams to the 10th inning in a tie instead of the Phillies losing and being eliminated right then and there.

"That was a crazy game," Brusstar said. "Every game was crazy in that series."[9]

The Phillies lived to hit another day, or at least another inning. Rose, the second man up, singled with one out in the 10th. With two outs, Luzinski pinch-hit for McBride and his clutch double sent Rose home for the lead. Trillo followed with another double, scoring Luzinski. That made it 5–3 as the Astros came up to bat.

Sometimes history repeats itself—not in a matter of years, but in a matter of days. Elia, who chastised himself for being reticent to urge McBride home in a key situation earlier in the series, was again at third as Rose steamed past for the plate. Elia said he knew it was going to be a close play at home, but wasn't sure if Rose would have even paid attention if he tried to stop him.

"When Pete gets that look in his eye, he wants it," Elia said.[10]

Rose said he would have respectfully stopped if Elia ordered him to, but he believed the situation favored the runner. Bruce Bochy, later the long-time manager of the San Francisco Giants, was the man waiting at the plate.

"If the catcher had the ball waiting for me, he could have planted me," Rose said. "Bochy had to concentrate on catching the ball—a tough play because of the short hop—and he wasn't braced for the collision." Bochy dropped the throw and suffered bruised ribs from Rose's slide.[11]

Brusstar was still the pitcher of record after throwing two full innings, but Green sent McGraw out for the 10th. By this point in the fall, October 11, McGraw admitted he was tiring. But if his energy was flagging, no one could tell. Joe Morgan took a called third strike for the first out, and both Jeffrey Leonard and Art Howe returned to the dugout on fly-ball outs.

The winning pitcher was Brusstar, the only postseason win of his career (though he made other appearances without decisions). "I'm pretty proud of that," he said of being the winning pitcher.[12]

There was joy in South Philadelphia and South Jersey. Game Five loomed, and the series was now tied, not decided. Brusstar said his and the team's attitude in Houston was to be prepared for desperate, creative measures to claim another win.

"When you go to Game Five, it's all hands on deck," Brusstar said. "You're sitting there ready to go." There being a Game Five at all, after trailing 2–1, was special enough to a team that could have been killed off. "It was a huge relief."[13]

Just about all of Green's moves in Game Four worked out well. Taking out Carlton when he did was OK. The other pitchers all performed. Even Brusstar, who gave up a big run but took home the victory the hard way. Lonnie Smith got two hits and when Luzinski came in cold off the bench, he basically won the game with a big blow, much as he had back on Opening Day and in Game One of the NLCS.

Rose, Schmidt, McBride, and Trillo each had two hits. Trillo was quietly outshining the bigger name players, his contributions coming at key moments at bat, opposed to just in the field. But the ruling by umpire Bob Engel calling Woods out was a big plus as well.

"Did I think this would be called in the playoffs?" Green said. "No-o-o."[14]

The play, the extra-inning scoring, the win-or-go-home situation with such high stakes on such a big stage, probably caused numerous heart attacks back home in Philadelphia.

"There has never been a game to compare with that one," McGraw said. "There has never been a game that I've ever witnessed that was more exciting, more controversial, more interesting, than the game I just saw."[15]

Of course, one must remember that McGraw, awarded a save, was on the winning side. Chances were that not too many people were exulting in such a manner in the Houston clubhouse.

The Phillies were rescued for a day, but now the series was 2–2, and they were still in Houston. It seemed they had been there long enough to register to vote. They had to overcome the scrappy Astros once more, a third time in a row. But certainly there were many more believers in Philadelphia—and the players had to feel a certain lightened load.

"I've got the feeling," Larry Bowa virtually sang in the clubhouse after the game. "I've got the feeling."[16]

17

THE CLINCHER

THE WAR BEGAN at 7 p.m. in the Astrodome. Two teams that did not want their season to end on October 12, but wanted it to go on and on as long as it took to win a world championship, were trying to sort out an even series.

By this point, the Phillies had truly absorbed the problems the Astrodome presented with its configuration and sound waves.

"Going into Houston, it was sort of notorious as a tough place to play, a tough place to hit," said Greg Gross. "It was without a doubt the loudest place I've ever been in for a game. It was just vibrating. I had a good playoff series. That was my highlight parade. I didn't have the best of years season-wise. But I had the playoff year that made up for it."[1]

Gross was wary of Game Five after all the ups and downs of the first four games.

Houston's starting pitcher would be Nolan Ryan, the best they had. The Phillies' starting pitcher was a wild-card choice by manager Dallas Green: Marty Bystrom. The same Bystrom who had parachuted in from the minors to own September, who then had to await a special ruling from the game's leadership to even learn if he would be eligible to take a seat on the bench during the Championship Series, was back in the spotlight.

Legend versus Rookie, as if Game Five needed any more storylines to juice it up. Could the Astros win their first pennant in franchise history? Could the Phillies win their first pennant in thirty years? This was a die-trying game with managers being counted on to employ quick hooks if a pitcher was faltering, and they would keep pinch-hitters and pinch-runners on speed dial.

It took almost no time for Ryan to retire the first three Phillies. Meanwhile, Bystrom gave up a single to the first man he faced, Terry Puhl. After Puhl stole second, and with two outs, Jose Cruz doubled to right field, scoring Puhl for the first run of the game. That had to be a little demoralizing for the Phillies, but if they felt that way, were able to rapidly shrug it off.

In the top of the second, Manny Trillo singled with one out, followed by a Garry Maddox walk. And voila, the Phils had something going. When Larry Bowa grounded out, both runners advanced into scoring position, which was handy when Bob Boone singled to center. With both guys coming around, that shifted the balance on the scoreboard. It was 2–1, Phils after two.

Bystrom then settled down, regaining the sharp form he'd had for much of September, though Ryan would not rate this performance on a list of his top 100 games (or maybe top 324 games). However, they danced around baserunners and no one scored again until the bottom of the sixth. Houston tied the game in the home half of that inning after Denny Walling reached on an outfield error and was driven home on an Alan Ashby single.

That was enough for Green, who removed Bystrom for Warren Brusstar after 5 1/3 innings. Brusstar took care of the last two outs in the sixth, and the game was tied going into the seventh. At this point, it was pretty much still a pitchers' duel—even if the cast of pitchers was changing. The Astrodome was a climate-controlled facility, but the atmospheric conditions were about to change, too.

To begin the bottom of the seventh, Green reached out for starter Larry Christenson to take the mound. Over his 11-year career, Christenson appeared in 243 games, starting 220 of them. He had been on the money during the latter stages of the regular season and in his playoff showing, but his stuff looked all too familiar to the Astros this time. Puhl started the inning with a single. Enos Cabell sacrificed him to second. After a Joe Morgan ground out, Jose Cruz was intentionally walked and Denny Walling singled to score Puhl. When Christenson threw a wild pitch to Art Howe, scoring Cruz, Green pulled him from the game in favor of Ron Reed. *Thwack!* Howe tripled, scoring Walling. The fans were pretty much dancing in the aisles of the Astrodome as Houston now led, 5–2.

This time, the Phillies' bats quelled the celebration very quickly. Ryan came out for the seventh inning and Larry Bowa, Bob Boone, and Greg Gross all singled. Then, with the bases loaded, Ryan walked Pete Rose to make it 5–3. Houston manager Bill Virdon inserted Joe Sambito in Ryan's place. Green replied by sending Keith Moreland in to pinch-hit for Bake McBride, and although Moreland did not kill the ball, his ground out scored another run.

Ken Forsch replaced Sambito and got Mike Schmidt to strike out, but Del Unser singled and Manny Trillo cleared the bases with a triple. Before the Astros sat down, the Phillies had put up five runs and now led, 7–5. Philadelphia had responded with a big inning and, entering the bottom of the eighth, had to feel good about the likelihood of closing out the series.

"When we got ahead again, I felt we were going to win," Gross said. "Even when we went to extra innings, I had a good feeling. They were pretty pesky, that's for sure. They never wavered. It was two very determined teams."[2]

Polishing off the Astros was even more difficult than it promised to be. Tug McGraw was entrusted with the 7–5 lead, but lost it. He was not clobbered, but rather pecked to death. Craig Reynolds singled, Puhl singled, Rafael Landestoy singled, Cruz singled, and, presto, the lead was gone—7–7.

Neither team could score in the ninth inning. Only the Phillies managed baserunners, both off Frank LaCorte. Dick Ruthven retired three in a row for the Phillies, another starting pitcher taking a turn in late relief. Next stop, extra innings … for the final time.

"They played great," Boone said of Houston. "Four of the five games were in extra innings. We had that huge comeback against Nolan Ryan."[3]

That's what propelled the Phillies back into contention, but it was déjà vu with the 10th inning, with time running out and pressure to score. If anyone was a nail biter, they probably had none left by then. Likewise if they were a tobacco chewer.

In the top of the 10th, LaCorte was still hurling for Houston and struck out Mike Schmidt to begin the inning. Though their big slugger could not get on base, Del Unser stepped in and belted a double to right field. The Phils dugout was alive with optimism. Trillo was next up and flew out to *deep* center.

One could almost imagine the Philadelphia fans home in their living rooms half-lifting out of their seats as the ball soared, only to plunk their rear ends back down when it was caught. Now with two outs, Garry Maddox followed and caught a pitch square, smacking it to center. Deep, deep, deep. This shot fell in, Maddox scampered to second, and Unser crossed the plate for an 8–7 lead.

That's how things stood when the Astros came to bat in the bottom of the 10th. Ruthven was still on the mound for the Phillies. Danny Heep pinch-hit for Gary Woods and popped out to the shortstop. One down. The dangerous Puhl was up next, but lined the ball to center, where it was grabbed by Maddox. Two outs. Cabell stepped in, the prayers of a city on his back. Cabell hit a 3-2 pitch to center, too, and Maddox caught that one as well. Remember the muff in a past playoff? Full circle for Maddox. The Phillies did it. Final score, 8–7. Winning pitcher, Dick Ruthven. Winning city, Philadelphia. Unreal, surreal, at very long last.

After the tribulations of the regular season and the challenges of the playoff series against the Astros, the 1980 Phillies were going to the World Series.

"It was such a grind," Boone said. "That series was an unbelievable grind." One reason Boone may have thought that way was because it was a particular challenge for him over the last several innings—he was playing with a possible broken bone in his foot. X-rays afterward showed not quite a fracture, only a severe bruise. "We thought, 'We have to win this.' We never had that feeling before."[4]

It was a very real feeling, and the Phillies did rise to the occasion when it was absolutely necessary, taking those three straight games—all on the road. Boone said the foot "didn't bother me too much" when he was in the field, but as soon as the game ended, "I went right to the trainer's room and didn't get to celebrate."[5]

Everyone else did.

Maddox was all over the place at the end of the game, making the big hit, making the final catches. It had not been completely forgotten that he made the big mistake in the 1978 playoffs, dropping a fly ball. As down as he was back then, that's as high as he was now. Higher, perhaps, since teammates hoisted him in the air.

"I've never had a feeling like it," Maddox said. "This was such an emotional series. There were so many turns, so many comebacks. You just ached on every pitch."[6]

Many laughed when Bowa poured champagne over manager Green's head with television cameras recording. Bowa said the bench was always alive over the three games in Houston, refusing to get down, refusing to yield the high ground of hope when things looked bleak—such as when Nolan Ryan was cruising with a three-run lead.

The series combined all of the suspenseful elements of Agatha Christie and Ellery Queen. No one was murdered, but one team died. For once, it wasn't the Phillies. Taken to the brink, they dug down and answered some of their long-time critics who accused them of choking in past championship series. Some of the players definitely had that on their minds after the victory, offering this result as a rebuttal.

"When we got to the playoffs, we dedicated ourselves to one thing and that was going all the way," Maddox said. "We knew we wouldn't be satisfied—and our fans wouldn't be satisfied— by anything less than the National League pennant. We adopted the motto, 'Whatever it takes.'" It did take a lot of gumption to sweep Houston in Texas and make comebacks on demand. "I think we proved something to a few people. I think we showed we have a lot of character on this ball club."[7]

It was definitely hard to argue with any analysis stating the Phillies had no quit in them, that's for sure. Greg Luzinski was a member of those teams that lost the NLCS, and was now part of a Philadelphia club that won one. He remembered the city-wide angst, disappointment, and, yes, even blame affixed to those three teams that couldn't hurdle the championship series to claim a pennant.

"Let them say we don't have any heart anymore," Luzinski said in the locker room. "We proved to the world that we don't have a quitter on this team."[8]

Both columnist Frank Dolson and his headline writers back in the sports department at the *Philadelphia Inquirer* completely grasped that change of tide in perception. The headline on Dolson's column read, "Phils Rewrite the Philadelphia Story," a play on the name of the famous movie starring Katharine Hepburn, Jimmy Stewart, and Cary Grant. In part, Dolson wrote, "After the heart, the character, the spirit—call it what you will—that the Phillies displayed last night in the Astrodome, that's the least anybody can do." While any Phillies win would have been memorable, the style in which this was accomplished, Dolson wrote, "should be the new standard by which all post-season baseball games are measured. It took 20 Phillies players to win this storybook game and to forever put to rest the notion, widely held before last night, that this Phillies team lacked what it takes to win a championship."[9]

Yes, twenty players played, but some deserved extra credit for the win. Maddox was high on the list, Boone for his stoic endurance of pain in his left foot while getting two hits, Bowa's two hits, Rose in the field, Unser slicing two hits, and NLCS MVP Manny Trillo, who banged out three hits. And that didn't count the rescue pitching of Ruthven.

When Ruthven was informed he might be saved for a World Series–opening start a couple of days later, his reaction was: "To hell with Tuesday. We gotta win this one first."[10]

Ruthven's attitude was right on. Everyone had to be ready for emergency service, whatever nature it took. He threw more than once before going into the game. "When I first got up to warm up," he said, "I felt OK—not great, but OK. The last time I felt super. Now I just feel spent, exhausted." Maybe so, but with a tired smile on his face, he added, "I don't know who's going to pitch Tuesday, but who cares?"[11]

The Astros might have cared, but no longer, since their next official game would be the following April.

"One thing that I can't begin to comprehend is that I'm not going to put this uniform on tomorrow," said Puhl, who did so many things to help his team almost win. "It hasn't hit me yet. I'll go home tonight and tomorrow morning I'll be wondering what time our workout is. And hey, there aren't any more. I want to cry about that."[12]

The Astros earned the right to be morose. They endured a crushing defeat when they thought they should have walked off with triumph. They led the series, 2–1, but in both home games lost they had a good chance of reversing the outcome. It couldn't have been much closer. Four extra-inning games out of five by definition means his team was right there at the end.

It was not merely the players so wound up in the contests with their hyperfocus and an atmosphere of supreme pressure who saw the series for what it was—a stunningly dramatic play that riveted theatres that held 45,000 or 65,000 people rather than the usual Broadway holding pens of hundreds per performance.

"That was probably the most exciting championship series ever played," said commissioner Bowie Kuhn. "I don't see how anything could top it. I'm sure the whole country was tuned in and excited by it."[13]

Caught up in the moment, and perhaps overlooking a World Series here or there, Tug McGraw raised the ante even higher than Kuhn.

"I've never been more proud to be a major-league baseball player," McGraw said. "It was a thrill to be on this field with the Phillies and Astros. This series showed you what a great game baseball is. To me, this was the most dramatic event in baseball history."[14]

Often mentioned as the greatest World Series game ever played was the sixth game of the 1975 Series between the Cincinnati Reds and Boston Red Sox. Well, Rose was part of that, and part of the Houston series. He didn't directly compare them, but did not underrate this playoff's drama, either.

"I believe the Houston-Philadelphia playoff was the best ever played," Rose said. "Just the competition. Us coming back against Nolan Ryan. Every game was a one-run game. When you play three-out-of-five, that's a lot more pressure than four-out-of-seven. The only pressure I ever felt in baseball was in the playoffs, playing for the right to go to the World Series."[15]

Eliminating the Astros, grabbing that NL pennant with two hands, celebrating with champagne, seemed to be a major release for the Phillies. They took that giant step beyond playing in the NLCS. It was a freeing of the soul moment, placing their names on the pennant, even though the World Series still loomed, most assuredly a bigger prize at stake.

"Every game with Houston was extra innings," Larry Bowa said. "There really wasn't any pressure after we got past Houston. Once they led at two games to one, it was 'Uh, oh, here we go again.' Game Five was beyond huge. I never did think we were going to lose. Us beating Nolan Ryan. Us coming back to tie the series at 2–2, it was the perfect storm."[16]

While the Phillies had a New Year's Eve–type party in the clubhouse, a few toasts, some champagne down the gullet and poured over heads, fans in Philadelphia were less restrained. They partied in a bigger venue: the great outdoors. Drivers on city streets honked their horns. Fans on foot dashed through neighborhood streets. Fans ignited fireworks. They participated in their own toasts and not all drank champagne. Other fans, an estimated 5,000, began lining up to buy World Series tickets hours before Game Five began, never mind after the Phillies even won.

Capturing the National League Championship Series was such a release. If only for a moment, the World Series was on the back burner for some players. "It didn't matter who we were playing," Bowa said of their American League opponent.[17]

At least, not for a day or two. Then the Phillies had to remember there was a team named the Kansas City Royals out there, another group like Houston that had never won it all, another group like the Phillies which had put its own demons to bed while defeating the New York Yankees.

PHILLIES 1980!

Was there any reason to think overcoming Kansas City in seven was going to be any easier than taking out Houston in five? Nobody wanted to think about that just yet. The Phillies deserved the opportunity to bask, if only for 24 or 48 hours. Then they'd hold a World Series.

18

THE WORLD SERIES

AFTER WHAT SEEMED like an eternity in Houston, the Philadelphia Phillies returned home to prepare for the first World Series visiting the town since 1950 when the Whiz Kids claimed a pennant, but could not go all the way. Neither could the 1915 Phillies go all the way. Remaining members of the 1950 team could watch and root for this bunch of Phillies. Members of the 1915 team were all long dead.

Same for the fans of those two eras, including local businesses which had been around for a century or so themselves. Although now defunct, Strawbridge and Clothier was founded in 1868, predating the creation of the Phillies by fifteen years. On the eve of the 1980 World Series, Strawbridge's—as it was first called for short, and ultimately officially—took out advertising that read, "Sure, we've waited a long time. Thirty years to be exact. But now it's official: the 1980 Phillies are the National League champs. Like a tight-knit family, they came through when it counted most. So from Philly's Family Store to the super

Phillies' family, CONGRATULATIONS! And best of luck in the Series."

Even before the games began at Veterans Stadium on October 14, the town was giddy with excitement and anticipation. The leaves were falling, Halloween was on the horizon, and the baseball team was still playing! Fans were buzzing, and everyone had something to say about a World Series in Philadelphia. Even the Phillie Phanatic mascot wrote an opinion column on special assignment for the *Daily News* for the duration of the Series.

Noting he was only three years old, in his first commentary, the Phanatic could hardly stop gushing about the thrilling playoff series against Houston. "Even if I'm still dancing on the dugout roof when my green feathers start to turn gray, I'll never again experience the emotions of last weekend. Have you ever seen a five-game playoff series you thought no one would win?" In the World Series, "I'll be leading cheers. The Phanatic is where he belongs, and the Phillies are where they belong—in the World Series!"[1]

Where they belong: the World Series. The idea was growing on people in a hurry. Royals players, as well. After all, they hadn't been to the final playoff round, either.

"We had a really close team in 1980," said John Wathan, who as a utility man batted .305 that season for Kansas City. "We had gone through a lot." They were as excited about beating the Yankees as the Phillies were over ousting the Astros. "It was as if we had won the World Series. I think that hurt us. We had like three days off. I don't know if we were as prepared as we should have been."[2]

Survival to the next round was paramount for the Royals, too, and it was sweeter because they polished off their longtime nemesis from the Bronx.

"That was a big one," said designated hitter Hal McRae. "We wanted to reach that next step. We felt we could win it all. We were not satisfied just being there." Sounding much like Pete Rose, he said, "The World Series was a lot more relaxed than the playoffs."[3]

By sweeping the Yankees, Kansas City finished its ALCS on October 10. The Phillies didn't win until the 12th, so the Royals had a couple of days to watch Philadelphia-Houston on television—and to set their pitching rotation, with just about everyone rested.

The Phillies had a day off hanging around Veterans Stadium before the Series opened, and had barely come down from the high of disposing of the stick-like-glue Astros.

As prelude to the World Series, a Kansas City disc jockey bet a Philadelphia disc jockey a quart of whiskey and a strip tease against a six-foot-long hoagie and a case of Schmidt's beer. US senator Bob Dole, a future presidential candidate, wagered 25 pounds of Kansas beef on the Royals, while Pennsylvania senator John Heinz bet 25 pounds of pretzels with mustard in a counteroffer. Kansas City mayor Richard Berkley and Philadelphia mayor William Green also went one-on-one, steaks versus pretzels at stake in this showdown.

Naturally enough, demand outstripped supply for tickets to Game One in Philadelphia. That sent scalpers into action, hoping to profit from their transfer of ducats from their hands to others' eager hands. The biggest problem the ticket sellers faced was a lack of good seats. Mostly, they were offering seats that were so far from the action—600 and 700 level—occupants needed binoculars to call balls and strikes. These were the professionals who came by fistfuls of tickets somehow, ones that had a face value of just $15. They were doing their best to hustle them for $80, laughably low prices compared to the modern world of resale. Once in a while a better ticket would be offered, located closer to the action, for something like $300.

Most of the sellers claimed to have waited in line from eight to sixteen hours to legitimately purchase the tickets at the Veterans Stadium box office. They had no intention of attending the game, only doing business. One seller said he sold most of his stash of way-up-there tickets for $50 each. Some optimistic buyers flashed a billfold of $20 bills, an indicator they would go high for a better seat. Since the sellers situated themselves off stadium property, security didn't bother to intervene. For the most part, neither did police, despite a strong blue-uniformed presence on the scene. Maybe everyone was in too good a mood and it was looked at as a no-harm, no-foul operation. Anyway, much benign neglect for this rare special occasion occurred.

A World Series in town was something new for much of the populace that hadn't been born or of age when home games during the last one were contested in old Shibe Park a few years before it was renamed for Connie Mack. Shibe-Connie Mack Park opened in 1909, and its last season hosting the Phillies was 1970. Veterans Stadium replaced it in that role the following year.

For that matter, most of the Phillies' players were less than thirty years old, too, or were of elementary-school age the last time the Phillies played a Series game in Philadelphia. Pete Rose, at thirty-nine, was the oldest and had competed in his share of playoffs with the Reds.

Many Phillies players were like their fans. They had never seen a World Series game in person before, only on TV.

"I used to dream of pitching in it," said Marty Bystrom. "I could picture myself in it and winning a ball game. I just want to get the chance to pitch in it."[4]

Backup John Vukovich had never witnessed a live World Series game, but was riveted as a youth when it was on the tube. Growing up in nearby Sacramento, he followed the San Francisco Giants and recalled intently following the Giants-Yankees Series of 1962. But he also remembered watching some of the classics, including Pittsburgh's Bill Mazeroski finishing the Yankees in 1960 with a walk-off home run in Game Seven.

Coach Herm Starrette was in a unique position. He already owned two World Series rings from his association with the Baltimore Orioles, but wasn't at the games. In 1969 and 1970, he was stuck on the road evaluating the organization's prospects in the Florida Instructional League.

"I'll be like a 10-year-old kid," Starrette said of stepping on the field for Game One.[5]

Of course, since it was a national-caliber sporting event, there was legal betting on the World Series in Las Vegas, where odds-makers make a living. Once it was established the combatants would be the Phillies and Royals, the option to choose one over the other by laying down cash was made available. The selections varied. Although KC won 97 games in the regular season and the Phillies 91, some gave Philadelphia a slight edge. Others leaned toward Kansas City. Sportswriters did not deal in those types of statistics, but rather in what their trained eyes told them about the comparative strengths of each team.

The *New York Times* selected two managers to write scouting reports on the World Series teams: Earl Weaver of the Baltimore

Orioles did a study of the Kansas City Royals, while Chuck Tanner of the Pittsburgh Pirates discussed the Phillies.

Tanner described Philadelphia as having "a solid and talented team. Their two greatest assets should be Mike Schmidt and Steve Carlton."[6] That was stating the obvious. Any fan could have picked them off the stat sheet. Schmidt would soon be named the 1980 National League Most Valuable Player and Carlton would soon be announced as the 1980 National League Cy Young Award winner.

Beyond the two prominent stars, Tanner liked the Phillies lineup top to bottom. "The rest of the Phillies are aggressive and talented at bat and in the field. Their defense may be the best in baseball. At bat they hit line drives, run swiftly on the bases and come through with important hits."[7]

The turnaround between the end of the NLCS victory over Houston and the start of the World Series was quick enough that poor Manny Trillo probably never really got his due. It was Trillo, the regular second baseman, who was voted the MVP of that series. He hit .381 with four runs batted in and made some exceptional plays in the field, including throwing Luis Pujols out at the plate in Game Five. Trillo was no power hitter, but for once, home runs were not a factor in a playoff series.

Of course, without being able to read the future, outfielder Bake McBride and Trillo actually practiced completing sharp relay throws in pregame warmups, ready for the possibility.

"We were working on that," Trillo said. "All of a sudden, it happened during the game. I was happy we worked out. It's something you never expect to happen. The playoff was exciting. It usually is when you win. You cannot win the MVP if you do not have good teammates. I put them in that category. I believe they were all MVPs in the playoff."[8]

That tiny window between the end of the playoff and the start of the Series brought forth all sorts of predictions, opinions, and impressions tracked down by the four Philadelphia newspapers.

Jeane Dixon wrote a syndicated astrology column, and was a nationally known psychic. Generally, she did not engage in too many sports predictions, but this time she ventured a guarded comment about the Phillies' chances.

"I am picking up heavy positive vibrations on the Phillies," Dixon said. "I hope it's not just because I'm here." Maybe she was swayed by the aromas wafting from pretzel vendor carts in the streets or by a visit to sample the wares at Jim's Steaks. On the other hand, if she didn't want to go out on a limb (though going out on a limb was pretty much her profession), Dixon may not have conducted a press conference at Philadelphia's Warwick Hotel.[9]

Majority opinion was tilting in favor of the Royals, however, so it can be said Dixon was not taking the easy way out. The reason for the Royals advocates was the belief that they had superior pitching, as Carlton could not pitch in every game. When her comments went public, she also mentioned the Phillies were going to win the thing in six games.

Tanner had suggested in his analysis that Carlton, as the ace, might start three games for Philadelphia—but that was not how manager Dallas Green saw it and it was ultimately his call. If Carlton was going to start the opener, he would be doing so on two days' rest because of his appearance against the Astros when that was the paramount business to be accomplished. He factored in Carlton's 304 innings during the regular season and the fact he was thirty-five years old. Dick Ruthven, the No. 2 starter, had been used in relief against Houston in the deciding game.

Pete Rose, as usual, expressing his enthusiasm vehemently, scoffed at suggestions the Phillies could be fatigued from the dramatic series against the Astros. But then, he was a position player, not a pitcher.

"You can chain me to a pole for two days and nights and then tell me to play ball in the World Series," Rose said. "And no matter how emotionally drained I may be, I'll be ready."[10] Yep, that was Pete Rose all right.

Royals manager Jim Frey did not have the same dilemma as Green. His staff was much better rested. And Dennis Leonard, who went 20–11 during the regular season and won a game from the Yankees in the ALCS, had not been chained up for a couple of days. Frey anointed Leonard as his Game One starter. As the team's biggest winner of the year, it was no surprise.

Green was pretty much in a corner, though. He finally chose righty Bob Walk to start the first game of the World Series. It should be recalled that Walk did not make the team out of spring training, but then came on to win 11 games during the regular season.

As the arms were being used up against Houston, Walk recognized he was probably going to be the only fresh starter left if the Phillies moved on. "I saw all our other starters [Marty Bystrom and Larry Christenson in addition to Ruthven] go into the game last night," Walk said on the day off. "So I figured it had to be me"[11]

In reality, it did not take a genius to decipher that Walk was likely to be the man in the opener against Kansas City. During Game Five, he said he was told by the coaches, "You're not going to be in this game," he said years later. When he was officially announced as the starter and he participated in a press conference, Walk said, "I don't think it had really sunk in to me. I didn't think about what a big deal it was."[12]

Such a callow rookie. He learned soon enough just what it was to be the chosen one as the starting pitcher for the Phillies first World Series game in thirty years, and as a rookie.

19

WORLD SERIES: GAMES ONE AND
TWO IN PHILADELPHIA

L ONNIE SMITH DIDN'T know what kind of atmosphere to expect in Philadelphia, at Veterans Stadium, for the first game of the 1980 World Series. He was a young outfielder, still technically a rookie, and was coming off the hullabaloo of the National League Championship Series, which had been as suspenseful as any in memory. So how could the World Series be bigger?

Well, it was. When Smith walked into Veterans Stadium, he sensed a ratcheting up of emotion in everybody, from fans to ushers. "For the first game of the World Series," he said, "it felt like three times the number of people."[1]

Although the players had other things on their minds, the *Philadelphia Bulletin* suggested that holding a World Series in town was also a potential financial bonanza worth about $8.6 million if it lasted the distance or close to it. It was estimated that 10,000 extra people would come to town, that ticket sales were going to be valued at $2.3 million, and Philadelphia fans would contribute $1 million to the local economy by spending money at restaurants, on transportation, and buying food and the like inside the stadium.

Del Unser felt the vibes from the fans as well, immediately noticing the difference from a regular-season game. Right away it seemed that this World Series was about more than winning and losing, but history. That was to be expected when playing for a team that had not won a championship in its ninety-seven years, and had not even won the right to play for one in thirty years. "You couldn't believe the fans," Unser said. "To me, it was 90 percent about the fans. They were saying, 'If only grandpa could be here.'"[2]

Grandpa, maybe pa, and other descendants, had likely gone to their graves without the chance to see a World Series, never mind see the Phillies win a World Series.

So there they were, at one of the most important games in the existence of the club, and counting on a twenty-three-year-old rookie right-handed pitcher to rule the day. Bob Walk hadn't sniffed the big leagues until five months earlier. Though he won 11 games during the regular season, his earned run average was 4.57. His teammates won the Houston series without his help. Now they were relying on him to come through on an even bigger stage. "He pitched very well for us," said catcher Bob Boone. "He was a great get."[3]

Smith remembers that leading up to the game's start, Walk stuffed himself with Tootsie Rolls, presumably to calm his nerves the way other players might use chewing gum or chewing tobacco. When it was time to pitch, though, Walk "stopped eating them."[4]

He was on his own, without artificial sweeteners.

It was neither his best game nor his worst, but Walk persevered for seven innings against the Royals in the opener. Designated hitter Hal McRae worked Walk for a walk in the first, but he retired Willie Wilson, George Brett, and Willie Aikens. Getting past Brett safely was always a good achievement for a pitcher facing Kansas City. The Phillies were put down in order in the top of the first, offering little resistance.

Kansas City veteran outfielder Amos Otis reached Walk for a two-run homer in the second after he gave up a base on balls to catcher Darrell Porter. Philly hitters did nothing with Dennis Leonard in the second inning, either.

Looking a bit on the shaky side, Walk again surrendered two hits to the Royals in the third inning, highlighted by an Aikens two-run homer following a McRae single. But it could have been worse. Otis and Clint Hurdle each knocked out a single after the homer, but Porter was thrown out at the plate on Hurdle's hit. Big play by Smith, who started in place of Greg Luzinski in left field since the latter could also start as a designated hitter. This was a bonus situation for manager Dallas Green, being able to use both of the players from the first pitch.

It was 4–0, Kansas City, and the 65,791 spectators were not as cheery as they had been a half an hour or so earlier. The score could well have left the Phillies grumpy, too, if they were unable to do something about it quickly.

The something showed itself in the bottom of the third. Heretofore in command, Leonard suddenly became very hittable. After one out, shortstop Larry Bowa singled to center, then stole second. It was a move that paid off, as Boone slugged a double, sending him home. Smith then grounded a single to left, scoring Boone. He probably should have remained at first, but was thrown out going for second on a play that was scored 7-5-6-3. Those were not winning lottery numbers, but losing baserunning numbers as the ball zipped from Wilson to Brett to U. L. Washington to Aikens.

That could have been a rally killer, but it was not. After everyone caught his breath, Rose was hit by a pitch, Schmidt walked, and Bake McBride blasted a three-run homer over the right-field fence. Rather than letting the Smith play affect them, and still being down by two runs, that turned things around with a 5–4 Phillies lead. Although KC manager Jim Frey's patience was tested, Leonard stayed in.

It was clear this game was not going to be a pitchers' duel. Walk looked sharper in the top of the fourth, avoiding putting on any baserunners. In the bottom of the inning, Manny Trillo singled. With Bowa at the plate, Leonard whirled and had Trillo picked off first, but an error led to him going safely to second. Trillo then went to third on a Bowa ground out. Boone cracked a double, though, sending him home for another Phillies run. That was the demarcation line for Frey. Leonard went to the showers after 3 2/3, and Renie Martin came on in relief, trailing, 6–4. Although Walk appeared the more vulnerable of the two starters in the beginning, he was still out there throwing after Leonard was exiled.

"I had some 1-2-3 innings," Walk said of his survival in the game after giving up those early runs and then being handed the lead. "Three or four of them."[5]

Some of his best innings followed those Phillies rallies. Walk set down the Royals in order in the fifth and the sixth. He probably would have been replaced by a reliever by then after allowing those four runs if the designated hitter had not been in use.

Martin, a right-hander, was not the best known of the Royals' pitchers, nor did he have a long career. But he went 10–10 in 1980, which gave Frey enough confidence to call him in for middle relief.

In the home half of the fifth, Schmidt walked, McBride singled, and Luzinski was hit by a pitch, loading the bases. Garry Maddox's sacrifice fly scored Schmidt, giving the Phillies a 7–4 lead.

Clearly under the influence of Tootsie Roll power at this juncture of the game, Walk seemed capable of giving Philadelphia a complete game, which would have probably irritated the heck out of Frey.

In the seventh, it was Martin who was in bigger trouble. Singles by Schmidt and McBride with one out made it appear the Phils would add more runs, but Martin closed out the inning without allowing any more scores.

Walk had not yet felt the George Brett Effect in the Royals lineup, nor did he have to cope with the same type of problems the American League had faced all season in trying to get him out. That changed when the third baseman led off the eighth with a double. Walk then threw a wild pitch, which ultimately didn't matter because the next batter, Aikens, whacked a two-run homer, his second of the game. Now the score was 7–6, and Walk's time was up.

With nobody out in a one-run game, closer Tug McGraw took the mound in the kind of late-inning situation he reveled. The Phillies had such confidence in McGraw at this point of the year they believed that, if confronted by a forest fire, he could guide them to safety.

For all of his fun-loving mannerisms, McGraw relished the big moments in the spotlight—not to show off his sense of humor, but to display his pitching smarts. Sure, he might flutter his glove against his heart, or tap it against his thigh if he got a strike call, but he was always aware of the magnitude of the moment.

"He's an artist out there painting a picture," said Phils pitching coach Herm Starrette. "When he goes to the mound, he's all business. Really, not knowing the guy, you'd think he was a hot dog. And he's not. He's Tug McGraw."[6]

In the cartoons, Mighty Mouse had a battle cry of "Here I come to save the day." McGraw was not hardly tiny at six feet, but seemed more of average height. Still, the slogan worked for him most times, too. He got Porter on a fly ball, but after Otis singled he turned it to an advantage, coaxing pinch-hitter John Wathan into an inning-ending double play.

Not everyone on the Royals might have agreed, but Wathan did not mind opening the Series in Veterans Stadium. Plus, the way the game began with those quick runs off of Walk, he thought his team was going to win and negate the Phillies' home-field advantage.

"To play in Philadelphia was the easiest place to play," Wathan said. "There were 60,000 screaming people. It was exciting. If you win the first game you get more out of it."[7]

One reason Wathan was content to play in Philadelphia was the Vet's reputation as a hitter's park. After the game, Bowa noted that the team's advance scout, Hugh Alexander, "said their doubles hitters would be home-run hitters in this park, and they proved it."[8] The Royals hit three homers in the first game, more than the Phillies and Astros combined in their championship series.

Since it was only a one-run game, the Phillies would have loved to add some insurance runs to avoid a ninth-inning scare. But the closest they came to jump-starting anything was a lonely single by Boone. They did get their first, brief look at Royals closer Dan Quisenberry, who obtained the last out.

McGraw did it again in the ninth, eliminating any threat of challenge when he got Royals second baseman Frank White to ground out, and then struck out Washington and Wilson to end the game. True to form in these playoffs, Game One of the World Series was not a no-sweat result, but the Phillies were up, 1–0.

After McGraw participated in all five NLCS games, some wondered if he would be strong enough to keep rolling on an every-game basis. He acted as if that was a silly suggestion.

"What it comes down to, simply, is the ability to do what you're paid to do," McGraw said. "The catcher has to throw the ball every day. So do the shortstops. What's so different about me throwing it?" A follow-up question approximately asked, Well, if it's not the power in the arm, is it the mental prep? "If that was true," McGraw added, "I'd be down in the trainer's room soaking my head in ice. I've never been paid a dime for my brains yet."[9]

Green confirmed suspicions when he said he would have pulled Walk early if he was hitting in the usual National League nine-spot in the order instead of the teams employing the designated hitter in this Series. He was glad he didn't have to make such a move.

"Going to the bullpen would have hurt us that early in all probability," Green said. "But I probably would have done it if Walk was the hitter. He had good stuff, and as we've seen him do in the past, once he got over that early hump, he gave us a good three-four innings."[10]

Walk was a little bit sensitive about being viewed mostly as a spare part.

Years later, when reviewing his role in the game, Walk said, "We got the win. That's always the important thing. Getting the first win was huge for us."[11]

* * *

There was no day off before Game Two back at the Vet before a similar 65,775-fan throng. The Royals eluded the Phillies' best pitcher, Steve Carlton, in the opener, but now he was rested and the natural choice to start against Larry Gura. This was what home-field advantage was all about: holding serve, as if in a tennis match, going up 2–0 instead of allowing the visitors to go home with a split.

However, Carlton never seemed completely settled in. George Brett and Hal McRae both singled off Lefty in the first inning, but were left stranded on the bases. Gura permitted no baserunners in the bottom of the first.

Carlton issued a walk to Willie Aikens in the second, but was also required to get four outs in the inning when his strikeout of Frank White (one of three) was a wild pitch on strike three, permitting him to reach first. Wathan flied out and Carlton fanned Jose Cardenal and Willie Wilson in the oddly extended inning. There was activity, but again no runs crossed the plate.

By the end of the second, Gura had retired six straight Phillies batters. Carlton again gave up singles to Brett and McRae in the third, but a strikeout and a double play got him out of that mini jam with his shutout intact. It was nine batters in a row set down by Gura one-third into the game, with the Phillies seeming baffled at the plate.

Carlton allowed still another hit in the fourth, a single to Aikens, but once again a double play erased the runner. Three more tries by the Phillies in their half of the inning and three more oh-fers were recorded. At that point, Gura was tossing a perfect game.

Like Carlton, Gura was a southpaw, but he did not garner the same kind of accolades. After winning the College World Series with Arizona, Gura spent 16 years in the majors and won 126 games with one All-Star appearance. His 18 wins in 1980 equaled his career season high. Through four innings, however, it was Gura—not Carlton—who looked more like a Cy Young Award winner.

It was the same kind of inning for Carlton in the fifth. Two men reached base, one on a walk and one on a single, but mixing in a couple of strikeouts kept the Royals off the scoreboard. Thus far perfect, it was in the bottom of the fifth when Gura ceased his Cy Young imitation and was victimized by anxious Phillies hitters. Keith Moreland singled with one out and Maddox doubled him to third base. Trillo brought Moreland home with a sacrifice fly and Bowa drove Maddox across with a single. It was the wake-up inning for the Phils and the fans. Philadelphia 2, Kansas City 0.

Carlton had been skating on thin ice all night. So in the sixth, when he gave up a single to Amos Otis and a walk to John

Wathan, he again had little margin of error. This time he did not pull it off. Aikens hit a grounder to second, which Trillo fielded, but then threw errantly to first. Aikens was safe on the E-4 and Otis came around to score and slash the lead to a single run. Again, the inning ended on a double play. Trillo may have committed the miscue, but the Phillies infielders were Carlton's best friends this day, converting a total of four double plays.

There was an unexpected development when the top of the sixth ended. As the Royals took the field, Brett did not go out to third base for the bottom of the inning, instead being replaced by Dave Chalk. In one of the strangest of pronouncements of an in-game injury in baseball history, Brett left the lineup because he was suffering from hemorrhoids and was in such pain he could not continue—even in this critically important game. While his problem was not a deeply shrouded secret, no one, least of all Brett, expected the situation to come to this.

After the game Brett issued one of the most unusual quotes in American sports history when he said, "It is a pain in the ass."[12] Unusual because this was probably one of the few times the words were spoken literally. This was no minor loss, of course, having a .390 hitter going to the bench.

Rather than act demoralized, the Royals went after Carlton with even more vigor in the top of the seventh. He helped them, too, issuing three walks by the time the first out was on the board. That was a direct invitation to catastrophe. Otis's double scored two runs, and a sacrifice fly by Wathan brought in another. Now Kansas City led, 4–2.

Frey went to his bullpen for the bottom of the seventh. Gura had allowed two runs in six innings on just four Philadelphia hits before being relieved by Quisenberry. It was still early in his career, but "Quiz" loomed as possibly the next great reliever. His personality somewhat resembled McGraw's, maybe an indication some closers had to remain light-hearted to cope with the pressure. The Phillies made three straight groundball outs on only nine pitches.

And, wouldn't you know it, Carlton's eighth was the mirror image of the previous innings. He allowed two singles and struck out two, but didn't allow a run. Quisenberry had to feel pretty good about himself in the bottom of the eighth, but was about to get whipped around Veterans Stadium like a pennant flag on a windy day.

Bob Boone led off the inning with a walk and Del Unser, pinch-hitting for Lonnie Smith to set up a more favorable match-up, doubled. Good hunch on Green's part. With men on second and third, Bake McBride singled to score Unser. Mike Schmidt followed with a double and Moreland singled as the hits just kept on comin'. When the roughing up of Quisenberry concluded, the Phillies had four more runs and a 6–4 lead.

Green assumed Carlton had done enough for the evening and when he removed him from the game in the top of the ninth, the big guy had thrown 159 pitches. In this era of managers living and dying by the pitch count, a manager might be fired the next day if he kept his starter in that long.

Ron Reed was the reliever, the marshal brought on to keep the peace. Although he gave up a one-out single to McRae, he cooled the rest of the Royals without incident. McRae had three hits on the night and Otis two. So did Brett, in only two at-bats. The Royals now trailed in the Series, 2–0, but Brett's rear end was the object of more attention than any other single play in Game Two.

"I'm frustrated, but there's nothing I can do about it," said Brett, who said he had been wrangling with the problem since the day after Kansas City eliminated the Yankees in the ALCS. "The more you move, the more it hurts."[13]

Brett was chipper enough to crack a joke or two as well, since he knew the rest of the known world was likely making fun of his butt.

"[Jamie Quirk]," Brett said of one teammate, "told me I could make commercials for Preparation H and make $100,000."[14]

Whether the fans recognized the significance of Pete Rose's welcome gesture to first base in the first inning after a single or not, upon further review it could be interpreted as a joke or the hard-nosed Rose looking for any little advantage. When Brett stood on the bag, Rose slapped him on his rear end. Brett's response was to admonish Rose, saying, "Oh, don't do that." Rose played that a little bit on the innocent side, but got serious after Brett left the game. "He must be hurt bad. It's a shame."[15] Rose felt for Brett because the Royals star had been in the sport for a long time and finally made it to the World Series, only to be too sore to move and become the butt of jokes.

When the Royals flew back to Kansas City to prepare for Game Three, Brett entered a hospital and underwent surgery to correct his "problem." The debate swirling in the baseball world was whether or not he would be able to play in the next game, although the actual operation took about 20 minutes and seemed as routine as trimming a hangnail. Brett was nowhere to be found; the Royals were not giving out any information. Yet, somehow, despite no such quotation being directly stated in the paper's story, the *New York Daily News* ran a headline reading: "Brett: 'I'll Play.'"[16]

Meanwhile, back at the just-completed game, others—both Phillies and Royals—focused on analyzing baseball more than theorizing about Brett's medical issues.

It was one of Quisenberry's worst outings of the season, and in retrospect he felt the avalanche of problems stemmed from walking Boone on a 3-2 pitch which he believed was a strike. He accused the umpires of being prejudiced against submariners because of their style.

"Umpires think we're freaks," Quisenberry said, "and that we belong in paddy wagons with lace wrapped around our faces and should be whipped." He paused, zeroing in on that four-run Phillies' inning. "I didn't think the script was going to end that way."[17]

Carlton off-days were Haley's Comet occurrences, but the Royals couldn't take advantage of this one and he got the win. It didn't hurt that he struck out 10, but he also gave up 10 hits.

"We should've scored 10 runs off Carlton tonight," Gura said—and he was not wrong. "We had him on the hook all night."[18]

It was the Royals' bad that they didn't.

For the Phillies, McBride had one of every type of offensive stat in the box score. One hit, one run, one RBI, and one walk. He was enjoying the heck out of being up 2–0 in the Series.

"I think the World Series has got me hyped up," McBride said.[19]

As it well should have.

20

WORLD SERIES: GAMES THREE, FOUR, AND FIVE IN KANSAS CITY

OF COURSE, EVERYONE wanted to know if George Brett was going to be able to get off his butt and play in Game Three, as the World Series moved to his home park of Royals Stadium on October 17. Would he be magically healed overnight, well enough to run and slide and throw and hit? Why, yes he was. Brett said he was going to be able to play and he reported for duty, assuming his usual spot at third base.

Although less widely noted, Phillies left fielder Greg Luzinski, who had been sent home with a 103-degree fever before Game Two, was still suffering from his ailment, running a temperature of 101 degrees. He would not start nor get into the game.

The Royals were back home, but the pressure was all on them being behind 2–0. Losing Game Three was untenable. Falling behind 3–0 was unacceptable. They would be toast.

For Kansas City's first home game in the Series, Jim Frey started Rich Gale. Dallas Green countered with Dick Ruthven. The right-handed Gale stood 6-foot-7, one of the tallest players in the game, and weighed 225 pounds. He went 13–9 that season with a 3.92 ERA, his last good one in seven years in the majors. Ruthven was rested after appearing in the final playoff game against Houston.

This was a fan base that was exhilarated when the Royals defeated the Yankees to advance to the World Series. The 42,380 fans agonized as the Royals lost the first two games in the Series, but they could perhaps make enough positive noise to tilt the outcome of Game Three Kansas City's way.

Lonnie Smith led off the game against Gale and hit a 1-2 pitch to right for a single. With one out, Mike Schmidt walked. One could almost hear those Royals fans' blood pressure rise, but Gale got out of the inning unscathed. Those fans were pretty loud when Brett stepped to the plate in the bottom of the first. When he slugged a solo home run, Kansas City led, 1–0. When the bat hit the ball, it was as if an earthquake had rattled the stadium. OK, Brett was healthy enough to approximate Brett of the summer.

"The pain is all behind me," Brett said after the game, showing his sense of humor had not been injured.[1]

Gale was uneven—not only in the first, but in the second as well. He could barely hold his team's lead for 20 minutes. After the first out on a grounder off the bat of Garry Maddox, he was unable to retire the next three Phillies. Manny Trillo and Larry Bowa each singled, and Bob Boone walked to load the bases. Smith was up again, and his simple ground out scored Trillo to tie the game.

Ruthven allowed a single to Amos Otis in the second, but that was it. Gale gave up a single to Bake McBride and a double to Trillo, meaning three innings in he had yet to set the Phillies down in order. Even so, he escaped without allowing a run.

Ruthven did go 1-2-3 in the third, and then Gale finally did, too, in the fourth. Gale's teammates gave him the lead back in the fourth when Hal McRae's single brought home Willie Aikens, who had tripled, making the score 2–1. Gale's smoothness proved to be a one-inning deal. Leading off the top of the fifth, Mike Schmidt bashed a home run deep to left. Philadelphia seemed ready to add a few more runs after a Keith Moreland single, so Frey used the quick hook on Gale. He was out after pitching just 4 1/3 innings. Renie Martin came on in relief, and Maddox singled. But then Trillo hit into a double play to end the threat. So it was tied again, now 2–2.

Twice the Royals had scored a run to take a lead, and both times the Phillies immediately scored to tie. "I'd be talking to the other outfielders between innings," Wilson, said, "and we'd say, 'Damn, we just can't hold a lead.'"[2]

Such things can work on a team's psyche. The Royals could become frustrated, thinking there was nothing they could do to hold the Phillies down. Ruthven gave Kansas City nothing in the bottom of the fifth. With Bowa and Smith each singling in the sixth, the Phils started treating Martin like Gale. Despite the baserunners, he held them off and Philadelphia did not add a run. Neither did the Royals in the bottom of the sixth. It was three up, three down with two outs coming on Ruthven strikeouts.

Martin pretty much cruised through the Phillies seventh, retiring all three batters on fly balls. Ruthven was not as sharp in the seventh as he had been in the sixth, and Amos Otis tagged him. The home run, with no one aboard, cleared the right-field fence, pushing Kansas City ahead by a run (again), 3–2. That was a big hit, but Otis was best known for his fielding (he won three Gold Gloves during his career) and in Game Three set a World Series record for an outfielder by making nine putouts.

However, the pattern for the Royals of score one, yield one, continued in the top of the eighth. Martin, who had pitched extremely well, was solved by the Phillies' bats. With one out, Larry Bowa managed an infield single. He then stole second, but Smith, hitting behind him, walked anyway, putting men on first and second. Pete Rose then singled to right-center and Bowa came around, tying the game for a third time, 3–3. After that single, Martin hit the showers in favor of Dan Quisenberry. Schmidt flied out to end the inning. While Brett cracked a double off Ruthven in the Royals' turn at bat, it didn't amount to anything on the scoreboard.

It was Schmidt's at-bat that was the most intriguing. Before flying out, the team's biggest slugger had counterintuitively attempted a bunt that the Royals did not figure to be prepared for. He gave a good tap, but the ball just rolled foul.

"The umpire told me my bunt in the eighth inning was just six inches foul," Schmidt said. "If it's fair, Smith scores and we win."[3]

The Phillies, who'd been producing comebacks throughout October, were used to these scenarios. This game resembled those of the championship series against the Astros. Never a suspense-free moment.

Bake McBride led off the ninth inning with a single off Quisenberry, then Moreland gave the home fans a scare with a deep fly out to left, caught by Willie Wilson. Strategizing to set up ground-ball force plays, the Royals intentionally walked Maddox. The plan worked, as Quisenberry induced two grounders, sending it on to the bottom of the ninth. Ruthven was still throwing, although it would not have been a surprise if Green pulled him after he allowed a leadoff single to McRae, his second hit of the game. But this time Otis, following in the order, went meekly, grounding into a double play. That hurt the Royals, as Clint Hurdle singled next. Then Ruthven finished off the inning as Darrell Porter flied out to right.

It was on to extra innings again, a regular occurrence for these Phillies in the playoffs.

In the top of the 10th, Boone led off with a single. Pinch-hitter Greg Gross moved him to second on a sac bunt, and then Rose was intentionally walked. Schmidt was at the plate, a lovely scenario for the Phillies. He got hold of a Quisenberry pitch with most of his bat, but lined it to Royals second baseman Frank White, who turned it into a double play.

Just as he had lamented his bunt rolling a few inches in the wrong direction, Schmidt was bugged because his smack did not zoom a few inches in another direction.

"In the 10th, if my line drive is six inches away from White, we get a run, or possibly two, and we win," said Schmidt, playing the "baseball is a game of inches" card.[4]

After Ruthven basically pitched a complete game, Green brought in Tug McGraw to pitch the 10th. It was a water-torture inning for the Phillies, starting when U. L. Washington led off with a single. Wilson walked on four pitches, Brett was intentionally walked, and Willie Aikens ended the game with a single to left-center to score Wilson. The final was 4–3, Royals, cutting the Series lead to 2–1.

Mulling the Phillies' resilience and how they kept trumping the Royals with answering runs, Wilson said, "Luckily, they didn't get a chance to bat again."[5]

Brett was actually still at St. Luke's Hospital up until four hours before the game. He had arranged for teammate Jamie Quirk to pick him up on the way to the stadium, but Quirk said he forgot. Brett ended up taking a taxi to Royals Stadium, costing him $11.

"It was a great satisfaction just to play," Brett said. "Just to hit a home run in the World Series is something special."[6] Not to mention winning the game.

But later, Boone said he did not believe Brett was back to 100 percent.

"George Brett had hemorrhoids and he wasn't the same guy," Boone said. "It was a different team without him. He didn't have as many at-bats."[7]

The Phillies probably should have won. They stranded 15 baserunners, many just aching to be driven home by a timely hit that didn't come. "If we'd have just gotten a couple of hits, there'd have been no contest," Green said.[8]

Phils pitcher Warren Brusstar definitely thought Philadelphia could have taken this game, providing a commanding Series lead. Putting that many men on base meant the Phillies were in good shape offensively, and they kept rebounding, but not sending those guys around to score. "We were on a pretty good roll," he said. "We were up late."[9] And then Kansas City was up later.

Obviously, the teams were going to be in Kansas City for a while, not with days off between games, but perhaps with time enough for a meal-time getaway to Arthur Bryant's for some barbeque.

"Game Three was a big win for them, instead of us going up 3–0," Bowa said. "We knew we were going to have a dog fight."[10]

While so much attention had been paid to George Brett's hemorrhoids and less focus was placed on Greg Luzinski's fever, another personnel matter was given short shrift: Kansas City management refused to allow the Phillie Phanatic to perform his act on the field. He had been welcomed in Houston and later praised Astros fans in his *Philadelphia Daily News* guest column. But the Royals did not accept the Phanatic as a member of the postseason roster. In another *Daily News* column, the Phanatic revealed his predicament.

"Last night," the mascot wrote, "the Phanatic was banned in Kansas City." He informed readers that Steve Carlton had soothed him, the same Carlton who did not speak to other newspaper reporters, saying, "Don't worry about it. They're still into Nehru jackets here. They'll be ready for you in about fifteen years."[11]

* * *

Game Four on October 18 was back at Royals Stadium. Kansas City was hopeful of tying the Series, the Phillies optimistic they could cushion their lead. The starting pitchers were Larry Christenson for the Phillies and Dennis Leonard for the Royals.

Pete Rose got a single in the first inning, but otherwise Leonard had no problem. There was one problem for the Phils, though. The Royals blew up Christenson right away, scoring four runs in the first. Brett belted a triple, Aikens homered, McRae doubled, and Otis doubled. Dallas Green could hardly have sprinted to the mound fast enough, as Christenson lasted 1/3 of an inning, surrendering five hits and four runs. Before fans could finish a beer, it was 3–0 and Dickie Noles was pitching.

The Phillies maintained their pattern of scoring in their next at-bat after a Kansas City score, but retaliated with just one run. A single and a KC error put Manny Trillo in scoring position and Bowa knocked him in with a single. This time, adopting Philadelphia's playbook, the Royals, too, scored promptly after the Phillies had, adding a run in the bottom of the second on a solo shot by Aikens.

Noles gained control of the game after that, putting the Royals' bats on silent mode for a while, only giving up a hit here or there. For a guy who barely had time to warm up, Noles was performing an impressive rescue mission. However, the Phillies were not disturbing Leonard much, as he was a different thrower than he had been in Game One. Schmidt had a single in the fourth and Boone had a single in the fifth, but there was no parade on the bases as runners died far from home plate. Noles, though, in a clutch showing, matched Leonard, giving no additional ground.

It was not until the visitors half of the seventh that the Phillies scraped together another run. A Trillo double, a Bowa single, and a Boone sacrifice fly produced a run. Boone's .229 average during the regular season bugged him, and so was trying to make up for it with solid hitting now.

"I was swinging the bat pretty well," Boone said.[12]

At the end of the regular season, when the Phillies had put away the Montreal Expos, a Philadelphia columnist had taken stock of Boone's contributions, singles that were more subtle than Schmidt's home runs, but were definitely table setters. Green teased Boone by saying, "Hey, Boonie, why don't you get a clutch hit before the year's over?" Boone replied, "It's early yet, Dallas."[13] Boone was right, and in the World Series he was making good on that promise. He would bat .412 against Kansas City before this thing was wrapped up.

Noles departed after tossing a very helpful 4 1/3 innings, giving up just one run while striking out six. In came Kevin Saucier for two thirds of an inning, and Brusstar entered with one out in the sixth. Brusstar recognized his role was to hold the Royals at bay so the Phillies had a better chance to catch up.

"They jumped on us early," he said. "They had all the momentum in their favor."[14]

Brusstar retired McRae on a ground ball to end the bottom of the sixth before the Phillies got that one run back. Leonard lasted into the eighth, but when Rose doubled, Frey went to the bullpen and summoned Quisenberry. In seven innings, Leonard allowed just two earned runs. Rose went to third on a McBride ground out and scored on a Schmidt sacrifice fly. The Royals had every reason to be concerned, as the score moved to 5–3. Brusstar overpowered the bats of Wilson, White, and Brett, who all made outs on grounders. That was excellent pitching in the heat of the moment, though much later Brusstar reminisced that the challenge of going up against a future Hall of Famer in Brett was memorable.

"Facing George Brett in the World Series," he said. "That was a thrill."[15] Brusstar provided everything Green could have asked for, throwing 2 1/3 innings without allowing a hit. Only Quisenberry polished the Phillies off in the same manner in the ninth, setting down all three hitters in order. The score stayed at 5–3, and now the Series was tied, 2–2. All advantages Philadelphia accrued at home had evaporated.

Christenson was the chief victim, not even surviving the first inning. He just couldn't get his stuff working. "They hit my mistakes and some good pitches, too," Christenson forthrightly confessed. "If you want to say I didn't do my job, that's correct. I didn't."[16]

Aikens, whose Series average was up to .423, drove in three with two home runs. Suddenly, he, and not Brett, was Public Enemy No. 1 in the Royals lineup. That made four home runs for Aikens, counting the two others he clobbered in Game One.

Aikens was wielding a dangerous bat, and there was a moment in the fourth that smacked of retaliation. A high, inside pitch thrown by Noles created major consternation. Frey ran out of the dugout to protest what he viewed as absurd headhunting. Green's reaction later was of the innocent, see-no-evil kind. "I didn't see any knockdown pitch," said Green, who must have been sipping at the water cooler at the time.[17]

* * *

The Series had a whole new complexion heading into Game Five. Playing for a third day in a row in Kansas City, there was no question the teams would be returning to Philadelphia for a Game Six. But the Sunday afternoon, October 19 game would determine who had the upper hand. It was a crossroads game, likely foretelling which team would become the next world champion.

The Royals trotted out Larry Gura, who had been so effective earlier, and the Phillies went with Marty Bystrom. That meant two of the five games to this point featured rookie pitchers for Philadelphia.

It was all outs for the Phillies in the first inning and the Royals also failed to score, though Brett singled. The second inning flew by with neither team obtaining a baserunner. Bowa tried to get something going for the Phillies in the third with a single, but was erased on a double play. Bystrom gave up two singles in the home part of the third—one to Darrell Porter and the other on a bunt by U. L. Washington—but no runners advanced beyond second.

The wake-up call reached the Phillies in the top of the fourth, as they benefited from a Royals mistake in the field and another mistake on a pitch thrown to Schmidt. Bake McBride was safe at first on an error and then Schmidt belted a 2-2 Gura pitch into orbit for a two-run homer. That was the first time the Phillies had led in a game since they left Philadelphia. Presumably, Bystrom thanked Schmidt because he needed the assistance. He did allow two singles (to Aikens and Otis) when the Royals took their turn batting, but no runs.

Gura showed that his bad pitch to Schmidt was an aberration by regaining command in the top of the fifth, as the Phillies were retired in order. In the bottom of the fifth, the Royals made some noise. While they didn't really bat Bystrom around, they instead nibbled their way to a run. Washington and Wilson both singled to start the inning, and Frank White sacrificed them ahead a base on a bunt. A simple Brett ground ball out scored Washington to make it 2–1.

It seemed fairly clear the Phillies were going to need some more runs to get out of this one alive, but a Boone leadoff single went for naught when Rose lined into a double play and Gura retired the side. Bystrom showed more vulnerability in the bottom of the sixth, as Otis led off with a home run, and that was just the start. When Clint Hurdle and Porter singled, Green summoned Ron Reed to replace Bystrom. A Washington sacrifice fly brought in a second run before Reed shut off the faucet. So now Kansas City led, 3–2, going into the late innings. There were 42,379 happy customers in Royals Stadium.

Feeling a sense of urgency, after Luzinski walked, Lonnie Smith pinch-ran for him and Keith Moreland came through with a single. Frey decided that was enough for Gura, and in came Quisenberry yet again. Kansas City definitely spelled relief with a Q, as a couple of ground balls sent the Phillies back into the field without a tying run. Following a similar relief strategy, Green brought in McGraw for Reed. Tug looked super sharp at first, striking out the first two Royals hitters. He wavered slightly when McRae doubled and the Phillies gifted Otis with an intentional walk, but was able to pitch out of the jam.

Both star relievers seemed in charge of the opposing lineups until the top of the ninth, when Schmidt said hello to Quisenberry with a single to open the frame. This was a rocket past Brett at third, who had been second-guessing Phillies batters with all the bunts they'd been flirting with. So Brett played Schmidt in and paid for it when the ball zipped into the outfield.

"I looked at him and smiled and he smiled back," Schmidt said of the moment before he stepped into the batter's box. "But there was no way I was going to bunt."[18]

The not-quite-secret pinch-hitting weapon Del Unser went to the plate for Lonnie Smith and cracked a double that scored Schmidt from first. Moreland, not famed for his short game, produced a sacrifice bunt to move Unser to third. Trillo then singled Unser home to cap the two-run inning.

Now the Phillies led, 4–3, and McGraw came out to close out the Royals in the bottom of the ninth. The stadium was rocking and rolling as the fans tried their best to will their hometown team into a comeback. Things definitely progressed to an intense level when McGraw walked three men to load the bases with two outs. There it was: hero time for someone. Jose Cardenal could win the game with any good placement of the ball, and McGraw had no wiggle room with the ducks on the pond. The count quickly favored McGraw at 1-2. Then he finished it, fooling Cardenal into a swing-and-a-miss to end the game.

That hero thing seemed real to Cardenal. "I knew I was going to be the hero or the bum," he said. "I struck out, so I'm the bum. You have to take the good with the bad."[19]

This was one of the periodic times McGraw named his pitch. "I got him on a Cutty Sark fastball," McGraw explained, initially confusing journalists. "Yeah. It sails."[20]

McGraw later subtly described how his stomach was churning with his comment, "No wonder Rolaids sponsored the award for Fireman of the Year."[21]

After an adventurous stay in Kansas City that felt more like three months than three days, the Phillies returned to Philadelphia with the World Series lead.

Winning that game, Greg Gross said, was special for many reasons. The win gave the Phillies a controlling position, back at home, with their ace scheduled to go. Gross liked Philadelphia's chances going into Game Six. "On the flight back you felt good," Gross said. "You knew you had Lefty going for you and he was well-rested."[22]

Unser, who smacked that big double as part of the winning rally, also did some thinking on the plane returning to

Philadelphia. Up 3–2, he could not help feeling good about the Phillies' chances to capture the World Series. "I was cautiously optimistic," Unser said.[23]

It did seem propitious that Steve Carlton was going to start in a possible elimination game, and back at Veterans Stadium, too. Not that Kansas City was about to forfeit out of fright. The pattern of this World Series left the Royals' Hal McRae believing anything could happen in the next game.

"The momentum shifted game by game," he said. "It doesn't matter how many games you're down."[24]

Not until the last out of the last game.

21

WORLD SERIES: GAME SIX IN
PHILADELPHIA

PEOPLE WHO ONLY follow sports casually, for entertainment more than out of passion, don't understand. They can't really feel it when the electricity crackles in a stadium when a championship is on the cusp of being seized. The trendy fan may not feel the atmospheric conditions that prevail at the World Series when time is running out, at the NCAA basketball championship, before the bell rings for the first round at a heavyweight title bout.

The air was ripe with heart-pounding anticipation on October 21, when the Phillies and Royals took the field for Game Six with Philadelphia ahead, 3–2, in a World Series that could end that night. It was not as if the 65,838 fans present at Veterans Stadium were unaware that this might be the night when nearly a century of waiting culminated, fulfilling the dreams of fans long dead, of fans who had grieved, of fans alive to see this moment arrive.

Game Seven carries the most pressure in any championship series, but Game Six was much like a Game Seven this time, as the Phillies had the chance they fought for with such spunk all summer.

Two days earlier, the Phillies captured Game Five. Then they flew home to Philadelphia, arriving at two in the morning, trying to quell the still-coursing adrenaline to sleep for a few hours before arriving at Veterans Stadium for a mini workout. Steve Carlton had been designated by manager Dallas Green to be the flag-bearer, starting the game to carry the Phillies home. Carlton, of course, had had nothing to say about that, keeping with his policy of staying mum. So Green spoke for him. "He's tired, there's no question about it," Green said. "He has every right to be tired. But he's also got the quality of a champion who's able to come back and get it one more time. All we need from him is one more time."[1]

The Phillies had an insurance-policy game in their pockets but, given this opportunity, who really wanted to play another one? The Royals were relying on right-hander Rich Gale again to counter Carlton. Listening to him discuss his situation, Gale sounded so blasé one might think he was warming up for an exhibition game.

"It's not a life-or-death situation," Gale said. "If I win, the sun will come up Wednesday morning. If I lose, the sun will still come up Wednesday morning."[2] There was a fierceness absent from Gale's comments. It may not have *literally* been a life or death situation, but it was assuredly do or die for the Royals. Is it possible Gale had not taken the pulse of fervent Kansas City fans?

Since it was going to be impossible for the Philadelphia spectators to hold their breaths for the game's entirety, they may have begun exhaling when Carlton threw the first pitch to Royals leadoff man Willie Wilson. Kansas City manager Jim Frey felt his players handled Carlton just fine earlier in the Series, but if Lefty was slightly off his game then, he exhibited a man-on-a-mission demeanor in the first inning of Game Six. Wilson went down looking, U. L. Washington went down swinging, and George Brett hit a grounder to Manny Trillo, who threw him out. Gale, however, was nearly as sharp in the bottom of the first with the exception of a Pete Rose single.

In the second inning, Carlton walked two men, but benefited from a double play to end a potential threat. Garry Maddox's double provided some Phillies excitement briefly, and he did advance to third, but no farther.

Carlton set down Royals in order in the third, two more of them on strikeouts. He struck out so many men in 1980 that he could have changed the spelling of his last name to "Karlton," and everyone would have understood.

Before the end of the third, Gale was gone, the Phillies led 2–0, and the needle rose on the excitement meter. Bob Boone led off the inning with a walk, Lonnie Smith reached on an error, and Rose bunted his way on with a single. The bases were loaded and fans watching on TV in Kansas City had trouble swallowing their dinners. Mike Schmidt strode in, briefly surveyed Gale's stuff, and slashed a single to right-center to drive home two runs.

"I can't get any bigger hit than that," Schmidt said later.[3]

When Frey went to the mound to chat with Gale, it was not about candlesticks. No small talk, à la *Bull Durham*, but instructions to take a shower. Renie Martin came in and continued his good work in the Series by retiring the next three Philadelphia hitters, stranding Rose on third.

After Washington singled in the top of the fourth, Carlton was aided by another double play and the Royals remained scoreless. Martin kept mowing down Phillies in the bottom half of the inning, disposing of all three hitters.

If Carlton was supposed to be weary at the start of the game, he was disguising it well. His fastball was humming and his slider was moving as he struck out the first two Royals in the top of the fifth, giving him six Ks. John Wathan, in at catcher, singled for one of his two hits on the night, but he wasn't going anywhere—except back to the dugout when Carlton closed out the inning.

"[Darrell] Porter and I took turns against some of the left-handers," Wathan said of how he happened to be starting. "You are always nervous before a big game. But we knew it was win or go home. That was nerve-wracking. We gave it our best shot."[4] Carlton, though, was too stingy to do more than shrug off best shots.

In the bottom of the fifth, the Phillies began to solve Martin. Lonnie Smith hit a leadoff double, and although Rose flied out, he hit it so deep that Smith was able to tag up and go to third. When Martin walked Schmidt, with whom he couldn't be too careful, Frey was out of patience and brought in Paul Splittorff. To that point, Splittorff was Kansas City's forgotten man in the Series. The left-hander, who won 166 games in his career, went 14–11 for the Royals that season and had pitched 5 1/3 good innings against the New York Yankees in the ALCS. Manny Trillo hit a routine ground ball to short for an out, but the swift Smith scored anyway. Greg Luzinski followed with a ground out as well, but the score had moved the lead up to 3–0.

Splittorff was back out on the mound in a jiffy for the home portion of the sixth because Carlton whizzed through the Royals batters in the top half of the inning, adding another strikeout when he fooled Washington into swinging at a third strike. It was probably not his favorite inning of the night, for despite pitching solidly, Splittorff was still touched for another Philadelphia run. Maddox opened the frame with a single, but Splittorff threw a double-play ball. Whew, right? Not quite. Larry Bowa doubled. Then with two outs, Boone singled him home to make it 4–0 before Smith made the last out.

The game was two-thirds into it, the Phillies had a four-spot of a lead, and Carlton was cruising. Phillies fans had been burned before by unfortunate come-from-behind defeats, but faith seemed to be stronger this time. They all knew what Tug McGraw ran around saying: "You gotta believe." He believed, and it always seemed to work for him.

Brett, no stranger to base hits, led off the seventh with a single, but nobody helped him. Carlton kept reminding people what made him Steve Carlton. Kansas City was not only running out of time, but the Royals could not afford to give up any more runs. When Rose, the first batter up in the bottom of the seventh, managed a single, Splittorff was removed from the mound and replaced by Marty Pattin. Pattin had been a starter for most of his career, but now, at thirty-seven, in his final big-league season, was a regular reliever. Seeking to pad the lead and maybe surprise the Royals, Rose attempted to steal second, but was thrown out. The Phillies were not zeroed in on Pattin. Trillo reached base on an infield error, but that wasn't the pitcher's fault. Luzinski then struck out, so no added runs for the Phils.

In the top of the eighth, Wathan led off with a walk. When Carlton allowed a single to Jose Cardenal, Green decided it was

Tug McGraw Time. McGraw did not throw as many innings as Carlton had, but did appear in 57 regular-season games, 19 more than Lefty. He also pitched in all five games against the Astros, and in four thus far against Kansas City. "In McGraw We Trust" was a Phillies motto, but it should be remembered that his outings were often two innings at a time, not something seen much—if at all—in today's game.

"Tug was pitching in every game," said catcher Boone. "Everything he was throwing was high. He said, 'You've got to fix me quick.' He was looking at me with fear in his eyes."[5]

If McGraw said, "Don't tell anyone else," Boone never said. But sometimes athletes can respond to pivotal moments even if their bodies do not feel 100 percent.

Royals designated hitter Hal McRae knew if Carlton did not pitch a complete game, they would see McGraw again. "Tug McGraw was the guy they went to for the win," he said.[6]

McGraw got Frank White on a foul-ball pop to first base, but then walked Wilson to load the bases. This was the Royals' chance. The good news was that McGraw induced Washington to hit a fly to Maddox in center. The bad news was it was a sacrifice fly, scoring Wathan. The out hurt, but at least the Royals were on the scoreboard. There was a little bit more unease when the next batter, Brett, singled to again load the bases. McGraw took a deep breath and, in an eight-pitch at-bat, finally retired McRae on a grounder. Not so much damage. Just one run, and the Phillies still led, 4–1.

Closer Dan Quisenberry came in for Pattin for the eighth, and Philadelphia did not come close to adding a run. That set up a dramatic top of the ninth. Three more outs, and the Phillies would be World Series champions. Three more outs, and they didn't even have to bother about a bottom of the ninth.

McGraw, as was his job, was game to go out for the ninth, but was no more rested than he was before pitching the previous inning. Could the Royals score three runs or more and break Phillies fans hearts yet again? He did not advertise how he was feeling, but McGraw was not feeling so peachy.

"I was so tired, I didn't think I could make it," McGraw said after the game. "The last inning had me so shook up, I can't remember too much about it."[7]

Usually, it's the losses pitchers want to forget. But this win came hard.

Amos Otis led off the Kansas City ninth and McGraw caught him looking, a strikeout for out number one. Willie Aikens worked McGraw for a walk and was replaced by pinch-runner Onix Concepcion. Wathan, who was on base three times that night, placed a single to right field. First and second, one out. Cardenal then stroked a single, but Concepcion couldn't score and the bases were loaded. Sometimes pitchers wouldn't mind being beamed up, as in *Star Trek*, to another planet or solar system for respite, but McGraw eventually had to throw another pitch to the next batter, Frank White.

On the first pitch, White got a piece of the ball. Not much of it, but enough to pop it up down the first-base line in foul territory. What ensued was the most heart-stopping fielding play of the Series for the Phillies. Catcher Boone seemed to have the ball in his sights, but first baseman Rose darted over to serve as a potential emergency backup. Well, the emergency occurred. As fans yelled "Yikes!" the ball nicked off Boone's nice large catcher's mitt and was on its way down to the Veterans Stadium turf. Rose reached over with his glove and speared the ball for the dramatic out.

"When it was hit, it could [have] been either of us making the play," Rose said. "I couldn't hear him, but I happened to see him make the call. Normally, it's his ball, and with a man at third I'd be the cutoff man to home. [Meanwhile, McGraw ran to home to cover the plate.] But with all the cameras over there near the dugout, all the equipment and stuff, I thought there was a chance he might trip or something. I stayed there. I normally don't do that."[8]

It wasn't clear if Boone was joking or not, though he said it lightheartedly nearly forty years later when discussing the crucial pop-up catch. It was a counterpoint comment to what Rose said right after the game.

"Did he say how he screwed up the pop-up?" Boone said. "It should have been his all the way. He's heard it from me many times. I knew we were both going into the dugout. I am the one who hustles down the line." Boone was briefly horrified when the ball ricocheted off his mitt, but there was almost instantly a reprieve. "I saw the glove [Rose's] come right into my face. I wanted to kiss him."[9]

McGraw was just happy someone caught the ball. That was the second out. Sometime near game's end, Boone remembers Schmidt saying aloud that when the Phillies won the World Series, he knew exactly what he was going to do first. "He said, 'If we win this thing, I'm going to jump into his [McGraw's] arms,'" Boone said.[10]

Kansas City loading the bases was not the swift, culminating inning Philadelphia fans sought. They were at least as worried as any of the players on the field. Even Dallas Green was on edge. He trekked to the mound to chat with his favorite reliever. Green said, "Hey, Tug, let's not make this SOB as overly exciting as we're trying here."[11]

McGraw was looking for a quick escape route, not any prolonging of the strain on his weary left arm. "My arm was so tired in the ninth all I wanted was for the Royals to please hit the ball at one of our guys," McGraw said. "I could see the security people lining up, all the animals behind home plate. Tired as I felt, I wasn't about to go to the dogs."[12]

Royals left fielder Willie Wilson was ready for his turn at bat. The possibilities were endless for what could result from it. A hit knocked in a run. A home run put the Royals ahead. If he made an out, the Royals were kaput.

He made an out.

McGraw struck him out, and ninety-seven years of frustration and impatience finally ended for the Philadelphia Phillies. They won Game Six, 4–1, and they won the first World Series in franchise history.

There was only despair on the faces of Royals players who missed out on their first chance at a World Series crown. "I was on second base when the game ended," said Wathan, who had an excellent view of the first moments of the party.[13]

Noise the fans made could have been heard on the moon. McGraw leapt in the air, as high a jump as his tired legs would allow, his arms outstretched above his head in the iconic pose photographers caught him in for all time. Schmidt did as he had promised, running from third base to the mound. It was a giddy, championship dog pile. Fans stood and applauded and yelled and cheered and let everything out into the night air. It was an end-of-movie scene of joy.

Yep, there was Schmidt "jumping on everybody," Boone said.[14]

There were the Philadelphia police, not really jumping on everybody, but standing guard just in case those happy fans got a little too rowdy. Their dogs were also on alert. As he mentioned, McGraw noticed the dogs edging onto the diamond before he even threw the last pitch. Talking to himself, he thought the scene was weird, that the K-9 dogs didn't really belong. He was distracted for a moment, then let the dogs lead him back to his task. "The K]in K-9] reminded me of a strikeout," McGraw said.[15]

Wilson was among the top players on the Royals Frey would have wished to be in the crucial situation if given the choice. He batted .326 in the regular season with 230 hits. But after hitting .308 against the Yankees, he hit just .154 in the Series and was 0-for-4 in the finale.

"I was flat the whole Series," Wilson said. "I just couldn't get anything. I'm down. I'm depressed."[16] In other comments, Wilson seemed to already be accepting being blamed as a scapegoat, although no such word had been uttered out loud. "I know a lot of guys would have liked to be here," he said. "But it was terrible to be here and play bad. All people will remember is the end, not the season. And who knows if I'll ever get into another Series to live it down."[17]

It is possible Dallas Green smiled more and longer in the clubhouse after the vindication of a World Series title than he had all year long. For months he had frequently roasted his guys, singeing them with pointed comments as he cajoled and demanded that they play better. They lived through a lot together, the Phillies manager and his troops, spending hot months coming together to rally in September, squeaking past the Houston Astros in a memorable NLCS, and at last grasping the biggest prize in the sport. He went man to man in the locker room, thanking those same players.

His tour of the facilities and imbibing champagne was interrupted by a congratulatory phone call from president Jimmy Carter. On his end of the call, Green said in part, "I tell you, we've waited a long time in Philadelphia. A lot of people thought this baseball team couldn't do it. But I think we proved we are the best baseball team in America."[18]

Didn't Green tell them that all along?

After his opening game, pressed-into-service start, Bob Walk never threw another pitch in the Series. Knowing the personnel and the likely way the game might unfold, Walk said, "Carlton was going to end it that night. With Tug it was like a script."[19]

That night Carlton went seven innings, allowed four hits and one run, and struck out seven Royals. He did exactly what his teammates expected, not just Walk.

"With Lefty on the mound as a rested starter, it is over," said fellow pitcher Warren Brusstar. "I knew he was going to win. You just have the confidence in him. We had had some failures, but this was what we wanted to accomplish. At the end of the game, they had us up throwing in the bullpen. But they're going to take Tug out and bring us in? No way."[20]

That's where Brusstar was when McGraw fanned Wilson to end it, still in the bullpen.

"I went crazy," Brusstar said. "Just absolutely ballistic."[21]

This was not a group of players who had championships stacked up on their resumes. There were many rookies and many veterans who had been with the Phillies for years, been to wars for the Phillies, but lost them. Take away Pete Rose and the feeling of owning the world, literally owning the baseball world, was a new sensation for most of them.

"You just kind of let go of everything," said Del Unser, who had been in the majors since 1968 and never experienced anything approaching the deep-down satisfaction of being proclaimed the best by the known world. "It's a wonderful, wonderful thing."[22]

Although there was competition for the title, probably the most raucous corner of the Phillies clubhouse was Mike Schmidt's locker. He was named Most Valuable Player of the Series and was surrounded by sportswriters to hear his take on it all. Schmidt hit safely in all six Series games and drove in the winning runs in the final one with his two-run single.

"It [the MVP] could have gone to any number of guys on our team," Schmidt said. "My performance didn't stand out. I just did something every game."[23]

While the rest of the Phillies were whooping it up, Schmidt was slow to loosen up. His emotions seemed to be on hold. "I'm still sort of in a coma," he admitted. Only until Green hoisted the championship trophy high and shouted, "Look at this. Look at this, Schmitty!"[24]

Schmidt looked and smiled and suddenly it seemed to sink in: the Philadelphia Phillies were champions of the world. It was real.

22

LONG NIGHT INTO MORNING

THEY DIDN'T WANT to go home. Not the players, who wanted the clubhouse celebration to last forever. Not the fans, some of whom screamed as loudly as they could as they exuberantly exited from Veterans Stadium into the streets where revelers partied as if it was New Year's Eve.

There was a sense of unreality spreading through players' heads and fans' minds, a slow-to-sink-in attitude that was part shock, part pleasure, part a desire to relive every minute of the regular season, playoffs, and World Series all over again.

When the impossible dream comes true, it takes some time to settle in. So many felt this day would never come and now it did and oh how crazy it was to savor reality that was sweet, not bitter, at the end of a baseball season.

Dallas Green had been the stern schoolmaster and his pupils resented every other word out of his mouth. There was sniping and snarling, suggestions the Phillies were a snakebit team that could not, would not ever win the big prize. When leading margins on scoreboards and as series narrowed and played out, people said they were chokers, that they could not, would not win. But they did.

"We couldn't imagine winning," said outfielder Lonnie Smith. "Once we won everybody was becoming best friends."[1] Yes, the cure-all was winning, a many time delivery of a truism in professional sports.

For months, they didn't seem to want to live with one another. But presto, they now wanted to relive it all. How Lefty won whenever needed. How Schmitty clubbed opponents into submission. How Tug seemed to dance on a tightrope in all the big games, but without falling. How Pete Rose made a difference with all his experience, with the approach he brought to each and every game.

Warren Brusstar didn't go home until the sun began to shine. He remained at Veterans Stadium, refusing to surrender to fatigue or sleep, a champagne glass or beer not far from his fist, talking baseball, talking about how the Philadelphia Phillies, the team he played for, were champions of the world.

"We talked about how lucky we were to be there," Brusstar said. He and other players, and even members of the grounds crew also hung around. Brusstar has always remembered the date, October 21, and as the years pass he always takes a little bit of time to reflect on the anniversary. "It is like a holiday for me. It's a great memory. I think, 'Boy, I did that one time.' That's a memory you have for the rest of your life."[2]

The locker rooms of losing teams empty quickly. Players can't wait to get on the bus, get away from the scene of the crime. Winners linger. But these winners lingered longer than most.

The players had never been in this position before, so they were in no hurry to do anything else but savor the moment.

There was so much pressure on the team from the start of spring training throughout the long, drawn out, up-and-down pennant race, during the hyper-intense championship series against the Astros, and of course with the eyes of the world focused on every play through television.

Greg Gross, who said he remained in the clubhouse until at least three in the morning, could feel the tension evaporate, feel weightlessness take over.

"I just felt like it was a big relief," Gross said. "I thought, 'It's all good.' You can just relish it. It finally culminated with us being at the top. It's great to be part of a team that wins a World Series. That's never taken away."[3]

The players who stayed in the clubhouse communing were oblivious to how the outside world reacted to their triumph. These were the days before cell phones and texting, so they remained in a cocoon while the world beyond their doors went insane.

Somehow, over time, the response to a home team being victorious in a championship match veered across some invisible line. It was not enough to repeatedly bark out cheers, to pump one's first in the air, to share the moment with friends and family all hugging, to down a beer in a favorite bar. It makes no sense to go on a rampage through the streets, doing damage in celebration, but that has begun to happen with regularity. The rank and file wanted a bigger part in it, even if they had no connection to the Phillies payroll. The excitement and joy were expressed in inexplicable ways.

PHILLIES 1980!

It was late at night, but the switchboard was sizzling at City Hall. Once the Phillies won, telephone calls poured in from across the land. The basic message was a simple one: Congratulations. Some were transplants, longtime Phillies fans in exile. They were far away, but wanted to feel as if they were there.

Newspaper reporters not inside Veterans Stadium fanned out across the city, seeking to capture the mood of the populace. They slipped into bars, sharing glimpses of the action on TV with drinkers. They monitored the police radio. They mingled with fans on the street.

"We've been tagged the City of Losers too long," said one bartender.[4] Many not able to obtain tickets went to Veterans Stadium anyway, massing on Broad Street near the ballpark. Police on horseback were a major presence, prepared to stifle unruly behavior. When it was official, last out, game over, fans jumped up and down and signaled, "We're No. 1."[5]

Not all was so benign throughout the city. Some felt compelled to loot businesses. Some fired off guns. In some areas crowds attacked police and firefighters. Arrests for drunk and disorderly were common, though there were many happy drunks glued to television sets for postgame reports. Sadly, there was one homicide a couple of hours after midnight. These were not-so innocent celebrations. There were said to be 1,000 police officers working that evening. There were enough for containment inside the Vet. Outside, things were tougher to control. Many people climbed over parked cars as if they were so many boulders on the way to a mountain summit, rather than 2,000-pound metallic hunks.

The Phillie Phanatic, who was definitely on the home side, explored the stands during the game, as usual, but quickly retreated from sight after a second-inning appearance. The enthusiasm ran too high for him, even while accompanied by a bodyguard carrying a billy club. "It just wasn't safe," the Phanatic wrote in his column. "It was scary. The people were just so hungry for the title, they were going crazy. In the second inning!"[6]

By the time anyone and everyone went to sleep, every fan knew what transpired: the Phillies had become the kings of baseball. But they wanted to snarf up every morsel of information, purchase souvenir newspapers that would confirm for eternity what they had seen with their own eyes and heard with their own ears.

There was not a citizen of the region who was not blind who could misunderstand the *Philadelphia Daily News'* main headline about Game Six and the World Series. It read: "We Win!"[7] The only time letters probably ever ran larger in the paper was a day after drastic action was taken against a foreign power and the message was: "War!" Another headline in that paper, perhaps half as tall, read: "Phillie-mania!"[8]

In comparison to the "We Win" declaration, the *Philadelphia Inquirer* was more subdued. The headline font for "Champions!" was pretty darned big, but couldn't match the *Daily News.*[9] Newspapers almost never employ exclamation points to emphasize a headline's message, but both papers did so on this day.

This was such a civic occasion, the Phillies invaded the *Inquirer* editorial page as well, with the top of the editorial column announcing executive editor Gene Roberts and editorial page editor Edwin Guthman as the keepers of the newspaper's editorial philosophy. In a rarity, a sports team was the focus of the lead editorial.

The headline atop this editorial read, "The Day of the Phillies; Champions of Grit and Guts." The opening sentence read,

"The Phillies are champions of the baseball world! Some may have thought they'd never live to see the day, but it's here and it's great."[10] The ninety-seven years of waiting was NOT worth the wait, the next passage realistically said, but "it is fitting and proper that the entire Delaware Valley has exploded with pride and is exalting the team's indomitable comeback."[11] A prediction followed: "Oh, how it will be remembered."[12]

At Veterans Stadium, the 65,000-plus fans were ushered out, but nobody was going to kick out the players. After a time, most of the lights were shut off, but there remained a bright glow from high above where the sportswriters kept typing, trying their best to immortalize the moments of this game and this championship and explain what it all meant. When the stakes are great and a city is enthralled, that is the best of all times to be a professional eyewitness. The scribes, too, were under pressure to be great and live up to the moment. Deadlines loomed and they would gradually run short on time, knowing that their fans, the subscribers, and even more than usual a number of passersby feeding change into boxes, would read their words.

After considerable time passed, with the press box still illuminated, Bob Walk wandered from the clubhouse back to the playing field. He had made one gigantic contribution to this gigantic triumph to highlight a rookie year that included 11 regular-season wins. He now had a World Series win on his résumé, too, from Game One.

"I ended up walking out on the field," Walk said. "I wanted to look around one more time. I went out in front of the dugout." There was nobody else out on the turf, not another soul at field level. "It was an eerie, weird feeling. I thought, 'We did it.'"[13]

Shortstop Larry Bowa had been a Phillie since 1970 and lived through those disheartening playoff losses. Influenced by his father, Paul, who was in attendance for the deciding game, Bowa had always wanted to be a ballplayer. When the game ended and the Phillies went berserk on the field and then adjourned to their lockers, Bowa's entire life in baseball ran through his thoughts. It was not so much that he dwelled on the near misses of past league championship series, but that he paused to remember all of his steps to the big leagues.

"Everything froze for me," Bowa said. "I remembered growing up in Sacramento, throwing balls off the garage door. Seeing all the hard work you put in. All that stuff was going through my mind."[14]

Like many of his teammates, there was nowhere else he would rather be than spending some extra time in the clubhouse for the last time in 1980. He shared that time with other Phillies, and with his dad.

"We stayed there to the wee hours of the morning," Bowa said. "About two a.m. We were up all night. I didn't get any sleep. In fact, I didn't sleep for like 48 hours."[15]

Some players might have spent a week secluded in the clubhouse if it was possible, but Philadelphia had scheduled a victory parade for the very next day. Cities throw these kinds of parades for all of their professional championship teams these days, but they generally schedule a day off in between.

Mayor Bill Green and other city fathers expected no less jubilation than had been on exhibit at the stadium and in the streets after the win, so it is probable police officers got less sleep than players as they absorbed their own preparation plans. When the moment arrived for the parade, it was estimated there were one million people lining the route, ready to fete the Phillies as they passed on floats.

Such massive civic outpourings get repeated in major professional sports towns when their team wins, but in 1980 they were less common and attendance for this one was overwhelming, a crowd of humanity bigger than Phillies players had ever seen.

Even the Phillie Phanatic was impressed, as he explained in his parade postmortem column. The thrill seemed to make up for his difficulties in the stands during Game Six when he feared for his green-feathered well-being.

The parade, consisting of thirteen flat-bed trucks masquerading as floats, the Phanatic wrote, was "something that no one involved will ever forget. Everyone was just in a great mood, and they were so excited, they cheered anything. Any move the Phanatic made along the way, the response was unbelievable."[16] And he was only the mascot. The mood was so upbeat, if a Phillies player sneezed, he would have been cheered.

The sheer mass of people floored Phillies players. They expected a mob to turn out and they got a crush.

"I never saw so many people," said Del Unser. "It was solid people all the way. I'd say the fewest was about five deep in some places."[17]

Catcher Bob Boone was a late stayer in the locker room, too. But he had a morning responsibility. Phillies public relations chief Larry Shenk had arranged for him to appear on a morning talk show. When Boone returned to his home in Medford, New Jersey (Greg Luzinski also lived in that town in South Jersey at the time), the first thing he saw was a congratulatory sign erected by his neighbors.

"That was pretty special," Boone said.[18]

Boone went to sleep at about 4:00 a.m., and when he awoke he was hungover. There were some frantic doings in the early morning when Boone's scheduled limousine ran late. Finally, he was driven to Veterans Stadium, ran onto the field, and was told, "Oh, Bob, we had to go on without you."[19]

Luzinski did the driving to the parade start, but even though they were borderline late, Boone said Bull insisted on stopping at a McDonald's. Then it really was parade time, the kickoff at 18th and Market Streets in Center City at 11:30 a.m. Boone was ridiculously tired and worried he would not even be able to stay awake for the slow-but-steady meandering through the city's streets as he sat in a comfortable chair riding on the flatbed truck.

"When we turned right onto Broad Street, all you could see was a sea of people," Boone said. "Police on horses were holding the people back. One guy ran the whole way to JFK Stadium." Rather than nod off, Boone was energized. "I'm standing up with my hands out [as fans reached towards him]. It was very special."[20]

John F. Kennedy Stadium in South Philadelphia, opened in 1926 with a capacity of 102,000 for football, was the destination. Fans who skipped the parade route showed up at JFK, first trickling in early in the morning, but later just about filling it up, with an attendance figure of 100,000 given for the 1 p.m. start at the stadium, and no charge for the events. When the trucks carrying the Phillies entered the stadium and circled the track, fans responded with a 12-minute standing ovation. However, it was selective applauding since Mayor Green and governor Richard Thornburg were booed. Thornburg did not even receive any love for proclaiming it Phillies Day across the entire state of Pennsylvania.

The microphone was passed around to Phillies, whose words were more warmly greeted. Owner Ruly Carpenter even tweaked the fans for their fickle support in the past, noting that few of the many thousands present believed these Phillies would go all the way. "But here we are," Carpenter said.[21]

There were reminders the journey had not always been a smooth path. Mike Schmidt, the National League and World Series MVP, did not overlook those moments or pretend they had never existed.

"We had so many low points," Schmidt said, possibly including those 1970s playoff losses in this statement, too. "And they all came in front of the world."[22]

But those most glorious of high points, outlasting the Houston Astros in the NLCS and fending off the Kansas City Royals' challenges in the World Series, were also achieved in front of the world.

While most thanked God for living to witness this once-in-a-century accomplishment, the *Daily News'* Chuck Stone, an African American, had more than sports on his mind. He wrote, in part, of winning the World Series, but a possible coming together. "A grateful city promptly held funeral services," Stone said. "Once and for all, we could bury the image as a city of losers, a city whose racial tensions have made a mockery of its sobriquet, 'the City of Brotherly Love.' But last night we were united on the proposition that 'we hold these truths to be self-evident' that all Phillies are created superior, that they are endowed by their Creator with certain inalienable skills and among those pitching, clutch-hitting and the ability to come from behind in a win."[23] Even in the city's African American neighborhoods, Stone opined, the residents were euphoric.

Yes, another *Daily News* columnist wrote, despite the players enduring much in the way of ups and downs, teases and defeats, this win was for fans who had been following a team that had let them down for longer than the players had been alive. One of them, Ray Didinger wrote, was his grandfather, in his sixties, who had rooted for the Phillies since the 1920s, and was present at the Vet to see the 4–1 win. Until then, "all he had to show for it was a pacemaker and a TV chair with a busted arm." Didinger was speaking for grandpa and the millions like him throughout the region who represented "the spirit of this city."[24] They woke up with a fresh bounce in their step on October 22.

Boone played in the majors for 19 years, then managed and worked in front offices. He not only never won another World Series on the field, he never again got into one in uniform. For all of the baseball he played and saw, the grandest day of all for him occurred in 1980.

"It was the best moment of my career," Boone said of riding on that flatbed truck past a million fans who treated he and his Phillies teammates like royalty. It was Princes for a day. "People ask me if winning the World Series was the best moment of my career. It was the parade."[25]

EPILOGUE

WHEN ROOKIE BOB Walk reviewed his 1980 baseball season, he was pleased. He had progressed from a pitcher who could not make the Philadelphia Phillies regular-season roster out of spring training to a player who won 11 games on the mound and then not only pitched Game One of the World Series, but was the winner. His best souvenir of the season was a world championship ring.

Walk knew he definitely needed to improve, but felt he had proven himself at the big-league level and could count on being a key member of the rotation in 1981. "I was very happy," Walk said years later. "I didn't realize what a big deal it was at first. I didn't realize how big this was in my career. As far as I was concerned, I was going to be in Philadelphia for life."[1]

That did not track with management's thinking, as Walk never pitched another game for the Phillies. He was stunned when on March 25, 1981, shortly before the start of the next season, he was swapped to the Atlanta Braves for outfielder Gary Matthews.

"It was hard on me," said Walk, saying he even met with owner Ruly Carpenter to dispel trade rumors and was told he was not going anywhere else. "For a lot of years I held that against the Phillies."[2]

The development left his head spinning. Walk did little for the Braves that year, going 1–4, but bounced back to go 11–9 for Atlanta in 1982. He spent as much time back in the minors as he did in the National League until the Braves released him in 1984. Picked up by the Pirates, Walk remained with Pittsburgh through the 1993 season when he retired with a 104–81 career mark.

However, he quickly experienced a new beginning in the sport, joining the Pirates' broadcast team. Walk was still affiliated with the club, and on the air, through the 2019 season. "Since 1984, I've been getting a paycheck from the Pirates twice a month," Walk said.[3]

Over the rest of his 14-season pitching career, Walk threw for several division winners, but no more pennant winners.

"I played on four more first-place teams," he said, "and I never got back to the World Series. It's something that will never go away." Neither will his Series victory. "It's one of the proudest moments of my life."[4]

The rookie who would have been voted most likely to succeed over the long-term from that Phillies team was Marty Bystrom. However, his whirlwind 5–0 September with the 1.50 earned run average was the apex of his six-year, 29–26 career.

"The whole World Series ride was just an incredible blur to me at the time," Bystrom said when he was in his forties and in the business world, "and the celebration in the city afterwards was unbelievable."[5]

A third 1980 rookie pitcher for the Phils, southpaw Kevin Saucier, went 7–3 that season. In a five-season career—four in Philadelphia—this was his best performance. His lifetime record was 15-11.

Righty Scott Munninghoff got into four games with a 0–0 record and never pitched in the majors again. Infielder Luis Aguayo got into 20 games that year and hit .277. That started a 10-year career in the majors, mostly with the Phillies. He stuck on rosters, although he never played in as many as 100 games in a single season. Outfielder Bob Dernier appeared in 10 games for the Phils that season, spent 10 years in the bigs, but did most of his best work for the Chicago Cubs. Dernier did have seven double-figure steal seasons. Jay Loviglio's 16 games represented the only time he played for the Phillies. He saw very limited action over three more years elsewhere. Catcher Ozzie Virgil played one game that year, but later, in his twenties, had several solid seasons for the Phillies and spent 11 years in the majors.

Keith Moreland was a few seasons into a solid big-league career. In 12 seasons he batted .279 with 121 home runs, but most of his achievements were recorded with the Cubs. His nickname was "Zonk."

One of the young players who made major contributions and then did have a long, big-league career was outfielder Lonnie Smith. Smith, then twenty-four, batted a career-high .339 in 1980, played in 100 games, batted .600 against Houston in the playoffs and .263 against the Royals in the World Series. In 17 seasons, Smith appeared in 1,613 games, batted .288 with a .371 on-base percentage, and stole 370 bases for six teams. Fortunate in his affiliations after trades, Smith won another World Series ring with the St.

Louis Cardinals in 1982 and a third with, of all teams, the Royals in 1985. He replaced Amos Otis in Kansas City's outfield.

Smith, who lives in the Atlanta area, relishes playing a part in all of those championship runs, but the Phillies' crown stands out because he was young and just breaking in.

"My first year in the big leagues and I won a championship," Smith said. "That was when I felt I really belonged there. I remember it going crazy in the streets. [That year], it rates as the No. 1 highlight."[6]

Greg Gross was a 10-year veteran already when the Phillies won it all. He spent 17 years in the majors, all but the last season after 1979 with Philadelphia. In 1,809 games he batted .287 and was renowned as a pinch-hitter. Gross ranks fifth on the all-time major-league pinch-hitting list with 143. He has remained in the game, mostly as a hitting coach, and in 2019, at sixty-seven, was spending his season in that capacity for the AAA Reno Aces, an Arizona Diamondbacks affiliate. The 1980 season was Gross's only World Series title.

Once the Series win was accomplished, it was as if the entire attitude of the city was uplifted, almost as if clouds had turned to sunshine. "Everybody is in a good mood," Gross said. "That winter, everywhere you went, people talked about it."[7]

Del Unser, who was approaching seventy-five in 2019, ended his 17-year on-field career in 1982 with the Phillies, playing in 1,799 games and compiling a lifetime .258 average. He hit .500 in the 1980 World Series, his only one. After a year away, he remained as a coach in baseball for most of the next thirty-five years. Of the 1980 success, he said, "it was kind of the apex. It only happened once in my career."[8]

Right-handed reliever Ron Reed completed his 19th year in the majors at forty-one in 1984, and won 146 games in his career. Larry Christenson pitched through 1983, but never had another winning season. Dick Ruthven appeared in his last big-league game in 1986, and won 123 games in the big leagues.

Warren Brusstar's career concluded in 1985 after nine seasons. His record was 28–16 with a 3.51 earned run average. He pitched in 340 games without ever starting one.

Steve Carlton wanted to pitch forever. Lefty was thirty-five in 1980, and was the best pitcher in the National League. The next season, 1981, was screwed up because of a labor strike, but Carlton finished 13–4 in the shortened campaign. He went 23–11 in 1982, struck out 286 batters, and won another Cy Young Award—the fourth of his career. Carlton began to fade after that and even after going 1–8 for the Phillies in 1985 and being cut loose, he caught on with other teams. When he retired in 1988 at forty-three, Carlton had 329 victories on his résumé, the second most by a left-handed pitcher in history to Warren Spahn's 363. And he struck out an astounding 4,136 batters, fourth all-time behind Nolan Ryan, Randy Johnson, and Roger Clemens.

In 1994, Carlton was elected to the National Baseball Hall of Fame—and he spoke up. "I led a sheltered life for twenty-three years," Carlton said, describing his time in the majors. "I've had a lot of catching up to do."[9] Living on a 400-acre farm in Durango, Colorado, with his wife, Carlton occasionally called himself a recluse.

A *Philadelphia* magazine story in April 1994 by noted author Pat Jordan blew up on Carlton, discussing his bunker-like fortress of a home which Carlton said protected him from gamma rays and gave shelter to his storehouse of weapons. At various points in their conversation, Jordan quoted Carlton as suggesting such organizations as the Skull and Bones Society of Yale, the World Health Organization, or the International Monetary Fund could foment revolution and added, "The Elders of Zion rule the world," unless it was "Twelve Jewish bankers meeting in Switzerland rule the world."[10]

Carlton denied making the antisemitic remarks that were attributed to him, but apologized and the American Jewish Congress accepted the contrition after previously urging the Hall of Fame to ban him from acceptance in the planned ceremony that year.

Lefty successfully negotiated his way through his Hall of Fame induction speech without mishap, and a year later found himself in Anchorage, Alaska, making a personal appearance. He spoke to Little Leaguers about pitching and signed autographs for them.

He referred back to his Cooperstown talk and admitted, "There was pressure. Making a speech is not my bailiwick." He offered pitching advice to twelve-year-olds without creating controversy, and when the then fifty-year-old was asked if he could come out of retirement and help the near-to-his-home floundering Rockies, he made a joke. "I could do it," Carlton said. "I could commute."[11]

Right-hander Dickie Noles was out of baseball at thirty-three. But the man who had such difficulty holding his liquor became a respected crusader against substance abuse. Noles became a sought-after speaker on substance abuse prevention and presided over numerous seminars and programs around the Philadelphia and New Jersey area. He worked for the Phillies community relations department, and while describing himself as a recovering alcoholic, spread his cautionary message.

He developed a program called S.A.V.E.S with the Phillies' assistance, the breakdown reading, "Students, Attitudes, Values, Education, Substance Abuse." In 1994, the State of New Jersey acknowledged his work with a resolution of praise, in part reading, "Therefore Be It Resolved that the Governor's Council on Alcoholism and Drug Abuse recognizes and commends Dickie Noles for all he has done and continues to do to support and enhance the Municipal Alliance throughout New Jersey."[12]

After 11 years in the majors, outfielder Bake McBride retired with a lifetime .299 batting average, his career ending with the Cleveland Indians in 1983. McBride won the Rookie of the Year Award, was chosen for one All-Star Game, and was an integral part of the 1980 Phillies world champions.

Center fielder Garry Maddox lasted 15 years in the majors with a lifetime average of .285 and a reputation as one of the best fielders of his generation. His eight outfield Gold Gloves ranked behind only Willie Mays and Roberto Clemente in the National League. New York Mets broadcaster Ralph Kiner, a Hall of Famer for his slugging, said of Maddox, "Two-thirds of the world is covered by water. The other third is covered by Garry Maddox."[13] After leaving baseball, Maddox had a career not managing a baseball team, but managing money. He served as a director of the Philadelphia district of the Federal Reserve.

Second baseman Manny Trillo, the NLCS MVP, spent 17 years in the majors. The native of Venezuela batted .263, made four All-Star teams, and won three Gold Gloves before retiring in 1989.

Before the 1981 season, the Phillies shipped Greg Luzinski to the Chicago White Sox, where he rebounded with some good years before retiring in 1984. The Bull hit .276 lifetime with 307 home runs. Luzinski was also awarded baseball's Roberto Clemente Award for community service in 1978. In recent years, Luzinski operated "Bull's BBQ" in Citizens Bank Park.

As catcher, Bob Boone moved from team to team during the latter stages of his 19-season major league career. He played for some winners, but never returned to the World Series. He batted .254 lifetime, managed for six seasons, and stayed in baseball in various other roles.

Boone was forty-two years old in his final on-field year, and was playing for the Royals, the team he did so much to defeat with his .412 World Series average in 1980.

"My last year I was older than the manager," Boone said while laughing. The World Series emotion ran so high, was so intense, he almost wanted it to hurry up and end. "It was a fantastic time. I hated to have all that adrenalin going for so long. It was almost, 'Thank goodness it's over.'"[14]

Shortstop Larry Bowa made it through 16 big-league seasons, the last few with other teams. The bulk of his success came with the Phillies, for whom he made five All-Star teams and won two Gold Gloves. He finished with a lifetime batting average of .260. Bowa was a baseball lifer, spending his post-playing days managing the San Diego Padres and the Phillies, and serving as a coach for the Phillies for years. He also worked in broadcasting.

Bowa always kept the World Series championship close to his heart, though. "That's the one thing you want as a big leaguer," Bowa said when he was seventy-three. "It's the ultimate." For Bowa, the glorious victory occurred after he had been in the majors for a decade. "It made the long wait worth it. We could beat you a lot of ways. Our main objective was the Series. We finally got there."[15]

The year after the World Series title was secured, Mike Schmidt won the National League MVP award again in the strike-shortened 1981 season. He won a third MVP in 1987. When Schmidt retired after 18 seasons in 1989, he had 548 home runs and 1,595 runs batted in on his résumé. He led the NL in homers eight times, was selected for 12 All-Star teams, and was about as respected as a fielder as he was as a slugger. Schmidt won 10 Gold Gloves covering territory at third base.

Over the following years, Schmidt was elected to the National Baseball Hall of Fame, was voted by Phillies fans as the greatest player in franchise history, and had his number 20 retired by the team on May 26, 1990. *The Sporting News* anointed him as baseball's player of the decade of the 1980s.

On the occasion of his jersey being retired, Schmidt said, "All kids need heroes. Not only mine, but every young child. This is especially important now when children are more vulnerable than during any other period in history. I hope I have touched kids in a positive way."[16]

Dallas Green never particularly wanted to be a big-league manager. He was more interested in management and building teams, not running them. He took the job to placate his bosses. Even in the immediate aftermath of winning the World Series crown, there was speculation about whether or not he would even return for a second full season at the helm.

Green only stuck around the Phillies dugout through 1981. Then he slipped away to the Chicago Cubs, hired as executive vice president and general manager, given the mandate to bring the long-moribund team to life. The Cubs did acquire contender status, but by 1987 fell back into last place. That ended Green's stay in Chicago. He also managed the New York Yankees for one year and the New York Mets between 1993 and 1996, but Green's teams never approached his Phillies' success and his career managerial record was 454–478.

Much later, when Green wrote a memoir, he reviewed some of his relationships with players on the World Series team. He called Pete Rose "the heart and soul of the '80 team." Green wrote that he thought Ron Reed was the only player "who held a real grudge against me."[17] He acknowledged Luzinski's disappointment when Green played Lonnie Smith ahead of him in some crucial games, but felt they had smoothed things over with time. "Most of the other fences have been mended," Green said.[18] He passed away on March 22, 2017, at eighty two.

John Vukovich was a unique figure in Philadelphia Phillies history. A member of the 1980 World Series championship team, but one who rarely played and hit poorly, he made other contributions. Vukovich later became the longest-tenured coach in team history.

A tremendous fielder and a player admired for his attitude in the clubhouse, Vukovich managed to play 10 years in the majors while recording a batting average of .161. Called "Vuk" by almost everyone, Vukovich had a special relationship with the Phillies. He coached from 1988 to 2004, outlasting several managers, and was briefly interim manager. After 2004, he moved into the front office as a special assistant to the general manager. There are some individuals who are simply baseball men in their hearts, and Vukovich was one of them.

"Good coach, bad coach, I'm just a coach," Vukovich said when he moved upstairs. "That's the thing that drove me, that atmosphere. You were going to get a response every inning, good or bad. I love that aspect of coaching."[19]

Vukovich would have been happy to return to the field, but he never got the chance. During the 2006 season, he began experiencing headaches and other physical problems. He was diagnosed with a brain tumor and died on March 8, 2007, at fifty-nine, a sad denouement that deeply affected those in the Phillies' organization.

"John was an incredibly integral part of my life, my career, and a very, very close friend of mine," said former Phillies pitcher Curt Schilling.[20]

That season the Phillies competed with a black patch on their uniforms and the abbreviation "Vuk" on it to honor John Vukovich.

No one had a more dramatic, complicated, and unusual post-1980 Phillies life in and out of baseball than Pete Rose.

If anyone was a surefire Hall of Famer, it was Rose. He spent 24 seasons in the majors, first as a star for the Cincinnati Reds and then as an important element in the Phillies' 1980 success, when he was part of his third World Series championship. A lifetime .303 hitter, Rose owns several records, but his signature mark, the thing for which he is best remembered on the diamond, is his ownership of the all-time hits record with 4,256. He spent a career lifetime in pursuit of Ty Cobb, and ultimately surpassed him. Rose remained with the Phillies through the 1983 season, a year he hit only .245. The Phillies informed him the best he could expect for 1984 was to be a part-time player, so he moved on.

Known as "Charlie Hustle," Rose broke into the big leagues as the National League Rookie of the Year in 1963, and played his final game on a second go-around with the Reds in 1986 at forty-five. A 17-time All-Star, Rose epitomized hard work and grit on the field.

However, in 1989, while managing the Reds, Rose was accused by Major League Baseball of gambling on the sport, one of the paramount rules in effect for decades. Ultimately, in a stunning development for someone who gave so much to the game, Rose incurred a lifetime ban from the sport. That kept him from even being considered by voters on the Hall of Fame ballot. He appealed for reinstatement, but it was never forthcoming through more than one commissioner's tenure.

The season of 2019 marked thirty years of Rose's banishment and his seventy-eighth birthday. That season, in an amazing reversal, baseball, which had been the sternest of opponents of any type of gambling on the game, abruptly entered into a joint venture with a gambling outfit to help set odds and profit from bettors on baseball. This astonishing switch came about because of court rulings that gave the power to states other than Nevada to set up sports books. Rather than fight anymore, MLB jumped in seeking to make money from these operations. This provided the appearance of being hypocritical in the continuing banishment of Rose, and begged the question of how soon he might be reinstated after all.

In all of those intervening years, Rose could not take a job in baseball as a manager or coach. He set himself up with a regular gig signing autographs on the Las Vegas Strip and, thousands of baseball fans stopped in to chat with Rose and purchase autographed baseballs and other items.

Thinking back to 1980 in 2018, Rose said of the Astros series, "I believe the Houston-Philadelphia playoff was the best ever played. Every game was one run." Winning the World Series, he said, was received almost as a gift by the Philadelphia fans. "I think we understood what the fans had gone through. When we won, it was the most awesome sight I ever saw in baseball. After that, people would just come up to you and say, 'Thank you.' They had been waiting a long time. I was a small part of it. I'll never forget the parade. You're talking about a million people on Broad Street. You understood how big it was that night [when the Phillies eliminated Kansas City], but you never understood how big it was until you were on that float. Everyone had the same look on their faces of joy. Including me."[21]

After breaking and improving on Cobb's hit record, Rose's nickname became "The Hit King." It is a moniker he enjoys. When he signs his name on those pieces of memorabilia in Las Vegas and elsewhere, he usually writes "4,256" next to his name.

"Not many people say, 'What's that?'" Rose said. "They know I'm the hit king. I've been the hit king a long time and I'll die the hit king. I don't think there's going to be another one."[22]

There will probably never be another Tug McGraw, either. The clutch pitcher who was so full of whimsy and who not once, but twice proved to professional baseball fans in different cities that "Ya Gotta Believe," lived out his shortened life clinging to that motto.

McGraw retired from the Phillies—and from baseball—at thirty-nine in 1984 after 19 seasons in the majors. His lifetime record was 96–92 and he collected 180 saves. In a surprising and very public development, it was revealed that McGraw was the father of renowned country singer Tim McGraw, stemming from a one-night stand in 1966. Tim McGraw was seventeen when he first began developing a relationship with his father, and they later became close.

In a situation very similar to John Vukovich's, but just prior, McGraw was involved in spring training for the Phillies in 2003. He did not feel well, had tests, and was diagnosed with a brain tumor. It was first said he might have only three weeks to live. Son Tim McGraw and his wife, Faith Hill, also a successful country singer, researched alternative treatments.

After undergoing a six-hour surgery, and receiving radiation and chemotherapy treatments, it appeared McGraw was on his way to a dramatic recovery. Appearing bald, with a scar on his head, McGraw conducted a press conference during which he said, "I'm supposed to be alive for a long time. I'm not fearful. I have confidence."[23]

Despite his optimism, it was learned the tumor was not completely eradicated and when the cancer returned, it was in inoperable form. All of baseball ached along with McGraw, who had exhibited such an irrepressible personality that he not only made believers out of teammates, but made fans of baseball out of casual watchers.

At the end of the season when McGraw became ill, Veterans Stadium was going out of business, soon to be replaced by Citizens Bank Park. To say farewell to the Vet, the Phillies conducted a special event on September 28, 2003. It turned out to be Tug McGraw's public valedictory, too. On that day, McGraw recreated the final out of the 1980 World Series, his strikeout of the Royals' Willie Wilson.

A few years earlier, when giving a talk, McGraw said of his last pitch of the night of October 21, 1980: "It took ninety-eight years for that fastball to reach home plate."[24]

Tug McGraw died on January 5, 2004, nine months after doctors gave him three weeks to live. He was fifty-nine.

* * *

In 1985, the Kansas City Royals won the first World Series in team history, beating the St. Louis Cardinals. Frank White, Onix Concepcion, George Brett, Willie Wilson, Hal McRae, John Wathan, and Dan Quisenberry were all part of it. The manager was Dick Howser, who joined the team as a coach in 1981. Howser and Quisenberry, like Vukovich and McGraw, also died from brain tumors.

The Philadelphia Phillies won a second World Series in 2008. Ryan Howard hit 48 home runs and knocked in 146. Chase Utley hit 33 home runs and drove in 104. The best starting pitcher was Jamie Moyer with a 16–7 record. The closer was Brad Lidge with 41 saves.

Phillies fans finally had a pair of World Series championship trophies to admire, but the 1980 team will always be remembered for being the first.

ABOUT THE AUTHOR

Lew Freedman is a prize-winning journalist who has worked for the *Chicago Tribune, Anchorage Daily News* and the *Cody Enterprise* in Wyoming. In 1980, when the Phillies won the World Series for the first time, he was a sportswriter for the *Philadelphia Inquirer.*

Freedman is the author of more than 100 books, including *Warren Spahn, A Summer to Remember,* and *Knuckleball.* He resides in Indiana with his wife Debra.

ENDNOTES

Chapter 1

1   Lewis Freedman, "Forever Young: McGraw Enjoys His Life, His Job, Himself," *Philadelphia Inquirer*, August 5, 1980.

2   Ibid.

3   Ibid.

4   Ibid.

5   Ibid.

6   Rich Hoffman, "Game Six: McGraw Strikes Out the Mighty K.C.," *Philadelphia Daily News*, October 23, 1980.

7   Ibid.

8   Ibid.

9   Ibid.

Chapter 2

1   Dallas Green and Alan Maimon, *The Mouth That Roared* (Chicago: Triumph Books, 2013), 103.

2   Gross, Greg, personal interview, February 20, 2019.

3   Hal Bodley, *Philadelphia Phillies: The Team That Wouldn't Die, World Champions 1980* (Wilmington, DE: Serendipity Press, 1981), 166.

4   Bodley, 166.

5   J. Daniel, *Phinally! The Phillies, the Royals and the 1980 Baseball Season That Almost Wasn't* (Jefferson, NC: McFarland & Company, Inc., 2019), P. 14.

6   Bob Boone, personal interview, February 22, 1019.

7   Bob Walk, personal interview, February 14, 2019.
8   Ibid.
9   Ibid.
10 Ibid.

Chapter 3

1   Gordon Forbes, "Phils' Season Tickets, $25,000; Sorry, There's a Waiting List," *Philadelphia Inquirer*, April 10, 1980.
2   Del Unser, personal interview, February 13, 2019.
3   Fran Zimniuch, *Philadelphia Phillies: Where Have You Gone?* (Champaign, IL: Sports Publishing 2004), 74.
4   Seamus Kearney, "Richie Ashburn," Society For American Baseball Research (no date).
5   Bodley, 333.
6   Ibid., 331.
7   *Philadelphia Inquirer*, advertisement, April 10, 1980
8   Cheryl Gordon, "Ththe Phanatic Returns, and with a Contract, Yet," *Philadelphia Inquirer*, April 10, 1980.
9   Jayson Stark, "Schmidt Has the Stats, but He's Missing Something," *Philadelphia Inquirer*, April 10, 1980.
10 Danny Robbins, "How's this for Openers?" *Philadelphia Inquirer*, April 12, 1980.
11 Ibid.
12 Frank Dolson, "Phillies To Play By Green's Set Of Rules—Or Else," *Philadelphia Inquirer*, April 12, 1980.
13 Ibid.

Chapter 4

1   Joseph Durso, "Cards Trade Carlton to Phillies for Wise in Pitcher Exchange," *New York Times*, February 26, 1972.
2   Cosme Vivanco, "Steve Carlton," Society For American Baseball Research (no date).
3   Bodley, 239.
4   Walk interview.
5   Hal Bodley, "Reed Finds Plush Lifestyle in Phil Bullpen," *The Sporting News*, May 19, 1979.

6 Walk interview.
7 Ibid.
8 Ibid.
9 Ibid.

Chapter 5
1 Pete Rose, personal interview, November 12, 2018.
2 Ibid.
3 Ibid.
4 Ibid.
5 Ibid.
6 Ibid.
7 Larry Bowa, personal interview, February 13, 2019.
8 Rose interview.
9 Ibid.
10 Ibid.
11 Ibid.

Chapter 6
1 Gregory H. Wolf, "Dallas Green," Society For American Baseball
   Research (no date).
2 Ibid.
3 Ibid.
4 Sam Carchidi, "the Mouth That Roared," *Philadelphia Inquirer*, July
   10, 2005.
5 Wolf, "Dallas Green."
6 Carchidi, "The Mouth That Roared."
7 Green and Maimon, v-vi.
8 Ibid, vii.
9 Lindsay C. Prichard, "Billy the Kid DeMars: Former Teenage Phenom
   Spent 50-Plus Years in Pro Ball," *Sports Collectors Digest*, May 6,
   1994.
10 Philadelphia Phillies press release, November 7, 1978.
11 Bill Conlin, "Interim Label Clouds Pilot Wine's Future," *The Sporting
   News*, September 9, 1985.
12 Bill Conlin, "The Daze Of Wine And Rose," *Philadelphia Daily News*,
   October 23, 1983.

13 Dave Williams, "Mike Ryan," Society for American Baseball Research (no date).

14 Wayne Drehs, "Fans Won't Let Elia Forget Meltdown," ESPN.com, April 29, 2008. (Originally recorded by Les Grobstein, WLS-AM Radio, April 29, 1983).

15 *Around The Horn*, ESPN, July 1990.

Chapter 7

1 Lewis Freedman, "They Keep On Earning Their Keep," *Philadelphia Inquirer*, May 29, 1980.

2 Ibid.

3 Ibid.

4 David M. Jordan, *Pete Rose: A Biography, Baseball's Greatest Hitters* (Westport, CT: Greenwood Publishing Group, 2004), 91.

5 William C. Kashatus, Mike Schmidt: Philadelphia's Hall Of Fame Third Baseman (Jefferson, NC: McFarland & Company, Inc., 2000), 24.

6 Ibid, 7.

7 Ibid, 17.

8 Mike Schmidt and Glen Waggoner, *Clearing the Bases: Juiced Players, Monster Salaries, Sham Records, and a Hall of Famer's Search for the Soul of Baseball* (New York: HarperCollins, 2006), 47.

9 Hal Bodley, "More Muscle Lifts Schmidt's HR Total," *The Sporting News*, May 31, 1980.

10 Ibid.

11 Chris Cauley, "Larson Returns Home to Pass on His Expertise to the Next Generation of Baseball Players," *Sports Collectors Digest*, April 25, 1997.

12 Ibid.

13 Hal Bodley, "Pen Time Helps Lerch Write New Chapter," *The Sporting News*, June 14, 1980.

14 Ibid.

15 Lewis Freedman, "Phils Erupt for 7 in First, Stay Hot to Batter Padres," *Philadelphia Inquirer*, June 14, 1980.

16 Ibid.

17 Lewis Freedman, "Carlton Defeats San Diego, 3-1, Striking Out 13," *Philadelphia Inquirer*, June 15, 1980.
18 Hal Bodley, "Runs and RBIs More Important Than Home Runs, Says Schmidt," *The Sporting News*, August 25, 1979.
19 Bodley, *Philadelphia Phillies*, 151.

Chapter 8
1 *Around The Horn*, ESPN, July 1990.
2 Bowa interview.
3 Jack Carney, "Bowa at War; Clubhouse Battleground," *Philadelphia Journal*, August 11, 1978.
4 Ibid.
5 Hal Bodley, "Bowa Blows His Top, Pay Is Near Bottom," *The Sporting News*, March 22, 1980.
6 Bowa interview.
7 "Pitcher Who Retired Tells of the Pressure," *New York Times*, April 13, 1983.
8 Bus Saidt, "Rose May Lead the Phillies; Bowa Just Does Everything Else," *Baseball Magazine*, August 1979.
9 Bowa interview.
10 Joe Henderson, "Trillo, Not Rose, May Prove to be Phils' Best Acquisition," *Tampa Tribune*, March 21, 1979.
11 Ibid.
12 Bill Conlin, "NL Beat", *The Sporting News*, September 6, 1980.
13 Henderson, "Trillo Not Rose."
14 Frank Litsky, "To Err Is Rare for Trillo of the Phillies; It's His First in 89 Games," *New York Times*, August 2, 1982.
15 Steve Serby, "Serby's Sunday Q&A with Larry Bowa," *New York Post*, July 16, 2006.
16 Ibid.

Chapter 9
1 Neal Russo, "Card Rookie Was 800-to-1 Shot," *The Sporting News*, December 14, 1974.
2 Bodley, *Philadelphia Phillies*, 131.
3 Ibid., 131-32.

4   Hal Bodley, "Bake's Knees Ache, but His Bat Smokes," *The Sporting News*, August 16, 1980.

5   Bodley, "Bake's Knees."

6   Ray Kelly, "Agent Orange Concerns Maddox," *Camden Courier-Post*, July 10, 1981.

7   Ibid.

8   Sam Carchidi, "A Quiet Man Persevered in a Wild Year," *Philadelphia Inquirer*, July 12, 2005.

9   Hal Bodley, "Phillies Give Maddox Combination To Vault," *The Sporting News*, May 3, 1980.

10 Stan Hochman, "Maddox Helps Run a Clinic," *Philadelphia Daily News*, December 18, 1979.

11 Ibid.

12 Jack Hartman, "Goats," *St. Louis Globe-Democrat*, October 10, 1978.

13 Hal Bodley, "Quaker City out of Patience With Slump-Ridden Bull," *The Sporting News*, July 7, 1979.

14 Daniel, 38.

15 Ibid.

16 Ron Rosen, "Phillies Cleared in Drug Case," *Washington Post*, November 22, 1980.

17 Lonnie Smith, personal interview, March 9, 2019.

18 Ibid.

19 Bodley, *Philadelphia Phillies*, 159.

Chapter 10

1   Unser interview.

2   Rory Costello, "Del Unser," Society For American Baseball Research" (no date).

3   Wire services compilation, "Pinch HR Puts Del Unser In Record Books," National Baseball Hall of Fame archives.

4   Dave Anderson, "Del Unser: The Nonpareil Pinch-Hitter," *New York Times*, October 20, 1980.

5   Costello, "Del Unser,"; Milton Richman, "Now Everybody Wants Del Unser," United Press International, October 16, 1980.

6   Unser interview.

7   "Gross Still Finds Himself Stymied by Phillies' Talent," Associated Press, National Baseball Hall of Fame Archives, 1979.
8   Hal Bodley, "Phils' Gross Just Great as Fill-in for the Bull," *The Sporting News*, August 11, 1979.
9   Gross interview.
10 Ibid.
11 Bodley, *Philadelphia Phillies*, 224.
12 Gross interview.

Chapter 11
1   Ray Kelly, "Return of McCarver Revives Phils' Ace Carlton," *Camden Courier-Post*, August 2, 1975.
2   Hal Bodley, "Tough To Say Goodbye, Says McCarver," *The Sporting News*, October 27, 1979.
3   Hal Bodley, Boone Shatters Carlton-McCarver Battery," *The Sporting News*, May 26, 1979.
4   Boone interview.
5   Ibid.
6   Sam Carchidi, "A Quiet Man Persevered in a Wild Year," *Philadelphia Inquirer*, July 12, 2005.
7   Peter Gammons, "Baseball Is in His Blood," *Sports Illustrated*, July 4, 1988.
8   Ray Didinger, "A Classic Dallas Green Tirade," *Philadelphia Daily News*, August 11, 1980
9   Ibid.
10 Ibid.
11 Ibid.
12 Ibid.
13 Daniel, 125.
14 Ibid.
15 Allen Lewis, "Rifle Arm, Fast Glove; That's Phils' Vukovich," *The Sporting News*, July 10, 1971.
16 Hal Bodley, "Spare-Part Vukovich Plugs Phils Defense," *The Sporting News*, July 26, 1980.

Chapter 12

1   Bob Moskowitz, "Consolation Prize: A Perfect Game," *Newport News Daily Press*, September 2, 1978.

2   Warren Brusstar, personal interview, February 19, 2019.

3   Ibid.

4   Gross interview.

5   Hal Bodley, "Phillies' Bullpen In Good Hands—McGraw's," *The Sporting News*, September 20, 1980.

6   Tug McGraw and Don Yaeger, Ya Gotta Believe (New York: New American Library, 2004), 142.

7   Hal Bodley, "Phillies Have Stopper: Noles," *The Sporting News*, May 10, 1980.

8   Bodley, Have "Phillies Have Stopper."

9   "Dickie Noles on Headhunting, Fighting and Carousing," *Inside Sports*, July 1982.

10 Ibid.

11 Bill Koenig, "Noles Fights on vs. Alcohol," *USA Today*, July 19, 1988.

12 Smith interview.

13 Ibid.

14 McGraw and Yaeger, 143.

15 Ibid.

16 Brusstar interview.

Chapter 13

1   Susan Wood, "A Stone's Throw," *Washington Post*, May 17, 1981.

2   Baseball Almanac Quotes.

3   "Brett Tops .400, Improves Streak to 29 Games," Associated Press, August 18, 1980.

4   Ibid.

5   Vince Sweeney and Tim McBride, "Will Brett Hit .400?" *Milwaukee Journal*, August 24, 1980.

6   Ibid.

7   Ibid.

8   Hal McRae, personal interview, January 11, 2019.

9   J. R. Richard and Lew Freedman, *Still Throwing Heat: Strikeouts, The Streets And A Second Chance* (Chicago: Triumph Books, 2015), 137.

10   Ibid, 135.

11   Ibid, 5.

12   Ibid, 138.

13   Unser interview.

14   Lewis Freedman, "Dodgers Trip Astros, 2-1, To Stay Alive," *Philadelphia Inquirer*, October 5, 1980.

15   Ibid.

16   Lewis Freedman, "Astros Stumble Again, Forcing a Playoff," *Philadelphia Inquirer*, October 6, 1980.

17   Freedman, "Astros Stumble."

18   Ibid.

19   Ibid.

20   Lewis Freedman, "Astros Beat Dodgers For Title," *Philadelphia Inquirer*, October 7, 1980.

21   Ibid.

22   Ibid.

23   Ibid.

24   Ibid.

25   Ibid.

Chapter 14

1   Lewis Freedman, "Astros Beat Dodgers."

2   Jayson Stark, "Bystrom Gets OK; Saucier on Roster, Too," *Philadelphia Inquirer*, October 8, 1980.

3   Ibid.

4   Ed Fowler, "Astros: A Collection of Straight Shooters," *Philadelphia Inquirer*, October 7, 1980.

5   Brusstar interview.

6   Daniel, 160.

7   Hal Lundgren, "Virdon: That Other Coach in Houston," *Philadelphia Inquirer*, October 7, 1980.

8   Ibid.
9   Jayson Stark, "If It's Mind over Matter, Phils Are Headed in Right Direction," *Philadelphia Inquirer*, October 7, 1980.
10   Ibid.
11   Ibid.
12   Gross interview.
13   Smith interview.
14   Bowa interview.
15   Rose interview.
16   Peter Pascarelli, "The Thinking Man's Superstar: Mike Schmidt," *The Sporting News*, June 11, 1984.
17   Ibid.
18   Stark, "If It's Mind"

Chapter 15
1   "The Long Wait Is Over for Pete Rose," United Press International, October 7, 1980.
2   Bill Lyon, "Bull Silences Those Boobirds…His Way," *Philadelphia Inquirer*, October 8, 1980.
3   Jay Greenberg, "Astros' Forsch Patient in Loss," *Philadelphia Daily News*, October 8, 1980.
4   Lyon, "Bull Silences"
5   Greenberg, "Astros' Forsch Patient."
6   Ibid.
7   Dick Weiss, "Ryan Not Nervous as Tonight's Starter," *Philadelphia Daily News*, October 8, 1980.
8   Ibid.
9   Gross interview.
10   Frank Dolson, "Elia: 'I Screwed It Up,' and Win Vanishes," *Philadelphia Inquirer*, October 9, 1980.
11   Ibid.
12   Jayson Stark, "Astros Erupt In 10th, Even Series," *Philadelphia Inquirer*, October 9, 1980.
13   Dolson, "Elia."

14 Brusstar interview.
15 Ibid.

Chapter 16
1   Neil Hohlfeld, "Ex-Astro Joe Niekro Dies at 61," *Houston Chronicle*, October 28, 2006.
2   Daniel, 171.
3   Ray Didinger, "A Tale of Two Pities," *Philadelphia Daily News*, October 11, 1980.
4   Ibid.
5   McGraw and Yaeger, 145.
6   Daniel, 170.
7   Jack Chevalier, "Luck Is Finally Wearing the Phillies' Pinstripes," *Philadelphia Bulletin*, October 12, 1980.
8   Brusstar interview.
9   Ibid.
10 Chevalier, "Luck is Finally."
11 Ibid.
12 Brusstar interview.
13 Ibid.
14 Mark Whicker, "A Daring Dash by Rose Pushes Series to the Limit," *Philadelphia Bulletin*, October 12, 1980.
15 Ibid.
16 Chevalier, "Luck is Finally."

Chapter 17
1   Gross interview.
2   Ibid.
3   Boone interview.
4   Ibid.
5   Ibid.
6   Ray Didinger, "Maddox Takes Ride of His Life," *Philadelphia Daily News*, October 13, 1980.
7   Ibid.
8   Mark Whicker, "Phils End Frustration," *Philadelphia Bulletin*, October 13, 1980.

9   Frank Dolson, "Phils Rewrite The Philadelphia Story," *Philadelphia Inquirer*, October 13, 1980.

10   Mark Whicker, "With It Do-Or-Die, Ruthven Relieved," *Philadelphia Bulletin*, October 13, 1980.

11   Ibid.

12   Mark Hyman, "A Bitter End for the Astros," *Philadelphia Bulletin*, October 13, 1980.

13   Jack Chevalier, "Phils, Astros Do Baseball Proud," *Philadelphia Bulletin*, October 13, 1980.

14   Ibid.

15   Rose interview.

16   Bowa interview.

17   Ibid.

Chapter 18

1   Phillie Phanatic, "The Party Is Just Beginning," *Philadelphia Daily News*, October 14, 1980.

2   John Wathan, personal interview, January 8, 2019.

3   McRae interview.

4   Lewis Freedman, "Just Seeing the Series Will Be Something New for Some of the Phils," *Philadelphia Inquirer*, October 14, 1980.

5   Ibid.

6   Chuck Tanner, "SCOUTING REPORT: Carlton, Schmidt Hold Keys to Success," *New York Times*, October 14, 1980.

7   Ibid.

8   Michael Schwager, "Do You Remember? Manny Trillo: Sparkling Second Sacker Of 1980 Champions," *Phillies Report* (no date).

9   Scott Heimer, "Phils' Fate Is Crystal Clear," *Philadelphia Daily News*, October 15, 1980.

10   Joe Durso, "Phils Pick Walk In Series Opener," *New York Times*, October 14, 1980.

11   Mark Whicker, "It'll Be Bob Walk vs. KC's Leonard," *Philadelphia Bulletin*, October 14, 1980.

12   Walk interview.

Chapter 19

1   Smith interview.

2   Unser interview.

3   Boone interview.

4   Smith interview.

5   Walk interview.

6   Lewis Freedman, "Forever Young: McGraw Enjoys His Life, His Job, Himself; *Philadelphia Inquirer*, August 5, 1980.

7   Wathan interview.

8   Dick Kaegel, "Rose a Big Hit in Phils' Bakeoff," *The Sporting News*, November 1, 1980.

9   Rich Hofmann, "Using Walk in Opener Paid Dividends for Phils," *Philadelphia Daily News*, October 23, 1980.

10 Ibid.

11 Walk interview.

12 Dick Kaegel, "A Big Pain for Brett—and Royals," *The Sporting News*, November 1, 1980.

13 Ibid.

14 Ibid.

15 Fleischman, Bill, "Chats Not Off-Base with Rose," *Philadelphia Daily News*, October 16, 1980.

16 Bill Madden and Thom Greer, "Brett: 'I'll Play,'" *New York Daily News*, October 18, 1980.

17 Jay Greenberg, "Comic Relief for Quisenberry," *Philadelphia Daily News*, October 16, 1980.

18 Kaegel, "A Big Pain."

19 Ibid.

Chapter 20

1   Dick Kaegel, "Phillies Left Stranded as Royals Find Relief," *The Sporting News*, November 1, 1980.

2   Ibid.

3   Ibid.

4   Ibid.

5   Ibid.

6   "Brett Says, 'It Is All Behind Me,'" *Philadelphia Bulletin*, October 18, 1980.

7   Boone interview.

8   Kaegel, "Phillies Left Stranded."

9   Brusstar interview.

10   Bowa interview.

11   Phillie Phanatic, "Banned In Kansas City," *Philadelphia Daily News*, October 18, 1980.

12   Boone interview.

13   Ray Didinger, "Boone's the Clutchest .220 Hitter Around," *Philadelphia Daily News*, October 7, 1980.

14   Brusstar interview.

15   Ibid.

16   Dick Kaegel, "Phils Feel a Big Ache, Pounded by Aikens' Bat," *The Sporting News*, November 1, 1980.

17   Ibid.

18   Dick Kaegel, "Phils Renew a Patent on Rallies," *The Sporting News*, November 1, 1980.

19   Ibid.

20   Ibid.

21   McGraw and Yaeger, 147.

22   Gross interview.

23   Unser interview.

24   McRae interview.

Chapter 21

1   Bill Conlin, "Is Tonight THE Night?" *Philadelphia Daily News*, October 21, 1980.

2   Jack Chevalier, "Game 6 No End-All for Gale," *Philadelphia Bulletin*, October 20, 1980.

3   Bill Conlin, "Single Big Hit for MVP Schmidt," *Philadelphia Daily News*, October 22, 1980.

4   Wathan interview.

5   Boone interview.

6   McRae interview.

7   "Champs At Last, After 2-Inning Eternity," Binghamton (New York), October 22, 1980.
8   Phil Jasner, "Rose Was Johnny on the Spot," *Philadelphia Daily News*, October 22, 1980.
9   Boone interview.
10 Ibid.
11 Rich Hofmann, "McGraw Strikes Out the Mighty K.C.," *Philadelphia Daily News*, October 23, 1980.
12 Ibid.
13 Wathan interview.
14 Boone interview.
15 Dick Kaegel, "K-9: Strikeout Signal for Tug," *The Sporting News*, November 1, 1980.
16 Ibid.
17 Jay Greenberg, "Wilson Strikes Out at Scapegoat Role," *Philadelphia Daily News*, October 22, 1980.
18 Danny Robbins, "A Happy Green Makes the Round While Savoring His Moment of Glory," *Philadelphia Inquirer*, October 22, 1980.
19 Walk interview.
20 Brusstar interview.
21 Ibid.
22 Unser interview.
23 Lewis Freedman, "Hero Schmidt: Amid Storm, Calm," *Philadelphia Inquirer*, October 22, 1980.
24 Ibid.

Chapter 22

1   Smith interview.
2   Brusstar interview.
3   Gross interview.
4   Kitty Caparella, "Sites And Sounds," *Philadelphia Daily News*, October 22, 1980.
5   Ibid.
6   Phillie Phanatic, "Feeling Crowd-ed Was Scary, Fun," *Philadelphia Daily News*, October 22, 1980.

7   "We Win!" *Philadelphia Daily News*, October 22, 1980.

8   "Phillie-mania!" *Philadelphia Daily News*, October, 22, 1980.

9   "Champions!" *Philadelphia Inquirer*, October 22, 1980.

10 "The Day of the Phillies; Champions Of Grit and Guts," *Philadelphia Inquirer*, October 22, 1980.

11 "The Day Of."

12 Ibid.

13 Walk interview.

14 Bowa interview.

15 Ibid.

16 Phillie Phanatic, "I Loved the Parade," *Philadelphia Daily News*, October 23, 1980.

17 Unser interview.

18 Boone interview.

19 Ibid.

20 Ibid.

21 Ibid.

22 Bob Kennedy, "Parade Honors Philadelphia's Champions," *Camden-Courier Post*/Gannett News Service, October 23, 1980.

23 Ibid.

24 Chuck Stone, "A World Series for Brotherhood," *Philadelphia Daily News*, October 22, 1980.

25 Boone interview.

Epilogue

1   Walk interview.

2   Ibid.

3   Ibid.

4   Ibid.

5   Kevin Mulligan, "Whatever Happened to…Marty Bystrom?" *Philadelphia Daily News*, September 7, 2005.

6   Smith interview.

7   Gross interview.

8   Unser interview.

9   Michael Bamberger, "Baseball Hall of Fame Selection Ices Career Carlton Has Left Behind," *Chicago Tribune*, January 24, 1994.

10 Pat Jordan, "Thin Mountain Air," *Philadelphia* magazine, April 1994.

11 Lewis Freedman, "Lefty Shares a Few Tricks; Mellower Steve Carlton Gives Mounds of Advice," *Anchorage Daily News*, July 13, 1995.

12 State of New Jersey Resolution, October 18, 1994.

13 Jery Crasnick, "Gold Glover Now Manages Money," *Baseball America*, June 23-July 6, 2003.

14 Boone interview.

15 Bowa interview.

16 Rich Westcott, "Mike Schmidt: Phillies Retire His Number 20," *Phillies Report*, 1990.

17 Green and Maimon 315.

18 Ibid.

19 Todd Zolecki, "Loyal Soldier Out of Uniform," *Philadelphia Inquirer*, February 28, 2005.

20 "Longtime Phillie Vukovich Dead At 59," SI.com, March 8, 2007.

21 Rose interview.

22 Ibid.

23 Bill Finley, "McGraw Is a Believer in a Full Recovery," *New York Times*, May 30, 2003.

24 Sam Carchidi, "McGraw: Heart of a Champ," *Philadelphia Inquirer*, July 11, 2005.